EXHIBITING
DILEMMAS

EXHIBITING DILEMMAS

Issues of Representation
at the Smithsonian

Edited by
AMY HENDERSON and
ADRIENNE L. KAEPPLER

SMITHSONIAN INSTITUTION PRESS

WASHINGTON AND LONDON

Library of Congress Cataloging-in-Publication Data
Exhibiting dilemmas : issues of representation at the Smithsonian /
    edited by Amy Henderson and Adrienne L. Kaeppler.
        p.   cm.
    Includes bibliographical references (p.   ) and index.
    ISBN 1-56098-690-5 (alk. paper)
        1. Exhibitions—Washington (D.C.)   2. Smithsonian Institution.   I. Henderson, Amy.
    II. Kaeppler, Adrienne Lois.
    AM151.A96   1996
    069'.09753—dc20   96-16140

British Library Cataloguing-in-Publication Data is available

Manufactured in the United States of America
03 02 01 00 99 98 97   5 4 3 2 1

∞ The paper used in this publication meets the minimum requirements of the American
National Standard for Information Sciences—Permanence of Paper for Printed Library Materials
ANSI Z39.48-1984.

Contents

CONTENTS

DILEMMAS OF CURATORSHIP

Introduction

AMY HENDERSON AND ADRIENNE L. KAEPPLER

The modern museum has come a long way since its emergence in the nineteenth century as a "cabinet of curiosities." Instead of merely displaying objects, museum exhibits today draw on recent scholarship in art, literary criticism, and social history to offer broad interpretations about the origins, meaning, and value of objects, as well as theories about the thoughts and behavior of the people who made them and used them. Yesterday's cabinets of curiosities are today living, breathing founts of ideas—although some of these ideas have not always found favor with the visiting public.

The emergence of the idea-driven museum has forced curators, the men and women responsible for acquiring objects and mounting exhibitions, to confront a wide range of social, political, ethical, and cultural issues—issues that hardly affected their counterparts in the "cabinet of curiosities" days. Those issues—always challenging, sometimes vexing—are the subject of this book.

Exhibiting Dilemmas is about how exhibition issues are being played out at the Smithsonian Institution. Published to coincide with the 150th anniversary of the Smithsonian, the book, written exclusively by Smithsonian Institution staff, shows how curators, historians, exhibit specialists, and educators at the "Nation's Museum" have responded to the challenges of building a modern museum. But ours is also a shared journey, and the issues raised here are in many instances not exclusive to the Smithsonian alone. In that sense, this collection continues the dialogue that has recently appeared in a variety of works on museum studies.[1]

Each essay deals with a particular issue or dilemma of modern curatorship. Some engage the challenges inherent in exhibiting the recent past and popular culture. During the last thirty years, for instance, the "new social history," with its focus on history from "the bottom up" and its inclusion of previously marginal voices, has had a major impact on museum research, collecting policies, and exhibitions. This volume explores how decisions were made to begin collecting such objects as the Bunkers' chairs from *All in the Family*, the *M*A*S*H* set, or the Greensboro lunch counter, and how the acquisition of such symbolic objects—contemporary and cultural icons in their own right—reflects the growing tendency in museums to contextualize collections and to use objects to illuminate and interpret a wider history. In a similar fashion, *Exhibiting Dilemmas* assesses the impact of the "new art history," also largely contextual in interpretation, with art often being used to allude to a broad range of social and political issues.[2]

Other essays deal with questions about the authenticity of objects—about whether objects of dubious authenticity should be acquired, how it is determined if they are authentic or not—and if they should be put on exhibit in any event. In short, what is the real thing? And does it always matter?

Another issue has to do with stereotypes. Some collections present a virtual social history of how changing interpretations mark a journey from one stereotype to another and if so, how. Finally, other dilemmas center on the repatriation of collections, on when and to whom objects should be repatriated.

The transformation of the museum from reliquary to forum has forced curators to reassess their role as cultural custodians. Increasingly, curators must ask if museums retain the responsibility of validating and confirming tradition. Who has the authority to interpret history to the public—indeed, who "owns" history? Is an exhibition always the best venue to present diverse interpretations of complex historical issues, such as the *Enola Gay*? How does an exhibit best present an interpretation that reevaluates the sacred narrative of a culture in which the public feels a wide ownership? Perhaps even more basically, what are the implications of the public's willing partnership in the museum metamorphosis from a more removed and isolated existence to a very public and commercial one? Although such issues of contemporary curatorship and exhibition are far from resolved, this book is intended as a contribution to that ongoing dialogue.

Early Smithsonian curators did not have to engage in such a dialogue. At the time of the founding of the Smithsonian, in 1846, its commitment to the "increase and diffusion of knowledge" was characterized mainly in terms of

Fig. I.1. West Range of the Smithsonian Building (The Castle), ca. 1862. Courtesy Smithsonian Institution Archives.

research and the exchange of specimens. Little can be said about exhibitions, except to note their nonexistence. Only later, about 1858, with the acquisition of the Government Collections housed in the U.S. Patent Office, some of the materials belonging to members of the National Institute, the Washington Museum of John Varden, and the specimens collected on the U.S. Exploring Expedition, was exhibition deemed important enough to be considered. At the time, however, the objects and specimens were primarily just placed in cases for show in the Castle (Figure I.1), theoretically separating such displays from the research functions of the Smithsonian.[3]

Fig. I.2. The National Museum of American History's exhibition "A More Perfect Union" (1987–present), focusing on the internment of Japanese Americans during World War II, exemplifies the kind of idea-driven interpretation increasingly typical of modern curatorship.

Today, as exhibitions have emerged as a major focus of Smithsonian research and outreach, they have left their safely removed cabinets for arenas of often intense public scrutiny (Figure I.2). The dozen essays by Smithsonian curators included here deal directly with issues that have accompanied this transformation. Some are unique to the Smithsonian's particular status as the "Nation's Museum," while others present issues that have a broader application to the larger museum world. We have divided the essays into two sections: Part 1, "Dilemmas of Representation," and Part 2, "Dilemmas of Curatorship."

In Part 1, Steven Lubar's opening essay, "Exhibiting Memories," discusses one of the central quandaries of current museum curatorship: how to reconcile history and memory, and particularly how to combine history and memory in an exhibition. It explores how the curatorial voice takes account of memory and personal recollection in translating history to the public and how the curator shares authority with the public without abandoning the responsibility of the curator-historian.

The debate over history and memory has illustrated at least one truth: Today there *is* no single, overarching agreement on historical truth. And because there

4

are many histories, it follows that there are many ways of understanding. William H. Truettner addresses the ways in which the reinterpretation of historical truth has affected the emergence of the new art history in "For Museum Audiences: The *Morning of a New Day?*" Indeed, the new day of art history itself, in which interpretation is based on putting art in its contemporary cultural context, has led to a redefinition of what art represents. Consequently, the art historian today has to evaluate a painting on its historical as well as its aesthetic merits and then present this interpretation to a museum audience that may be accustomed to operating on a more traditional critical level, one that appraises works of art on the basis of what they appear to represent rather than as commentaries on contemporary culture.

Some dilemmas of representation are quite literal: the Hope Diamond, as Richard Kurin writes, is caught in an iconic no-man's (no-artifact's?)-land, "out of place, in the wrong collection, in the wrong museum." Its essential problem is that it has become a victim of its own fame: As a national icon swathed in the magic of its singular aura, the Hope Diamond, like the ruby slippers, has become its own symbol, representing nothing so much as its iconic self. Exhibiting such icons is both impossible (how could any display be adequate?) and uniquely simple (what difference could any particular pedestal make?) because they have come to represent a "parody on reality and illusion, myth-making and history-making, the valuing of museums and the museuming of value."

Mary Jo Arnoldi confronts a different dilemma in "Herbert Ward's 'Ethnographic Sculptures' of Africans." The original exhibition of these bronze sculptures at the Smithsonian in 1922 clearly reflected the abiding sensibility of the time, one imbued with interpretations keyed to the nineteenth-century Western invention of Africa, emphasizing a cultural hierarchy in which Africans were viewed as primitive and savage. The transformation in perspective over the last hundred years has brought into question the contemporary role that these sculptures can now play in representing African culture and their current value both to anthropologists and to Smithsonian collections at large. The debate involves their research value and the context in which they can be displayed: For example, even shifting them to an art museum may not be sufficient "to successfully historicize the images and to simultaneously communicate to the viewer that the artist's representations of Africans do not represent either philosophical or empirical 'truths.'" And how *would* these sculptures fit in many of today's art museums, in which, as William Truettner has argued, the bronzes would be seen not so much as art but as ideological vessels?

Issues of authentication have also presented curators with a variety of exhibition dilemmas. Tom D. Crouch discusses the Smithsonian's longest-running controversy in "Capable of Flight: The Saga of the 1903 Wright Airplane." In a dispute that outlived the primary participants—Wilbur and Orville Wright and Samuel Pierpont Langley (not only an aviation pioneer but secretary of the Smithsonian from 1887 to 1906)—the issue was to authenticate whether the Wright brothers' 1903 Flyer or Langley's Aerodrome would be recognized as the world's first "power-driven, heavier-than-air machine in which man made free, controlled, and sustained flight." The controversy, pitting proponents of the Wrights against those of Secretary Langley, lasted until 1948, when the Wright Flyer took its legitimate place as the world's first airplane. Today, the iconic Flyer is ensconced in the National Air and Space Museum's Milestones of Flight Gallery, floating near Charles Lindbergh's *Spirit of St. Louis* and above the *Apollo XI* command module that carried the first men to the Moon.

Jane MacLaren Walsh faces a different dilemma over authentication in "Crystal Skulls and Other Problems: Or, 'Don't Look It in the Eye.'" She delineates a classic problem about representing the controversial nature of an object—whether it should be accessioned if its authenticity cannot be proved, and whether it should be displayed even if authenticity is problematic. In the spirit of the Smithsonian's dedication to the "increase and diffusion of knowledge," Walsh argues that questionable—even outright fake—artifacts can prove useful. Whatever its status with regard to authenticity, the purported Aztec rock crystal skull that she discusses has already accomplished what all museum artifacts are intended to accomplish—the stimulation of curiosity and scientific inquiry.

In Part 2, the focus of the essays shifts to issues of curatorship and how curators are responding to particular dilemmas presented by contemporary exhibitions. The recent curatorial embrace of popular culture has provoked a new set of quandaries that, as would be expected in the exploration of heretofore uncharted territory, often produce more questions than answers. William Yeingst and Lonnie G. Bunch describe how they faced just such an issue in "Curating the Recent Past: The Greensboro Lunch Counter." In acquiring and then searching for the most appropriate way to display the lunch counter at the National Museum of American History, they found that this icon of popular culture became an analytical prism for interpreting contemporary history. Curating the recent past forces a reconsideration of the crafting of history itself, presenting challenges that expand the roles and obligations of curators. Arguing that today's history is clouded by an ambiguity that reflects "the legitimacy of multiple perspectives of the past and the fluidity of historical interpretation," they pose as a central dilemma the consequences of historical interpretations that can place curators and the museum public in a confrontation over the meaning and ownership of history. The nature of contemporary curatorial interpretation leads in turn to rock-bottom questions over who has the authority to interpret the past to the public, what the role of museums is in this new landscape—whether they remain primarily places of validation and tradition and, if not, how they balance public expectations with scholarly inquiry. Yeingst and Bunch are strong proponents of the idea that the exhibition of contemporary history is vital to the future of museums as "effective and contributing educational institutions." But the ramifications to the museum community are substantial, for if museums can no longer refuse to recognize the recent past, curators must discover new ways to untangle a web spun of such intricately interwoven issues as history and memory, meaning and representation, and a contextual interpretation framed by contemporary social and political ideologies.

Exhibiting the recent past is the focus as well of Ellen Roney Hughes's essay, "The Unstifled Muse: The 'All in the Family' Exhibit and Popular Culture at the National Museum of American History." Her exploration takes us into the ubiquitous realm of television and the impact wrought by the display of such popular culture icons as the Bunker chairs and the *M*A*S*H* set at the "Nation's Museum." The public outrage provoked by the initial display of the Bunkers' chairs in 1978 raised an immediate question: Do such artifacts possess enough lasting historical *gravitas* to warrant exhibition in a museum that much of the public views as a place of national enshrinement? In this instance, it is possible that the process of public acculturation was helped along by the familiarity that feeds popular culture. By 1983, when the *M*A*S*H* set was put on exhibition, the shock of the new had not only abated but had acceded to cheerful acceptance. Although questions remained about the validity of acquiring and displaying television relics as part of the museum's permanent collection, the tide had turned to the point that when many of the popular culture artifacts were taken off exhibit in 1991 because of funding shortfalls for maintenance, the public was incredulous: It was, one museumgoer wrote, "ridiculous that some dumb bureaucrat would eliminate Entertainment and Sports which are such an important part of American life." Indeed, within two decades, the curatorial advocacy of popular culture as an integral part of the museum's responsibility had transformed the public's perception of the museum from a temple into a virtual branch of popular entertainment itself.

The changing role of museums and evolving ideas about how the Smithsonian has curated its collections are at the heart of William L. Merrill and Richard E. Ahlborn's essay, "Zuni Archangels and Ahayu:da: A Sculpted Chronicle of Power and Identity." Originally, the acquisition of such Indian artifacts as the Zuni "war gods" reflected a curatorial tradition rooted in Euro-American ideas about organizing, studying, and preserving collections so that they would be available for research and public education. More recently, this view of museum curatorship has been challenged by members of contemporary American Indian societies who are dismayed by traditional museum practices of preservation and storage. As a result, Indian artifacts have become centrally involved in controversies over curatorial procedures, Indian access to collections for ritual purposes, and the repatriation of sensitive Indian objects. In choosing the carved Zuni images as an example of changing curatorial practices at the Smithsonian, Merrill and Ahlborn chronicle the lives of these religious images and the multiple identities ascribed to them "within the framework of contrasting Zuni and Euro-American concepts of objects, property, and knowledge." The interpretation of these distinct, culturally grounded concepts documents a century-long shift in Smithsonian curatorial practice from one that justified removing such objects to one that supported their subsequent repatriation. And although, as Merrill and Ahlborn suggest, this transformation of curatorship remains dependent for success on cooperation between Indian communities and Smithsonian scholars, even the return of the objects does not remove continued scientific, historical, and aesthetic significance for non-Indians. In their tenure at the Smithsonian, for example, the Zuni images have achieved an existence that transcends the cultural context in which they were originally created.

The evolution of curatorial relationships with native communities is also William W. Fitzhugh's topic in "Ambassadors in Sealskins: Exhibiting Eskimos at the Smithsonian." Fitzhugh analyzes the dilemmas faced by curators from the earliest days of "exhibiting Eskimos" at the National Museum of Natural History to the present, focusing on such issues as how to convey past and current views of culture and cultural history, how collections have influenced research and exhibition strategies, how to deal with recurrent problems of stereotyping, and how to achieve curatorial balance. He describes anthropology today as being at a crossroads, diverging from ethnographic exhibitions that froze native peoples in some late-nineteenth-century time warp to today's exhibits, which depict native cultures in their fullest form—integrating archaeological and traditional ethnographic displays with those that emphasize presentations of language, mythology, spiritual life, art, oral history, and modern social and political life. As we approach a new millennium and celebrate the Smithsonian's first 150 years, Fitzhugh with the Eskimos—like Yeingst and Bunch with the Greensboro lunch counter, and Merrill and Ahlborn with the Zuni images—finds a curatorial imperative for cooperation and understanding between museum curators and concerned communities, for working collaboratively to find ways "to keep the history, interrelationships, and diversity of cultural traditions alive and prominently exhibited, to the nation and to the world."

Sally Love's curatorial imperative posits a challenge that squarely identifies "Curators as Agents of Change: An Insect Zoo for the Nineties." As clearly happened with the introduction of popular culture exhibits that focused on sports and entertainment at the National Museum of American History, Love argues that exhibitions at the National Museum of Natural History can effectively influence public attitudes toward nature. Love traverses the shift in curatorial approaches by first describing nineteenth-century natural history exhibitions that kept people in touch with a world that lay outside their increasingly urban experience by presenting a "fragmented and exotic natural world, stuffed and mounted to show nature's curiosities and man's domination over them." Today, increased perceptions about biodiversity and global health have produced a new set of curatorial challenges that calls for change in the way we exhibit the natural world. Using the National Museum of Natural History's Insect Zoo as a case in point, she shows how its evolution reflects the transformation from depictions of insects as curiosities of nature "to their use as tools to teach the interconnectedness of organisms and the natural world." She establishes that the museum's traditional research mission—to discover, name, and classify the biological, geological, and human world—is today augmented by explorations of evolutionary processes that are responsible for the diversity of life. The key to the success of future exhibitions, she argues, lies with the curators' ability to use biodiversity research to inform the public about "how species extinctions dismantle ecosystems"—a challenge crucial to understanding the natural world today, when 99 percent of all species that ever lived are now extinct. In this the museum's educational mission assumes a primacy: If natural history museums have a twofold purpose (the acquisition of scientific knowledge and the dissemination of public information), the contemporary curatorial dilemma is to translate this research into exhibits and public programs that illustrate how the threads of nature's diversity are intricately woven into our own lives.

"And Now for Something Completely Different: Reconstructing Duke Ellington's *Beggar's Holiday* for Presentation in a Museum Setting" is an appropriate way to conclude these essays on Smithsonian curatorship. Here, Dwight Blocker Bowers asks the legitimate questions, What is a museum exhibition? and How do you apply the exhibition experience to research and collections involving the performing arts? Bowers fearlessly answers: by providing nontraditional "living exhibitions" that animate these collections to convey an immediacy not otherwise possible. Focusing on the Duke Ellington collection at the National Museum of American History, he describes how he transformed the Ellington musical *Beggar's Holiday* from its archival repository into a staged performance under the lights at the museum's Carmichael Auditorium. As with traditional exhibitions, this presentation was dependent on scholarly selection and a cogent interpretation congruent with an informed curatorial point of view; unlike traditional exhibits, the success of *Beggar's Holiday* relied on performers to breathe life into the historical data. Such living exhibitions, he argues, add a vital new dimension to the interpretation of collections, providing lively and accessible vehicles for scholarly research while attracting new audiences to the museum. For Bowers, the curatorial imperative is to restore research collections in the performing arts to the context for which they were originally created—to be interpreted and judged through live performance.

As a collection, *Exhibiting Dilemmas* illuminates a general state of curatorial being at the Smithsonian Institution as we celebrate our 150th anniversary. If the contemporary issues of curatorship and exhibition offered here seem to present as many questions as answers, our response should be enthusiastic, because there can be no overriding, monolithic point of view that speaks to the multiplicity of voices reflecting the diversity of American life and culture. Yet as these essays also make clear, there are central issues—and questions—shared not only by Smithsonian curators but by the museum world as a whole. It is the adventure of exploring these issues, and of discovering at least some of the answers, that will continue to define the curatorial imperative.

NOTES

1. See, for example, Ivan Karp and Steven D. Lavine, *Exhibiting Cultures: The Poetics and Politics of Museum Display* (Washington, D.C.: Smithsonian Institution Press, 1991); Ivan Karp, Steven D. Lavine, and Christine Mullen Kraemer, *Museums and Communities: The Politics of Public Culture* (Washington, D.C.: Smithsonian Institution Press, 1992); Steven Lubar and W. David Kingery, *History from Things: Essays on Material Culture* (Washington, D.C.: Smithsonian Institution Press, 1993); Candace Greene, "Discovering the Audience: A Reorientation in Museum Analysis," *Reviews in Anthropology* 24 (1995): 267–76; and Flora E. S. Kaplan, ed., *Museums and the Making of "Ourselves": The Role of Objects in National Identity* (London and New York: Leicester University Press, 1994).

2. Some objects, however, retain an iconic status that removes them from the trammels of change. For example, the Gilbert Stuart portraits of George and Martha Washington at the National Portrait Gallery are exhibited behind velvet ropes with little contextualization. And any rumblings about removing or changing the exhibition "The Elephant" at the National Museum of Natural History unfailingly provoke a great deal of consternation.

3. The saga of the National Institute can be followed in Douglas E. Evelyn, "The National Gallery at the Patent Office," in *Magnificent Voyagers: The U.S. Exploring Expedition, 1838–1842,* ed. Herman J. Viola and Carolyn Margolis (Washington, D.C.:

Smithsonian Institution Press, 1985), pp. 227–41. Already in 1853 the Smithsonian Regents noted that if the Smithsonian accepted an appropriation from Congress to take care of the collections, the arrangement would force the Smithsonian to become an annual "supplicant for government patronage, and ultimately subject it to political influence and control." See Nathan Reingold and Marc Rothenberg, "The Exploring Expedition and the Smithsonian Institution," in ibid., pp. 243–53.

DILEMMAS OF REPRESENTATION

1

Exhibiting Memories

STEVEN LUBAR

"We all remember World War II." That's the way a recent exhibit at the National Museum of American History welcomed visitors.[1]

At first reading, this seems absurd. Only those over fifty can remember the war. But in another, deeper, sense, we all do remember the war. We remember it in family stories, national mythology, the history we learned in school, and the movies we saw on television. "World War II: Sharing Memories," a temporary exhibit open from June through November 1995, was about the war—but its true subject was memory and history. We wanted our visitors to think not only about the war but also about how we know the past, about the ways that memory and tradition relate to history and historic artifacts. I think we succeeded. In this essay, after reflecting on the ways in which memory and history intersect in museums and describing the exhibit, I will look at some of the memories our visitors shared with us, considering especially the ways in which they thought about the past.

MEMORY AND HISTORY

Memory is how we connect with our individual past. It serves our own purposes: writer Stefan Zweig called it "a power that deliberately arranges and wisely excludes." History, too, partakes of this rearrangement of the past, but it must aim for a less personal point of view. Historians, Eric Hobsbawm wrote, are "the professional remembrancers of what their fellow-citizens wish to forget." How to combine memory and history in an exhibit? How to recognize and honor memories while at the same time moving beyond them? These were the problems I faced as curator of "Sharing Memories."

One difference between historians and the general public is the extent of critical distance we put between ourselves and our subjects. We share an interest in history, but the approach we take is different. Our sources are different also; historians want to use archives and objects, the public more often turns to memory, personal connections, and family stories. We use those sources in different ways; historians are careful to assess the bias of their sources, to question the evidence. And we consider different contexts; historians must cast a broader net. These factors help to determine our critical distance. Historians have no end of words to describe the degree of critical distance. Our stories of the past can be commemoration, remembrance, reminiscence, explanation, interpretation, or analysis. Objects move from keepsake to memento to souvenir to reminder to evidence. Our presentations move from celebration to memorial to exhibition.

All of these means of explaining the past have a place in our understanding of it. One can walk around Washington and find history presented in every one of these ways. Arlington Cemetery is properly the home of monuments. The Holocaust Memorial Museum has both an exhibition and, carefully separate, a Hall of Memories, a memorial. The Smithsonian encompasses a wide range of historic presentations. The National Air and Space Museum is, for the most part, a temple to technological progress. The National Portrait Gallery is a hall of heroes. Art museums show aesthetic masterpieces.

History museums have a different and, I think, more difficult task. The goal of a history exhibit is to move people from the ideas and information that they bring with them to the exhibit to a more complex, problematized, and nuanced view of the past. Exhibits should not be limited to reminiscence or commemoration; they should add perspective by aspiring to a greater critical distance and by putting the artifacts in context. Consider the exhibits at the National Museum of American History that examined aspects of World War II. The least successful, in my view, was "World War II GI," which told the public about the soldier's life by presenting objects and images without much context. Much more successful were "Women War Workers" and "A More Perfect Union," which told the stories, respectively, of women on the home front and Japanese Americans at home and on the battlefield, situating their stories in the context of changing American ideas about gender and race. An exhibit on wartime production posters explained the way they fit into the history of advertising and patriotism, analyzing the intentions and effects of the posters, which had often been presented in merely aesthetic terms. These exhibits are about history, mostly ignoring whatever memories visitors might bring with them to the museum or using those memories only as a hook to attract audience interest.

This disjunction between memory and history was the problem faced by the curators of the controversial "*Enola Gay*" exhibition at the National Air and Space Museum. Their first script moved too far for comfort from the veterans' memories, and the veterans had enough political clout to let the curators know it. The "*Enola Gay*" exhibition that finally opened has exactly the opposite problem: It focuses almost solely on the object, the airplane, with little context to allow it to move the visitor's understanding beyond memory. Its technological and restoration history is given in loving detail. Technological details are safe; they do not assume any responsibility for moving visitors beyond where they were when they came to the museum. Indeed, they seem, as presented here, to be beyond questioning, and they add the weight of their seeming inevitability to that of the actions that made use of the technology. (My guess is that the visual and technological authority of the airplane would have overcome even the strong message of the early script—something that readers of the script would have found difficult to judge.)

The authority of the artifact is reinforced by allowing the voices in the show to be only those of the plane's designers, builders, restorers, and, most important, crew. The crew's point of view is interesting and important, of course, but why it should be more privileged than, say, that of the residents of Hiroshima, or the atom bomb's makers, or, for that matter, the millions of Americans who grew up in the shadow of Hiroshima—that's a political issue. Each era—each community—nowadays, each political pressure group—emphasizes the history it thinks important. Each listens to the history that speaks to its concerns. The "*Enola Gay*" exhibit speaks in the veterans' voice.

"WORLD WAR II: SHARING MEMORIES"

The "*Enola Gay*" exhibit was very much in our minds as we thought about "World War II: Sharing Memories." It was clear, in the political environment that the "*Enola Gay*" controversy had brought to the Smithsonian, that we needed to move beyond the usual museum exercise of presenting history from a historian's perspective, beyond our usual techniques of displaying objects and providing explanations and interpretations; these techniques privileged historical analysis and depreciated the value of memory. We simply couldn't do that after the "*Enola Gay*" fiasco; we had to find a way to allow both memory and history to play a role. And so, in "Sharing Memories," we experimented with the ways in which memory and history allow us to comprehend the past. Memories are personal and specific; exhibits are general. Memories are incorporeal, exhibits show things. Memories stand on their own; a good history exhibit provides context. We had to somehow join the two. Just as important, from my point of view, we needed to allow thoughtful visitors to reflect on the very nature of memory and history. To allow our visitors to understand the value of both approaches to the past would be an important contribution to the ongoing history wars.

The way to do this was to share the job of interpretation, of creating meaning, with our visitors. To that end, we selected our artifacts to elicit a wide range of memories. We set aside a memorial area, a distinctive design indicating that it was intended for commemoration. And, most important, we asked our visitors to participate. We encouraged them to write down their memories of the war, and we displayed their contributions prominently, so that other visitors could share them.

Choosing artifacts was the first step. The objects selected for display were, mostly, everyday objects without a specific history. This is unusual; most recently mounted history exhibits aim for the specific, to tell a particular tale, surrounding an object with labels and photographs to provide the context that explains it both specifically and more generally. But in "Sharing Memories" we chose another approach. We wanted our visitors' stories, not ours. We wanted the visitors to supply their own context. The objects were to serve as aide-mémoire, not history lessons. We let them speak for themselves, allowing them to whisper something different to every visitor.

The exhibit started with "The Home Front." The objects here were the everyday things that touched American life in the 1940s. The symbolic object used to introduce the section was the most mundane artifact, but one that spoke to the all-encompassing nature of the war: a matchbook printed with a *V* for Victory. There were ration coupons and steel pennies and *Life* magazines and movie posters. Of course, there was selection here. There was a curatorial voice, but a quiet one, in a conversation with the visitors, not lecturing them. And so a few of the objects had a bit of a spin to them: the application for gas rations was signed "Mrs. Harry Truman," suggesting a level of equality in sharing the burdens of the war that might surprise some visitors. The *Life* magazine was open to an article titled "Negro Soldiers," reminding visitors that in the segregated 1940s equality went only so far. The section on production included union badges, suggesting that even during the war there was not unity in all things.

The curatorial voice was loudest in "The Things They Carried," part of "The Battlefield" section of the exhibit. The title was borrowed from a collection of short stories by novelist Tim O'Brien about soldiers in Vietnam, and the things the soldiers carried were, of course, symbolic of their thoughts. (Another title might have been "For Which They Fought.") And the things they carried, physically and metaphorically, were not the politicians' hoary clichés of patriotism. Rather, they were much more down-to-earth: candy bars and gum and pinup pictures and a picture of the girl back home. They fought for the everyday pleasures of American life. It would have been easy to simply drape this area with the flag, both literally and metaphorically—politicians, fifty years later, might suggest this—but there's good historical scholarship to suggest that what the GIs were fighting for was not God and country but mom, apple pie, and the girl next door. We chose objects that evoked those memories. These quiet objects suggested—but did not insist on—that historical truth. Historical analysis can bring to the fore some of the memories that individuals might forget.

How to deal with the front lines of the war? Here, I think, objects have less utility. In the "Tools of War" section of the exhibit, we displayed basic military equipment—an M-1 rifle, hats and helmets, a mess kit. Though they evoked memories for those who used them, these objects seemed to me insufficiently time-specific to evoke memories of World War II. For those who were not there, guns and helmets speak simply to the idea of "war," not specifically World War II. These objects, like those displayed in another exhibit at the museum, "World War II GI," had special meaning to those who were in the military during the war, but not to most of our visitors. Weapons, like other technologies, might be too specialized to allow visitors to see themselves or their pasts in them.

We might have used photographs of the war; there are wonderful images available. But most of them seem either too specific or too general. That is, some are pictures of specific scenes that mean everything to those who were there but little to those who were not. Others (the flag-raising on Iwo Jima, say) have a meaning that has become so enmeshed in our national memory that it's hard for people to see beyond the "official" story. Instead, we used wartime art—paintings from the collections of the army, navy, and air force. Visitors had not seen this art before, and so they had to figure it out for themselves. More than that, the paintings were in some sense generic. The artists were drawing specific individuals and situations, but paintings are more removed from the actual event than are photographs. They are therefore better at evoking memories than photographs would be.

Accompanying the paintings was a series of quotes taken from Bill Mauldin's *Up Front*. Mauldin, a cartoonist and writer who accompanied the infantry in Europe, captured the feel of the front lines. His words evoked for our visitors the boredom and fear of war and served to bring back memories for those who were there—but they also added some real-life complexity to the triumphal combat images of so many bad World War II movies, the list-of-battles sort of history that textbooks present, or the clichés in which politicians speak. Like so many of the other objects, Mauldin's words grounded our visitors in the day-to-day historical details. Perhaps they will shape future memories.

The section of the exhibition devoted to commemoration was set apart from the other sections by its design and by the tone of the words used. The area was carpeted, the structure was modeled loosely on the Tomb of the Unknown Soldier. There is a photograph of a Normandy cemetery. But here too, we did not go for the easy emotional tug on the heartstrings. To have done so would have moved the exhibit too far into the realm of memorial. On exhibit, in a window setting, was not a gold-star flag, symbolizing that a family member had died in the war, but rather a blue-star flag, symbolizing that a family member was in the armed forces. The symbol for this section was not the Congressional Medal of Honor but rather the Purple Heart—awarded to anyone who was injured in the line of duty.

The final element of the experience, and one that I think is essential, was music. We played, at a low background level, a Smithsonian Collection of Recordings CD, *We'll Meet Again: The Love Songs of World War II*. The love songs of the 1940s, the liner notes suggested, were "songs of love, loneliness, parting, and yearning." They were songs of memory—memory of better times, of lovers and love lost. Popular songs are both personal and general; they provide a structure for specific memories, yet at the same time they tell universal stories. That is exactly what we hoped the exhibit would do.

VISITORS' MEMORIES

The most interesting part of the exhibit was neither the objects nor the stories we told around them, but rather the visitors' own contributions. There were tables and chairs in the home front and memorial sections of the exhibit, and on the tables were spiral-bound books with "Share Your Memories" written on the cover. Our visitors responded enthusiastically, filling page after page of those books with personal and family stories of the war. These were available for everyone to read—some were mounted on a bulletin board—and it was these handwritten stories, a few paragraphs at most, that were the hit of the show.

I've read many of the several hundred memories that we collected. These stories suggested a fascinating complexity of memory and history and mythology that would delight anyone interested in the war, family traditions, and the process of remembering. In many of the stories visitors conveyed, in the space of a page, what the war meant to them, what was important, what they remember, or the stories that have been passed down in their families. They wrote down the stories to honor family in the war, to preserve memories, to let others know just how proud they were. The memories revealed a personal history that wasn't in the textbooks. Our visitors were fascinated too. They spent a long time paging through our "memory books," reading each other's stories.

Most of the men who were soldiers during the war told straightforward stories, a listing of assignments, bases, battles. Perhaps their deeper memories were too difficult to put down in a few words. But when their children or, especially, grandchildren told the tales, we get the purified essence of memory.

Consider one story, typical both in that it was a family story—probably 80 percent of the stories we collected come from children or grandchildren of those who lived through the war—and in that it nicely situated its hero in both the family and the war. "My grandfather was in the Canal Zone during the War," it began. It went on to describe the injury he received, the story he told the family about it—capturing saboteurs—and then the real story, admitted only years later—a car accident. The story was a gem. Like so many of the stories, it suggested the personal dimension to the war, and the family dimensions of memories. It was an everyday story, not a heroic one.

My grandpa fought in WWII. He was in the navy. His weapon was a 5 inch anti-aircraft destroyer. The name of the ship is U.S.S. Luce and the ship was sunk.

There were some fine stories tied to objects. Sometimes it was an object of memory:

My Grandfather. . . . He was a great man. I have his Bible which he carried in World War II.

My grandfather was an officer in the Pacific during the war and brought a string of pearls back for my mother. Years later I heard my father say that they were very special, expensive pearls. . . . I imagine a desperate Japanese family had to sell them cheaply to get themselves through the war. I never thought such a strange, disturbing detail of the war would touch me personally.

Sometimes it was an object left behind:

My father . . . served in Europe in the army's 3rd armored, Reconnaissance. In December of 1944 they were trapped in the Belgian village of Marcouray. Attempted supply drops all fell short. On Christmas they decided to leave under cover of darkness. He was a magician, specializing in slight-of-hand tricks involving thimbles. When they left, he left the thimbles behind. I have often thought about the possibility of a Belgian housewife sewing using those thimbles.

But most of the family stories were stories of humble heroism. You can almost imagine the stories being told over and over, passed down from father to son to daughter, sometimes expanding, sometime contracting. The big picture might be forgotten, but the details never are.

My Grandfather was one of those people who decode messages. He was stationed in a jungle somewhere and was attacked by a jungle cat. I am proud of him.

All I want to do is thank all the men and women who helped us win the war. All I know about it is my grandfather was in it and I saw him in a picture with his uniform on. He helped the court reconsider about sending a man to death for falling asleep on his shift. For that person and all of us he's a hero. Thanks.

My daddy was shot down on his first bombing mission. . . . He was the only man from 2 bomber crews who was not captured. He hid out for 6 months in Czechoslovakia being helped by partisans. After the war was over he had been declared legally dead and hitchhiked 1800 miles across Europe to be declared alive. This week he will be celebrating his 70th birthday with his family.

My favorite hero story, short and to the point:

My grandpa fought in WWII. He's awesome!

Some of these family memories were bittersweet:

My grandpa was a medic in the army. He helped save many peoples lives. I was very proud of him. He had a lot of nightmares at night. I pray that there is no more wars.

I am a late "Baby Boomer." My father went in to the service as the war was ending and was stationed in Italy. He is still, thankfully, alive today but continues to carry many of the emotional scars that have been too many years in the healing. My husband is a Viet Nam vet who has physical and mental scars—they are quite the pair—the men in my life.

And some proceeded from the family stories, moving or angry or bittersweet, to a moral:

My father was a Marine Raider
Has Three Purple Hearts, Should Have

Had Four, Worked Two Full
Time Jobs, Chicago
Policeman 26 yrs. And I am
Damn Proud He Is My Father.
   I am finally spending time with him now.
   You only have 1 father and 1 mother.

My grandfather fought in the Pacific in WWII. He was a ranger for the marines. He sat me down one day and told me stories of how it was his job (as he was in a field artillery unit) to direct the mortar shells. He told me, with a pained look on his face, how he saw people being blown apart. Very moving. He also told me how he had to jump into a fox-hole and slice a man's throat. He then saw a picture of the man's girl. "She was might pretty," he said. My God, war is sick. God bless all of the soldiers who fought for us.

Those who were on the home front remembered jobs, and rationing, and worry:

We remember the lonely times, the joy of letters, the rationing and the *pleasure* of our small sacrifices.

Those who were children during the war remembered mostly the small changes in their lives:

My vivid memories include selling Victory Garden seeds as students, riding the bus everywhere because of rationing, and having a milk horse named "Queeny" (dappled gray) because there was no gas for the milk delivery truck. . . . I thought black-outs were exciting—not realizing what they really meant.

But most of all, children seemed to remember the end of the war—specific events, images, stories:

In my memory V-J Day was a rush downtown where everyone was throwing torn up newspapers, hugging, kissing, yelling—and I could see only *knees.*

The whole family except me had ptomaine poisoning from bad (and rationed) hamburger. In the middle of the afternoon guns started shooting across the lake and my uncle drove down the lane honking the horn of his truck and yelling "The war is over!" My mother raised her head and said good! and then threw up.

I was born in 1939 and when the war ended I remember asking my father what would be on the news. As a child I thought news was only about the war. I also remember decorating my tricycle with red, white and blue crepe paper to celebrate.

VJ Day—August 14, 1945—Bklyn, N. Y. Party! Party! Party! Parents didn't care what time we got home. We passed a house on Ave. U and Brown St. 3! Three! Blue stars in the window. There was a bust out party of tears and joy. the mother of the house ran out grabbed us three 12 year old boys—hugged and kissed us and cried, "My 3 sons are coming home *and* you kids won't have to go in!!" That night we had our first beer in the crowded kitchen from a cold wooden barrel. "Yuk! How can they drink this stuff!"
 We cried with that happy mother!
 We went in 7 years later (Korea).

The fiftieth anniversary celebrations of World War II are over now. Memories remain. Reading these many memories gave me—and, I hope, our visitors—a new appreciation of the complex relationship between memory and history. Memories fill out the complicated story of the war. They make it personal, real. Indeed, in their own way, they are more real, because more strongly and emotionally held, than any well-researched history. But just as fascinating as what the stories tell about the war is what they tell us about the way we remember history. History is a personal story, a family story. Personal stories become family legend, a way of connecting to parents and grandparents. There are as many histories as there are memories.

In the post–"*Enola Gay*" world of history museums, curators must think increasingly carefully about the tone of exhibitions. Once we did not much worry about what the public brought with them to exhibits, but that is not the case anymore. The public is demanding to be considered a partner in the creation of meaning. This is good, but the trick is how to share authority with our public while not simply abandoning the job of the curator and the historian to those who have the political clout to demand that their own historical truths—their point of view—be given the museum's endorsement. I suggest that one way to accomplish this is to pay careful attention to the interplay of memory and history, reminiscence and research. The past holds many truths. There are many ways to understand it. Looking through the prism of memory as well as the prism of history gives us a fuller, more honest, and more interesting picture.

NOTE

1. A version of this essay appeared in the July/August 1996 issue of *Museum News*.
 The exhibit team also included Hal Aber as designer and a group of museum staff who contributed ideas and advice, including Eleanor Boyne, Betsy Burstein, Peter Liebhold, Jennifer Locke, and Margaret Vining. I am especially indebted to Betsy Burstein and Peter Liebhold for their initial proposal for an exhibit focusing on memories.

Fig. 1.1. As visitors entered the exhibition, they saw paintings that were the basis for some of the most famous posters of the war years, a classic Jeep, and in the background a U.S. flag and a large photograph of the scene in Times Square on V-J Day. The main label read:

> We all remember World War II. The men and women who fought in the war can never forget it. Nor can anyone who waited for them to come home. People under age 50 know the war secondhand. Their memories are made of family stories, songs and movies, politics, and from the way the war has reshaped the world since 1945. The entire nation cherishes the sacrifice and triumph.
>
> Several exhibitions and displays around the Museum explore aspects of World War II. In this exhibition, we want you to remember and tell your own stories. The paintings, objects, and photographs are here to evoke memories. Remember your past, your family's, or the nation's. Listen to the stories of other visitors. Share memories of the war, and think about its place in the nation's history and future.

Photograph by Eric Long, Smithsonian Institution.

Fig. 1.2. Objects that might remind visitors of life at home during the war were featured in this section, on the home front. "Men, women, and children who never left the country fought on the home front," the section label began and went on: ·

> For them, the war meant new kinds of work, waiting in line, walking rather than driving to save gasoline and rubber, doing without. The fighting war reached them, too, through the sacrifice of friends and family members, and in movies, radio programs, magazines, newspapers, and the war stories they passed along to one another.
>
> For many Americans the war brought dislocation and uncertainty: new places, new people, new jobs, a more complicated world. Millions of families moved during the war. Millions of others stayed put and endured the horrible wait for news of sons and daughters in the military and relatives lost in Europe or Asia. The war years at home held opportunity, mobility, scarcity, and dread.

Photograph by Eric Long, Smithsonian Institution.

Fig. 1.3. "Memorials and Memory" occupied the center of the show. On this wall were the public symbols of memory: a window with a blue star flag, an image of a war cemetery, a Purple Heart. Within were the simple things that soldiers carried to remind them of home: candy bars, pinup pictures, pictures of the girl back home. The label here read:

> Reminders of the war are innumerable. Cemeteries hold many of the roughly 300,000 American military dead, 15 million military dead from around the world, and 39 million civilians killed during the war. Monuments to local veterans stand in town centers and monuments to victory in national capitals. Holocaust memorials, battlefield parks, preserved concentration camps, and museums like this one keep the memory of the past alive.
>
> The war persists, too, in private memorials: gold star flags, uniforms, old photographs, and the accounts of men and women who endured the conflict on the battlefield and on the home front. The world must never forget.

On the walls surrounding this structure were paintings of the battlefront, scenes of the exhilaration and boredom, the heroism and horror of war. Photograph by Eric Long, Smithsonian Institution.

2

For Museum Audiences
The *Morning of a New Day?*

WILLIAM H. TRUETTNER

For many visitors to "The West as America," an exhibition of western art held at the National Museum of American Art in 1991, the comment book at the end was looked upon as the definitive gallery text.[1] The book (or books—four bound volumes of several hundred pages each were filled) became a battleground. Each contains the responses of viewers eager to challenge or affirm the curators' gallery texts, previous comments in the book, or whatever else struck them as noteworthy about the exhibition. Most of these responses, understandably, were attempts to sort out personal beliefs—usually but not always about art and history—after an emotional encounter with 164 works, redefined as narratives encouraging westward expansion.

How can we understand and put to use the charged commentary in these books that has already been the subject of a dozen articles, as well as chapters in dissertations and books? These have perhaps raised more questions than they have answered. On the one hand, few of those who wrote in the comment books seem to have come to the exhibition—which attracted widespread negative criticism only a few weeks after it opened—with an unformed response. So their subsequent commentary was to some extent influenced by what they thought they were coming to see. On the other hand, those who wrote nothing in the books (the great majority of visitors) may have encountered the exhibition in very different but equally important ways. And these are only a few of the problems that make it difficult today for art museum curators to gauge their audiences when planning new projects.

Despite these problems, "The West as America" comment books provide a helpful introduction to a debate that is stirring not only museum audiences but curatorial departments across the country. That debate is about how to view and understand works of art exhibited in museum galleries. For example, should they be seen as rare and beautiful objects, their appeal relatively unaffected by time or place? Or should they be seen in a narrower context, as objects no less pleasing but more closely tied to the time when they were made? Most museums, unsure of which way to turn, now offer an interpretive program that falls somewhere between these two approaches. But to sharpen the debate, which is the purpose of this essay, I have distinguished between the approaches by assigning to each a different voice—in this case the voices of two fictional art museum curators. They will debate the merits of three works prominently featured in the "The West as America," the last of which, *Morning of a New Day*, provides the title for this essay.

To begin, let us imagine the two curators standing before a large history painting called *The Founding of Maryland* (1861; Figure 2.1), by the German-American artist Emanuel Leutze. The painting serves to illustrate, with astonishing clarity, an important moment in the history of colonial Maryland. On the banks of a picturesque inlet off Chesapeake Bay, Leonard Calvert, governor and son of the founder of the colony, and the local (presumably Algonquian) chief have just concluded a treaty that apparently acknowledges the colonists' occupation of the site and simultaneously inaugurates a policy of peaceful coexistence.[2] A feeling of goodwill is shared by all who appear in the picture (except for one of the Indians), leading the viewer to assume that both parties will gain from the association. The Indians have taken on the role of providers, depositing at the feet of the colonists a locally gathered cornucopia: agricultural products (corn), a variety of game, and baskets overflowing with prime Chesapeake Bay oysters. The colonists, in turn, will bestow upon the Indians the institutional and technological benefits of civilization (ways of improving spiritual, communal, and physical conditions), such as Christianity, representative government, and a more comfortable domestic life. The cross and the English flag are the two most conspicuous symbols of civilization in the picture, followed by the colonists' clothes and the spacious dwelling or meetinghouse under construction on the hillside. (The Indians' tipis, situated between the tall cross and the new building, already have a diminished presence.) Other benefits soon to be acquired by the Indians are more efficient tools and weaponry, as well as livestock. The cow in the background, surrounded by jubilant colonists, is

Fig. 2.1. Emanuel Leutze, *The Founding of Maryland,* 1861, oil on canvas, 52 × 73 in. The Maryland Historical Society, Baltimore.

surely the beginning of herds that will eventually spread across the Maryland countryside.

What made viewers in Leutze's time believe this optimistic scenario, and what still attracts us to the painting today, is its descriptive detail—the hazy blue sky that arches above the crowd; the appealing contours of the landscape; the various activities of the settlers and Indians and their distinctive costumes; and the warm light that plays across the scene, falling in patterns that suggest late afternoon on a summer day. Each of these passages gives the scene a lively, realistic character. And yet the sense of an actual time and place that they evoke can be seen in quite different ways by our two curators. Both will probably assume that *The Founding of Maryland* (as well as the other two paintings under consideration in this essay) represents two different pasts: the past the painting is presumed to record (the events leading up to the founding of Maryland) and the past affecting the production of the painting (the events of the years immediately preceding the Civil War). Neither curator considers these two pasts to be entirely separate; information from one, they agree, affects how the other is understood. But how each curator proceeds to investigate the two pasts will determine the kind of information he or she is seeking. And therein lies the problem. Each curator will have questions about the past (or pasts) that the other curator constructs and therefore about the method used to construct it. And each will regard the conclusions that the other arrives at as somewhat beside the point; that is, one curator's conclusions will not always answer the questions the other curator is asking.

To begin the debate, let us assume that curator A wishes to regard *The Founding of Maryland* as a work in which colonial life in the mid-Atlantic region has been imaginatively portrayed but with some attempt at historical accuracy (an imaginative version of something "real," in other words). A's subsequent investigation of the subject, therefore, might entail gathering reliable data on the dress, customs, and dwellings of Indian tribes inhabiting the region during this period. These data he or she will compare to details in the painting, looking for a correspondence between the two. But we should not assume that curator A's more or less empirical approach will lead to believing that Leutze could re-create the colonial past, artifact by artifact. Instead, A probably sees the painting as offering another kind of window on the past—an assessment of colonial times that reveals how Leutze understood American history in 1861. The artist's concern for historical accuracy, whether or not achieved, is part of that assessment. It can be factored into the artistic process, A believes, and used to interpret *The Founding of Maryland*—to argue that the painting can be seen as reflecting (in the sense of openly describing) Leutze's beliefs at the time (and therefore providing some indication, because of Leutze's status as a major artist of the period, of how the nation understood its past).

Already, however, we encounter a problem that has long plagued art historians, no matter what methodology they favor. To maintain that art is simply a "reflection" of an artist's beliefs or that the meaning a work has in one era can be extended, virtually unchanged, to another (in this case from 1861 to 1996), is indeed problematic. It assumes that artists in the nineteenth century could somehow achieve historical innocence, screening from their minds all political associations with their present (and from their perception of the past), and that viewers today exist in a similar historical cocoon, unaffected by changing perceptions of their present or past. Clearly, that seems all but impossible; few contemporary scholars would argue that art can be understood in this way. And yet, some part of the reflection theory survives under the guise of artistic independence. Depending on how much a curator is willing to grant, a work can still be seen as a general assessment of the artist's own times (an assessment that is given further authority when a work is declared true to "the spirit of" those times). Thus judgments about the work's merit might ultimately touch on questions of individual procedure: Did the artist consult the right sources? Was he skillful enough to copy them correctly? Did he idealize the subject for aesthetic purposes? And so forth.

On either scale, as a factual or a more general description of the past, *The Founding of Maryland* will disappoint curator A. One glance will tell A that Leutze's Indians provide little helpful information about the dwellings, dress, or conduct of seventeenth-century Indians in the mid-Atlantic region. They did not, for example, live in tipis or wear fanciful adaptations of nineteenth-century Plains costumes.[3] But that is not the picture's only historical shortcoming. There is no real evidence that the founding of Maryland was ever celebrated in this way or that anything more than a brief woodland mass, at which no Indians were present, was held after the colonists landed. Leutze seems to have conflated several events from Maryland history into one "historical" moment, complete with actors—white and Indian—wearing "period" dress.[4] Although no one can say for sure what the event (if there had been one) would have looked like, we can assume that those willing to investigate (curator A, in particular) will conclude that *The Founding of Maryland* is a historical mirage, whose chief function, delighting the eye, also serves to obscure the past.

Once the curator reaches this conclusion, he or she will be judging the importance of the picture. Curator A has, after all, set out to understand the picture as a guide, however imperfect, to Leutze's view of American history. But at the same time that A is allowing for imperfection, he or she is operating on a theory that presupposes some degree of historical authenticity in the picture. And therefore, the more inaccurate the picture appears to be, the more it will assume the burden of a movie that strays too far from the book. The picture may or may not appeal to A's eye, but even if it does, that appeal will not entirely overcome his or her disappointment in its historical failings.

These so-called failings are of less concern to curator B, who is probably focusing more on how events of the years preceding 1861 affected the painting than on whether details in the painting match artifacts or events of the 1630s. One obvious approach, for example, would be to investigate how the painting mediates pre–Civil War social and political issues—that is, to examine it not only for Leutze's views but (despite its peaceful mood) as a battleground, encoding period conflicts. The fit between the painting and this new context will depend on how the painting addresses these conflicts. Some indication of that may be discovered in the ideological cast of images and texts that the artist consulted (the same "data" on Indians, perhaps, already gathered by curator A). Other clues may come from the beliefs of a patron class, or from commentary in period literature, histories, and the popular press. Curator B will regard the design of the painting as an additional guide to its meaning. A close look at how the narrative is composed might tell him or her why in 1861 Leutze chose or was commissioned to paint such a picture.[5]

The Founding of Maryland, for example, shows the figures, including the Catholic priest, loosely arranged in a circle around Governor Calvert and the Indian chief, a form that promotes union among those who compose it— whites, Indians, men, women, lords, commoners, a priest, and soldiers. Touches of color feature and distinguish this union—whites, blacks, an occasional red, and the tawny skin of the Indians. But within the circle, it is already clear that some are more equal than others. The demure colonial wife, her head covered by a blue shawl, looks askance at the three bare-breasted Indian women, raising not only racial but gender issues. The women, like the food they deliver, are made to look tempting and available. Almost as revealing is the comparison between the priest, elegantly attired in a long, dark cassock, and the shaman, or medicine man, at lower left, in more "savage" dress than the other Indians. The priest stands, blessing the assembly; the shaman sits cross-legged on the ground, having been both literally and figuratively cast aside.

What is the value of these observations? Why are they more germane to 1861 than to the 1630s? The most obvious answers are that (1) the observations shed new light on both the painting and the past, and (2) the race, gender, and sectional issues raised are those of 1861, despite presentation on a colonial Maryland stage. For example, the painting clearly addresses and seeks to ameliorate Indian-white relations, not in Maryland, where they were no longer an issue, but probably in the West, where bitter disputes over white encroachment had begun years earlier. Other meanings emerge from the settlement theme, with the West, especially the border states, again serving as the arena. North-South rivalry in these states during the previous decade had brought about open warfare, which the painting tempers, perhaps in an effort to encourage further westward migration. No doubt *The Founding of Maryland* was also addressing local problems. With the nation on the brink of civil war, and the state already divided by sectional issues, one can read the circular arrangement of figures as an enthusiastic plea for union, possibly issued on behalf of an old Maryland elite, represented by Leonard Calvert. Whatever meaning one prefers, the idea of union (or Union, considering Leutze's political allegiance to the North) runs through all of them.[6] Leutze's make-believe world, a stable, prosperous, and homogeneous colonial Maryland, serves to advance that idea, to justify on the basis of an ideal past a resolution of current problems. And yet embodied in that ideal past are divisions that would shortly precipitate a genocidal war against Plains Indians and a civil war that would shake the nation to its foundations.

To believe that *The Founding of Maryland* signals problems in the pre-1861 past requires us to understand how it combines the aesthetic and the historical—how formal strategies evident in the painting, such as the circular arrangement of figures, lead one to speculate about historical meaning. The same kind of inquiry can also lead to an alternate way of judging the painting. If, for example, it seems to convey a forceful message about its own culture, does it then become richer and more intriguing as a work of art? At this point, curiously enough, the gap between curators A and B appears to narrow. Both want to evaluate the painting on its historical as well as aesthetic merits. But the gap quickly opens as they proceed with the task. Curator A will probably discount the formal structure of the painting as an aid to understanding it, concerned that he or she will overinterpret it. Curator B, however, takes for granted that formal strategies encode historical meaning—that they will help him or her understand the cultural politics of 1861.

Our dilemma, then, is that we have two different ways of interpreting *The Founding of Maryland* and no apparent way to resolve them. Why is the difference so pronounced? Partially, of course, because I have made it so—because I have invented a dialogue that somewhat arbitrarily places the two curators in opposing theoretical camps. The camps, in turn, require the curators to assess *The Founding of Maryland* in different ways. But whim was not in full control: A similar ideological gap does exist among curators, as well as museum audiences, although it has been exaggerated in this essay to address a more fundamental problem.

At issue is the nature of art-making and whether it is an active or passive process. Curator B would contend that in the same way I have invented a dialogue to present the issue, an artist invents a painting. This theory delegates to the artist considerable control over the process of selecting and editing a subject. What the picture will look like, therefore, depends ultimately on what the artist thinks is important about the subject. The artist's eye becomes a two-way lens, sending as well as receiving signals, imposing his or her thoughts (often unintentionally) on whatever is observed. Thus whatever the artist observes and transcribes is not a "reflection"—it cannot "capture" a moment or an event or a feeling, simply because the art-making process does not allow it. What sets the process in motion is an artist who "claims" a subject: A "real" landscape becomes a painting after an artist has made it conform to laws governing the production of art at a particular time—after imposing on it a language understandable to a certain group of viewers. But an active art maker is never a totally independent figure. He or she is part of a culture and therefore subject to its beliefs and values. Those are shared with a wide range of peers (as well as a more narrowly focused group of patrons), and the art produced is deeply involved in framing and defining issues that are of immediate concern to the art maker's peers and patrons.

For curator A, the artist has a somewhat different status. He or she is presumed to be more disengaged—to be an observer rather than an agent of a particular culture. In this passive guise the artist floats free of encumbering temporal issues, which makes it possible to see both past and present in an objective light, or at least as a continuum. Art produced by an observer, then, has a more constant or fixed meaning; it rejects the mundane political arena of the so-called active artist, emphasizing instead what is essential and enduring about a given subject. This brings us back to the Indians in *The Founding of Maryland*. Had they appeared in proper costume (or at least in a documented historical narrative), curator A would have had more reason to take the painting seriously. Seventeenth-century Indians portrayed accurately in the nineteenth century would still appear as relatively authentic figures today. And the painting, despite its imaginative construction, might then have a greater capacity to reveal historical truth.

These two ways of conceptualizing works of art have in recent years complicated the job of art museum curators. In "The West as America" comment books, viewers were divided along similar lines.[7] Some saw artists as activists and their art as symbolic representation—as images, in other words, in which the iconography of the Old West represented a progressive national narrative. This group was more likely to discount literal meaning, asking instead how works commented on the artist's own times. The other group saw artists as *reactive*, and therefore more objective, observers of historical events. This group tended to appraise works of art in terms of what they appeared to represent and to value art as an inspirational, transhistorical medium. In general, when art curators try to appeal to one group, they often fail to engage the other, and vice versa. One is constantly reminded of ships passing in the night, unable to communicate because they cannot read each other's signals.

This dilemma is brought into sharper focus when we investigate a painting called *The Promised Land* (1850; Figure 2.2), in which the gap between past and present has been greatly reduced, and a Currier and Ives print with the more straightforward title *The Way They Go to California* (1849; Figure 2.3). The print is introduced as an aid to understanding the painting: Although done only a year apart, the two works address westward migration in very different ways. The painting presents it as a family affair—a narrative celebrating journey's end as a sentimental, uplifting domestic event. The Currier and Ives print shifts the emphasis to the beginning of the journey, to a mass departure from New York harbor that is raucous and disorderly. As a description of "getting there," neither

Fig. 2.2. William S. Jewett, *The Promised Land,* 1850, oil on canvas, 50⅞ × 65 in. Daniel J. Terra Collection, 5.1994 ©1996. Courtesy of the Terra Museum of American Art, Chicago, Illinois.

image can be taken seriously: The painting looks too contrived and respectable—the family ought to be more disheveled after a trip of several months across the country, and the print humorously exaggerates the haste of forty-niners departing for California. Still, curator A might wish to interpret the painting as representing the guiding spirit of California migration, at the same time that the print describes its devolution into a mob scene. Or A may conclude that somewhere in between lies the real history—the record of how people felt and what actually happened.

Let us assume, however, that curator B remains committed to a contextual approach—that he or she wants to compare the two images to discover why the Graysons (the family in *The Promised Land*) wished to have themselves portrayed in such idealistic circumstances. Andrew Jackson Grayson (1818–1869), it turns out, was an authentic California pioneer. In the early spring of 1846, he and his family left St. Louis and traveled west, part of the way in a wagon train with

THE WAY THEY GO TO CALIFORNIA.

Fig. 2.3. Nathaniel Currier and James Ives, *The Way They Go to California,* 1849, hand-colored lithograph, 10¾ × 17¼ in. Collection of the Oakland Museum of California, The Oakland Museum Founders Fund.

members of the ill-fated Donner party.[8] Business ventures and a few good years in California real estate provided Grayson with enough capital to turn an interest in birds into a full-time career as an ornithologist and illustrator, for which he is well known today.

In 1850, apparently to acknowledge his good fortune in California, Grayson engaged William H. Jewett, a New York portrait painter who had succumbed to gold rush fever, to "re-create" the moment on the overland journey when he and his family first caught sight of the Sacramento valley. Probably with the Graysons' approval, Jewett embellished that moment, making the California landscape into a spacious, light-filled Promised Land, and the Grayson family into a Holy Family, complete with a child in an ermine-trimmed robe. Thus the Graysons' good fortune comes not only from their bountiful surroundings but from having been appointed God's emissaries. They are part of a crusade, the portrait implies, a civilizing process that will gently but firmly bestow on California the benefits of an Anglo-Protestant culture. So filled with a missionary spirit is the portrait that it all but erases the offstage events of the previous

37

four years—that is, since the arrival of the Graysons—during which California had undergone momentous changes. The Graysons had barely settled in the Sacramento valley when an American force, operating under dubious authority, seized Mexican territory in northern California, precipitating the Bear Flag revolt and the eventual takeover of California by the United States. Three years later, in 1849, the discovery of gold in the Sacramento area brought more than eighty thousand miners to northern California, along with radically different economic and social conditions.

To allude to such events in a family portrait would have been highly unusual. And yet their erasure—the representation in 1850 of the Sacramento valley as serene and untouched—has the ironic effect of calling them back to life, especially when one learns that Grayson was deeply involved in both events. Indeed, he became part of the Bear Flag revolt so soon after arriving in California that it seems likely he had heard of plans to overthrow the local Mexican government before leaving St. Louis.[9] One can argue, therefore, that Grayson's high ideals were in part self-serving—and that the portrait subtly masks issues of opportunism and conquest, thereby naturalizing the process by which the United States acquired California.

Clearly less subtle are the motives of those crowding on board the ship in the Currier and Ives print. They lust after gold—their sole ambition is to get to California first, no matter what the cost. As the ship leaves the dock, one desperate argonaut decides to swim for it, with his pick and shovel still over his shoulder. Others appropriate airships to race across the country. They are a greedy, sordid lot compared to the Grayson family, almost absurdly at the opposite end of the social and moral spectrum. But, curator B argues, we should resist seeing the Currier and Ives print and *The Promised Land* as flip sides of the same coin, one real, the other ideal. Nor should the two works be considered extremes, between which lies a mean or "balanced" view of history. What they have in common is that *both* provide important views of westward migration. History, in this case, is revealed in the different ways in which a privately commissioned painting and a popular print make their arguments—and in how those arguments link the two images to their respective audiences.

The Graysons, for example, are above it all. Their dress and manners, as well as their "elevated" position, mark them as upper-class immigrants. They have come to California to civilize and refine it, to plant the seeds of Christian virtue in its rich soil. The gold rush crowd, on the other hand, consists of "common" people, whose objective is to exploit the land and to get rich quickly. Class differences were tied to regional issues.[10] The Graysons and Jewett had recently settled in California; their task was to justify their new existence, to make California as appealing and respectable in its own way as their previous homes were. (When *The Promised Land* was exhibited in San Francisco in 1857, it was said to represent "the high idea of the progress of civilization westward.") The Currier and Ives print, in turn, was the product of an Eastern establishment that wished to poke fun at the West. Therefore, it played to an Eastern audience—a conservative middle class that preferred to see itself a step above those who went off on get-rich-quick schemes. But this attitude may have masked other concerns of those who enjoyed Currier and Ives prints. Easterners were in fact deeply ambivalent about the West during those years, seeing it alternately as a haven for rustics and independents and as a nouveau East, with growing economic and vastly greater natural resources. The resources, of course, brought Easterners around to dealing with the West, but the former image never quite disappeared. So popular prints that ridiculed the West (or those drawn to it) made the process more palatable for Easterners. They could maintain their superiority—as well as their distance from questionable development schemes—even when their motives for exploiting the West were only marginally different from those of the forty-niners.

While our two curators have been debating the meaning of *The Promised Land,* museum visitors have been making similar distinctions. The art-as-observation group, for example, surely feels that an inspiring view of California migration has been unfairly tarnished. And curator A, after listening to B's lengthy analysis, will probably agree—claiming that such analysis is unsupported by information from the artist, by direct commentary from other period sources, or from what can actually be seen in the portrait. That, of course, will prolong the exchange. Curator B will reply, a bit peevishly, that knowing the audience for the portrait helps to determine its social use. And further, that the class and regional issues addressed in the portrait are sharpened when juxtaposed to those of the print. But visual comparisons, while helpful, are only part of the story that curator B needs to tell the public. *The Promised Land* must also be accompanied by extended written analysis. So curators espousing B's methods are now relying on gallery texts, more heavily than ever before, to get their message across. But that raises additional concerns: How should such commentaries be written so as not to put off those who are less persuaded by B's methods? And how can curators write labels that thoughtfully balance the aesthetic and the historical? Too little regard for the ways in which aesthetic strategies nuance historical arguments will flatten a work of art, causing it to be seen as a form of propaganda. On the other hand, too narrow an appraisal of a work's aesthetic merit—why *today* it is considered exceptional—will remove it from a useful historical context. And finally, gallery commentaries that are too numerous and too long will simply remain unread.

A close analysis of the title painting for this essay, *Morning of a New Day* (1907; Figure 2.4), by Cincinnati artist Henry Farny, raises further questions about how to exhibit historical works. At first glance, the painting seems easy enough to understand: It says, in effect, that the West (or the imposing, sparsely inhabited mountain landscape that represents an actual West) is changing. A New West, symbolized by the railroad train cutting across the landscape, is replacing an Old West, spelling hardship and eventual doom for the Indian tribes that inhabit the region. But by 1907, the date of the painting, not much of the Old West remained. And what had caused it to disappear (or at least caused Indians to retreat to reservations) was a series of events considerably more brutal than the nostalgic encounter that Farny depicts. Why then did Farny paint such a picture in 1907? And should it be seen as a gentle critique of progress, more sympathetic to the Indians than to technological change? Taking the second question first, curator B will, on the basis of two important facts, quickly challenge such a reading. The painting was commissioned or at one time owned by Melville Ezra Ingalls, president of the Chesapeake and Ohio, the third-largest railroad in the United States in 1907.[11] And, like the Leutze and Jewett paintings, *Morning of a New Day* refers to an earlier historical moment, playing that moment against the 1907 present. Our clue to understanding that scenario, curator B argues, is how Farny constructed the scene. Although not immediately apparent to our eye, the engine pushing flatcars through the mountain pass is old-fashioned for 1907. But viewers in Farny's time (like Ingalls) would undoubtedly have recognized it as a type of engine in use during the late 1860s, when the Union and the Central Pacific Railroads were laying track through such mountainous regions. In fact, the arrangement of engine and cars is that of a work train, which laid and tested new track along previously graded roadbeds.

Having established this historical setting, Farny then departs from it. In the late 1860s, Plains Indians (which those in the picture appear to be) were attacking railroad-building parties and tearing up track at numerous points along the line. Farny's Indians are not those disciplined warriors but their weary descendants, trudging through deep snow toward an uncertain destination. From their high, isolated position in the picture, they observe the train, cutting through the landscape on an almost level roadbed. The diminished size of the train only seems to make more efficient its passage through the landscape, toward the band of light that slants across the long diagonal hillside. Other diagonal lines crossing the landscape converge on the pass through which the tracks disappear.

The Indians proceed in the opposite direction, uphill and into deeper shadows, a forecast, one presumes, of their coming extinction. Thus they become the losers in an unequal contest, evoking the viewer's sympathy. But the picture

Fig. 2.4. Henry Farny, *Morning of a New Day*, 1907, oil on canvas, 22 × 32 in. National Cowboy Hall of Fame and Western Heritage Center, Oklahoma City.

also *sentimentalizes* that contest, making the Indians' defeat seem like a sad but inevitable consequence of history. No one can help them; they have simply become marginal to what Farny and his patrons would have called progress. The train, slicing through the mountains, gave pictorial form to their conception of progress. But, more to the point, the train challenges the Indians on their own terrain, suggesting that they, ill-equipped and raggedly dispersed along the trail, are unable to compete with white technology. By these standards, the Indians' retreat from progress—or civilization—is made to seem even more poignant, and yet more specifically a consequence of their failure to understand and adopt civilized ways.

Why were such paintings done so long after the fact? Perhaps because Farny was attempting to comment on the precarious state of Indians in 1907, when reservation life was at its lowest ebb and many thought that Indians were doomed. But surely the picture also elicits nostalgia for an Old West, not the proverbial wagon-train West but a railroad-building West, which had mostly vanished by 1907. By that time, passengers who could afford it crossed the great western divides in the comfort of Pullman cars. Those very cars, however, may have made them more concerned about losing touch with the past. *Morning of a*

New Day suggested a time when moving west seemed to involve more risk, more challenge, a more intense experience than was available through the windows of a Pullman car. And that perhaps was why Ingalls acquired the painting. It re-created for him the kind of Old West he thought he was missing.

At the same time, Ingalls was deeply committed to his own industrial age, to maintaining a prosperous lifestyle, and, after his retirement in 1905, to a host of civic duties. His postretirement quarters were probably high up in the Ingalls Building, a sixteen-story Cincinnati landmark named for him by admiring city fathers. No doubt his hard-driving style was only moderately checked in retirement. Indeed, one can imagine him in his new quarters—his air of authority complemented by an expensive cigar and a mahogany desk the size of a small freight car—advising the civic and cultural elite of Cincinnati that they ought to run their organizations more like railroads. In quieter moments, however, Ingalls liked to turn to the wall beside his desk on which he had hung *Morning of a New Day*. After gazing at the painting for a moment or two, he would swivel toward a large window in the opposite wall, through which he could watch sleek new passenger trains entering and leaving the C&O yards in Cincinnati. This unique vantage point perhaps gave him a new perspective on his railroad career, which had begun in Cincinnati in 1870 (a year after the completion of the transcontinental railroad). Farny's picture, in which the gutsy little work train makes clear why Indians had become marginal to a New West, captured perfectly the way Ingalls wished to remember the early days of railroading. And when he turned to look through the windows, the work train suddenly metamorphosed into its successor, a deluxe modern passenger train. Within his office, then, Ingalls could construct a career tied to this seemingly untroubled span of progress—his gaze literally swept over the massive social problems created by each new phase of railroad building. In the world beyond Ingalls's office, however, these problems were more evident. When modern passenger trains encountered "modern" Indians, as they did in other Farny paintings (Figure 2.5), the results were deeply disturbing.

At this point curator A and his followers are contemplating a quick exit from the galleries, not because they lack sympathy for the problems that Indians faced in those years but as a protest against curator B's methods. B's effort to explain Ingalls's fascination with *Morning of a New Day*, A maintains, is pure theater. And, indeed, much of it is—or, if not quite "pure," then another "artistic" invention. But three solid facts sustain the effort: Ingalls was president of the C&O from 1888 to 1899 (and then chairman until 1905); he did at one point own the painting; and an imposing Ingalls Building, completed in 1904, does occupy a prominent corner in downtown Cincinnati.[12] To get beyond those facts, to un-

Fig. 2.5. Henry Farny, *A Dance of Crow Indians*, after 1883, black and white gouache on paperboard, 13¹⁵⁄₁₆ × 19⅞ in. Cincinnati Art Museum; Gift of Charles Dabney Thomson.

derstand Ingalls's response to the painting, does take a bit of theater—or at least imagining how the painting might have functioned as a part of turn-of-the-century railroad culture. So, despite alienating curator A, B should perhaps get credit for confronting the problem of why in 1907 a subject that combined Indians and western railroad building raised important issues for both Farny and Ingalls. He or she has also tried to show how these issues become part of the design of the picture—how, for example, the arrangement of Indians in the landscape indirectly represents the attitudes of Farny and Ingalls toward Indians in 1907. Thoughtfully and patiently carried out, this method can offer viewers an understanding of how the aesthetic and the historical are imaginatively linked in a work of art (which, in turn, further undercuts two of curator A's favorite assumptions: A work can provide a truthful account of the past, and its meaning will remain the same for future generations). But the method is, unfortunately, antithetical to brevity. The more elaborately the interpretive stage is set, the more meaning a work of art will yield. But sooner or later strategies for constructing these meanings will surpass the tolerance of even those viewers sympathetic to curator B's methods. Raised on the assumption that works of art don't require so much explaining, and that gallery texts should be nonexistent or brief, they will be apprehensive about the number and length of texts that have appeared in recent exhibitions. And some will find an even more compelling reason to object: The new texts may subject them to an account of history that they find offensive and that they believe is demeaning to the work or works under consideration.

Curator B, therefore, faces a long uphill battle. For the past half century museums have taught visitors that most works of art (especially those done before the era of modernism) were only distantly affected by social and political issues. The lesson, moreover, was backed up by what visitors thought they could see for themselves. Most works *did* appear to be unaffected, to disregard everyday life in favor of expressing what was profound and lasting about the human spirit. Now curator B wants to bring art museum visitors back to earth, to make them believe that works have more-limited meanings and that these meanings change over time. The last is perhaps the most disturbing message of all. To assume a work of art has no fixed meaning is anathema to those who believe that culture must reside on firm, unchanging values. All arguments to the contrary, including those of curator B, they construe as risking a historical continuum. To overcome this concern, B will have to be very persuasive, well informed, and extremely patient—and, when all else fails, ready to leave town at a moment's notice.

NOTES

1. Thanks to Roger Stein and Alan Wallach for helpful comments on earlier versions of this essay.

2. Blessing the treaty is Father Andrew White, a Jesuit missionary who accompanied the first settlers to Maryland. Sir George Calvert, first Lord Baltimore and an English Catholic, had conceived of the colony as a commercial venture. But he also wished Maryland to serve as a haven for other Catholics, like Father White, who had been systematically discriminated against back home. Sir George died a few years after an exploratory voyage to Virginia in 1629, and his eldest son, Cecilius, took over the project. Under the command of Cecilius's younger brother, Leonard, two ships, the *Ark* and the *Dove,* carrying about three hundred people, set off to found the colony. They landed on a small island in the lower Chesapeake in March 1634 and then moved up the shore of the Potomac to establish St. Mary's, their first permanent settlement.

3. The pipe lying on the ground before the seated Indian at lower left; the headdress, shield, and spear of the Indian at the center of the picture; the beaded dress worn by the female Indian at right center; and the basket (or hoop) held by the female Indian at lower right all look like Plains artifacts. Generous advice on what Indian material appears to be authentic and what does not came from William Sturtevant.

4. See Thomas Scharf's *History of Maryland from Earliest Times to the Present Day* (1879; reprint, Hatboro, Pa.: Tradition Press, 1967), which describes a mass conducted by Father White in 1634, just after the colonists landed, and subsequent visits by Leonard Calvert to local tribes. A "romantic novel" about the "old colony," cited in Henry T. Tuckerman's *Book of the Artists* (1867; reprint, New York: James F. Carr, 1966), may have provided Leutze with descriptions of life in colonial Maryland. A trip to the lower reaches of the Potomac, presumably in the summer of 1860, also helped Leutze imagine the scene. See Barbara Groseclose, *Emanuel Leutze, 1816–1868: Freedom Is the Only King* (Washington, D.C.: Smithsonian Institution Press, 1975), pp. 57–58.

5. The provenance for the painting is incomplete. When exhibited at the Pennsylvania Academy of the Fine Arts in 1863, it was owned by C. M. Connelly of New York. The same Mr. Connelly, apparently, placed it on deposit at the Maryland Historical Society, where it has remained, at the turn of the century. But whether Connelly was the original owner of the painting or, indeed, who he was and what the subject would have meant to him, is at present unknown.

6. The Capitol mural, *Westward the Course of Empire Takes Its Way*, for which Leutze was sketching ideas in 1860, indicates how immersed he was at the time in national expansion issues. That some of these found their way into the Maryland picture should not be surprising. Leutze's views on expansion, none too subtly revealed in *Westward the Course of Empire*, were unequivocally pro-North and anti-Indian. See Vivien Green Fryd, *Art and Empire: The Politics of Ethnicity in the United States Capitol* (New Haven: Yale University Press, 1992), pp. 211–12. See also Leutze's correspondence with Montgomery Meigs, who became supervisor of the Capitol extension program in 1853, and comments by other friends of the artist in Raymond L. Stehle, "The Life and Work of Emanuel Leutze," unpublished manuscript (National Museum of American Art/ National Portrait Gallery Library, 1972), pp. 70, 72, 108–9.

7. Two examples from the comment books, representative of this division, follow. "The paintings are truly interpretive," wrote one viewer, "and without the commentary and discussion that was included alongside the paintings, visitors would not necessarily consider all sides of the westward expansion." This general approach was countered by another, affirming the vision of a heroic West. "I always thought painting was supposed to be about hopes, dreams, the imagination," a second viewer remarked. "Instead, you seem to say it's political statement at every brushstroke. Your tendentious opinions betray a . . . blindness to the paintings themselves . . . [and to what they say] about the appeal of the West to our collective imagination. Art is bigger than everyday logic."

8. Much of my reading of *The Promised Land* is drawn from Patricia Hills, "Picturing Progress in the Era of Westward Expansion," in *The West as America: Reinterpreting Images of the Frontier, 1820–1920*, ed. William H. Truettner (Washington, D.C.: Smithsonian Institution Press, 1991), pp. 97–100.

9. A behind-the-scenes diplomatic initiative, whose aim was to persuade native Californians that they would be better off under United States rule, had in fact been going on since 1845. The Mexican War began in May 1846, a month before the Bear Flag revolt, but California was not fully subdued until January 1847, when General Stephen W. Kearny defeated a Mexican army at Los Angeles. See Frederick Merk, *History of the Westward Movement* (New York: Alfred A. Knopf, 1978), pp. 356–58. Grayson had

begun recruiting troops for the Bear Flag revolt soon after settling in the Sacramento valley. When the gold rush came, he opened stores in both San Francisco and Stockton, profiting handsomely from the sale of supplies to miners. In time, however, the miners grew too numerous and rowdy, so Grayson joined a San Francisco vigilante group dedicated to keeping them off the streets and under control. See Joseph Kastner, "When Everything Became 'Too Tame in His Native Land,'" *Smithsonian* 19 (May 1988): 146–55; and Kevin Starr, "Grayson's Gift," *California Magazine,* December 1986, pp. 98–100, 112.

10. For helpful investigations of regional perspectives in western art, see Elizabeth Johns, "Settlement and Development: Claiming the West," in Truettner, *The West as America,* pp. 191–92, 201–6; and Angela Miller, "The Mechanisms of the Market and the Invention of Western Realism: The Example of George Caleb Bingham," in *American Iconology,* ed. David C. Miller (New Haven: Yale University Press, 1993), pp. 112–14, 121–23.

11. See J. F. Earhart, "Henry Farny, the Artist and the Man," *Cincinnati Commercial Tribune,* January 21, 1917. *Morning of a New Day,* credited to Mrs. E. M. Ingalls, is reproduced on page 1 of the magazine section. Her husband must have acquired the painting between 1907 and 1914, the year he died. Alex Nemerov kindly provided this reference.

12. Robert L. Fey, ed., *Railroads in the Nineteenth Century,* in the series Encyclopedia of American Business History and Biography (New York: Bruccoli Clark Layman/ Facts on File, 1982), pp. 196–99.

3

The Hope Diamond

Gem, Jewel, and Icon

RICHARD KURIN

The Hope Diamond
45.52 carats
The world's largest deep blue diamond.
Gift of Harry Winston, Inc. 1958.

—Hope Diamond label in the National
Museum of Natural History, 1995

The Hope Diamond is the largest and most beautiful diamond in the world. It is also the most famous. Its fame comes from the terrible luck it seems to bring to those who have it in their possession. Louis XVI and Marie Antoinette owned the famous diamond when the French Revolution began—and they were beheaded. A Russian prince loaned the diamond to a dancer who was wearing it when the prince shot her in a jealous rage. The prince was later stabbed to death. The diamond changed hands many times and with each owner its frightening reputation grew. When a wealthy American woman bought the Hope Diamond in 1910, she believed that bad-luck objects were lucky for her. But her life soon turned tragic and at the time of her death the legendary diamond was sold to pay off her debts. Today, the Hope Diamond is displayed at the Smithsonian Institute [sic] in Washington, DC where it attracts more visitors than any other gemstone. It also brings letters and calls from people who are afraid the diamond will bring bad luck to our country. What do you think? Would you want to own the Hope Diamond?

—Janet Hubbard Brown,
History Mystery: The Curse of the Hope Diamond

The Hope Diamond is one of the most well known of the Smithsonian Institution's holdings.[1] Interestingly enough, it is out of place, in the wrong collection, in the wrong museum. Hanging on a necklace, labeled with a simple caption, it has been sadly displayed and poorly interpreted since it arrived at the National Museum of Natural History in 1958. After almost four decades it will be redisplayed in a new, much improved Gem Hall to be opened in late 1996. And while Hope Diamond curator Jeffrey Post would insist otherwise, a better case could be made for its inclusion in the jewelry collections of the Smithsonian's Cooper Hewitt National Museum of Design in New York. A generation ago, the most logical place to display the Hope Diamond would have been at the Smithsonian's Festival of American Folklife, for it is as an object of folklore that the diamond has been most significant. But alas, given the diamond's current iconic place in American museum culture, perhaps the National Museum of American History has the best case for its acquisition.

THE HOPE DIAMOND AS GEM

The Hope Diamond, like every other naturally formed diamond, is made of carbon that has been crystallized as a result of immense volcanic pressures below the earth's surface for millions of years. Diamond is unique as a gemstone: it is the only one composed of a single chemical element. The crystalline structure forms around planes of carbon molecules and most commonly takes octahedron or rhombic dodecahedron shapes, though sometimes it forms cubes or even rough spherical shapes.

Unless the crystals are twinned, diamonds can be perfectly cleaved. The molecular structure makes the diamond the hardest mineral known (Mohs scale 10) and also impervious to heat below 2,700 degrees Fahrenheit. While "pure" diamonds are clear, or slightly bluish, diamonds may also be found tinted in a range of colors, from yellows and browns to the more common green and black, to the very rare pink, deep blue, red, and violet. Diamonds have an extraordinary capability to reflect, refract (refractive index 2.417), and disperse (index of 0.058) light. The realization of these properties depends upon the gem's quality—its color, flaws, and natural shape—as well as the way in which it is cleaved, polished, and cut.

From diamonds geologists gain information about the conditions in the earth's upper layers with regard to carbon composition and volcanic and seismic activity. Diamonds are formed below the surface, trapped in molten lava and forced upward through volcanic eruptions. To date, most of the world's diamonds have been found in India, Brazil, South Africa, and Russia. In India, where they have been known since about 800 B.C. diamonds have historically been found in alluvial soils. In South Africa, volcanic activity forced diamonds into subterranean "escape valves," out of which they must be mined. In a sense, a diamond is a chunk of biopsied earth that tells a dramatic story.

Contrary to sensationalized accounts of its fame or notoriety, the Hope Diamond is not the world's largest diamond. That distinction goes to the Cullinan diamond, found in South Africa and weighing 3,024.75 carats in its uncut state, and 530.20 carats cut and faceted—about twelve times larger than the Hope Diamond. There are many other diamonds larger than the Hope Diamond. And there is nothing particularly significant about the Hope Diamond that tells us more about the geology of the earth than most other diamonds do. The Hope Diamond is not in its natural state—it has been cut into a shape and placed in a necklace setting. Even in its unnatural state, it is still the largest deep-blue diamond known,[2] which makes it a curio—but is hardly sufficient reason for it to be the center of a scientific gem collection in the National Museum of Natural History.

THE HOPE DIAMOND AS JEWEL

The Hope Diamond is a piece of jewelry, as most viewers will certainly testify. It is currently set in a necklace surrounded by sixteen white diamonds and suspended from a platinum chain bearing an additional forty-six white diamonds. As jewelry, the Hope Diamond shares in a history common to many other diamonds.

Until the eighteenth century, diamonds were found and mined in India. Early Indian texts suggest several uses for diamonds, which were valued for their hardness, strength, and ability to contain light. Utilitarian swords were supposedly fashioned with diamond splinters to make for harder cutting edges. Diamonds were sometimes used to decorate temples and thrones or to serve as the eyes of divine statues. Indian rajahs and later the great Mughal emperors wore the gems as part of their royal costumes, set into turbans, necklaces, and brooches.

Gemstones in India were rubbed, ground, and polished. Cutting, when it occurred, was done mainly around the natural contours of the stone to preserve size and remove flaws. Simple cutting, grinding, and cleaving would produce cabochons, with relatively unsymmetrical and irregular planes around the bulk of the gem mass. Diamonds in India were sometimes cleaved, but they were not cut, ground, or faceted until the technology was transferred from Europe after the fifteenth century.

Diamonds were known to the Greeks and Romans. The expeditions of

Fig. 3.1. The Hope Diamond in its current jewelry setting. Dane A. Penland, Smithsonian Institution. ©1992.

Alexander the Great stimulated trade between India and the Mediterranean and brought more precious gems—emeralds, sapphires and diamonds, and pearls—to Europe. Familiar stones like lapis lazuli and turquoise could be polished, and other colored gems and pearls could be worked to show off their beauty, but diamonds resisted such attempts. Diamonds were generally mounted as natural or cleaved crystals—valued primarily for their hardness and strength, not their appearance.[3] Indeed, the term diamond is itself derived from the Greek *adamas,* meaning "untamable," and connoting "unconquerable," "unyielding," "resistant." Cognates include such words as adamant, dominant, and dame. In his Natural History, Pliny opines that the diamond has the greatest value among the objects of human property and is known only to kings and even to very few of these—presumably as a sign of their strength and indestructibility.

Romans mounted natural diamonds on finger rings. The tradition of mounting natural gemstones on finger rings continued among the papacy and church in medieval Europe as emblems of investiture and office. In 1194, Pope Innocent III issued specific instructions on the characteristics of such rings, including the importance of mounting uncut gemstones.

The Renaissance saw the translation of key works of antiquity, including Euclid's geometry and optics. Interest in the refraction and reflection of light affected painting, sculpture, and the arts in general. Leading figures turned their attention to mathematical studies of the movement of light, magnification, and the effects of angles, convexity, and concavity on the reflection, refraction, and dispersal of light. The new optics animated lens making, grinding, and the development of eyeglasses.

This knowledge was applied to diamond faceting. Diamond cutters in France were learning how to cut diamonds mathematically, in a regular, predictable way, in order to admit and reflect the maximum amount of light. The turning point in the development of diamond jewelry occurred in the early fifteenth century with the discovery of the technique of using another diamond to cut a gemstone and the use of diamond dust (with olive oil as lubricant) on a grindstone to help shape it.

Flemish paintings of that time depict Philip the Good, Duke of Burgundy, possessed of table-cut stones with flat, polished faces beveled by oblique facets, likely cut by his jeweler John De Leeuw. Transplanted Venetian Louis de Berquem was famous for cutting and grinding diamonds for French king Charles VII and later established a long-standing tradition of Jewish diamond work in Antwerp. De Berquem is reputed to have cut such famous diamonds as the Florentine (133.20 carats) and the Sancy (53.75 carats). With de Berquem's faceting and polishing techniques, diamonds were able to reflect about 30 percent of the light reaching their surface.

In the early sixteenth century, cutters under Cardinal Mazarin in Paris developed new forms of diamond cutting, among them the rosette and the single cut, which exposed the ability of the diamond to reflect inner light and to refract or bend light off its faceted surfaces. By 1690, Vincent Peruzzi in Venice developed the brilliant cut, which has become the most popular known today. The brilliant cut took full advantage of the octahedron crystal shape and involved the striking of fifty-eight facets. An upper table cut allowed light to pass into the lower reaches of the diamond and be reflected and refracted off the angular surfaces—so as to give the gem "fire"—a term for the sparkling brilliance of diamonds. Though the technique maximized the movement of light through the gem, it dramatically reduced the weight of the raw diamond, often by half.

European buyers tended to value brilliant cuts that "opened up the diamond" to release more light. Indian buyers, when exposed to European techniques, placed greater value on shallower cuts that retained more weight.[4] Many Indian diamonds were recut into new forms once they passed into the possession of western owners. Such reworking makes firm identification of particular stones more difficult.

Fig. 3.2. The brilliant
diamond cut, from top and
side views. Illustrated by
Joan Wolvier.

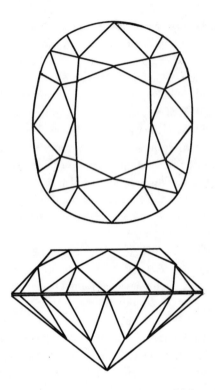

The round brilliant cut became increasingly standardized in the late 1800s
with the perfection of facets—thirty-three facets above the girdle (or lateral
midsection) and twenty-five below. To reflect maximum light, 29 percent of the
diamond should be between the girdle and the upper table cut, 71 percent below the girdle to the lower cutlet. Improvements to Peruzzi's technique have
enhanced the dispersal of light entering the diamond, i.e., the separation of light
into its colors. If the stone is too thick, it will appear "dark" or "sleepy" at the
center. Shallow stones are termed "fish-eyed" because the brilliancy surrounds
a black and empty center.[5]

The diamond that likely became the Hope Diamond was brought from India
to France by Jean Baptiste Tavernier, who visited Asia six times in the mid-
1600s. Tavernier traded pearls, bronze, gemstones, pistols, and other valuables
and sold his acquired treasures back in Europe. He knew a great deal about diamonds—about flaws, cleaving, and other lapidary techniques. He bought diamonds from the Mughals, including a deep-blue one weighing 112.19 carats.

Tavernier sold this diamond and others to Louis XIV, the French Sun King, in 1668. This diamond was cut, or recut, in a triangular shape in 1673 to a diamond weighing 67.50 carats and called the French Blue. Louis XV had the stone set in a piece of jeweled regalia known as the Royal Order of the Golden Fleece.[6] It does appear in a 1791 inventory of the French crown jewels, but it was stolen with other jewels in 1792 in the midst of the French Revolution.

It is thought that the diamond came into the collections of the English Crown in the early 1800s. It was likely recut into three portions, the largest of them a brilliant-cut oval-shaped 45.52-carat diamond eventually bought by English collector Henry Philip Hope in 1830 for £18,000. Today the Hope Diamond still retains this form and carries this collector's name.

Over time, diamonds as gems have been used in a variety of ways. Before the technique of faceting was developed, kings wore diamonds as symbols of power, signifying strength and permanence. The diamonds cut by de Berquem in fifteenth-century France reflected not only technical innovation but also a new social purpose for their use.

In the early 1400s, France was in the midst of change, with the campaign of Jeanne d'Arc, the retreat of the British from Normandy, and the reestablishment of Paris as a political and cultural capital. A key figure at this time was Jacques Coeur, a wealthy international trader, financier, and minter, who became chief financial adviser to Charles VII and a friend and patron of the king's mistress, Agnes Sorel. Through Coeur's trading, Parisians had access to luxury goods from the world over—linens, sables, pearls, ostrich feathers, coral, incense, tea, spices, dyes, and gems—including diamonds from India. Coeur was Louis de Berquem's protector and patron. With the jeweler's newfound ability to cut, and thus redesign, diamonds as eye-pleasing jewelry, Coeur sought to use diamonds for female ornamentation. According to Joan Younger Dickinson, Coeur "made Agnes Sorel his mannequin. Upon her lovely neck, he placed the first diamond necklace ever made; upon her bodice were pinned gold brooches set with diamonds; and the sash of her gown was held with a diamond belt buckle. . . . She became a showcase of jewels."[7]

Sorel became known as the Dame de Beaute, and Paris became a fashion center. A commoner who saw herself as following in the mission of Jeanne d'Arc, Sorel helped motivate the liberation of France and gave the king four daughters; her diamonds became part of the royal jewels of France after her death (which was falsely attributed to Coeur).

While Coeur and Sorel pioneered the use of diamond jewelry for the purpose of female ornamentation, diamonds were well beyond the reach of most Europeans. During the sixteenth to the nineteenth centuries, faceted diamonds came to decorate many of Europe's crown jewels in France, England, Russia,

Fig. 3.3. The French Blue
set in the Golden Fleece.
Courtesy Cooper Hewitt
Museum.

LA TOISON D'OR (FACE)

and the Austro-Hungarian Empire. Diamonds represented the wealth of monarchs and royalty, and as such, the wealth of their nations. They thus decorated the symbols of royalty—crowns, maces, thrones. And while diamonds were worn by queens, they were worn just as often by kings.

It was not until the late 1800s, when diamonds were discovered in South Africa, that the gems became available to a wider clientele. Men of means who occupied positions in high society increasingly acquired diamonds and other jewels, set in necklaces, brooches, and rings, to decorate women. In the late 1800s the Hope Diamond was set in a woman's necklace and used as part of a decorative motif that adorned the bodies of matronly women with conspicuous, even ostentatious wealth.

After being sold from the Hope family estate and changing hands several times between 1902 and 1910, the Hope Diamond came into the possession of the jeweler Pierre Cartier. He reset the diamond in a newly designed necklace and sold it in 1911 to Evalyn Walsh McLean of Washington, D.C. Some of Cartier's necklace designs of the time feature new and interesting filigree patterns, with a lightness and playfulness of form. Indeed, the designs of the early nineteenth century mirror the new, sleeker women of society, like McLean herself—women of greater independence, influenced by the suffrage, self-help, and self-discovery movements of the day, women who were more likely to decorate themselves than to be decorated by others.

Given its brilliant cut and its setting, the Hope Diamond could conceivably be legitimately placed in the collections of the Cooper Hewitt Museum as an example of designed jewelry. But the diamond's cut is neither original nor unique. Nor does the jewelry setting represent an extraordinary example of a particular type of design. And while it does participate in the general history of ornamentation, the Hope Diamond has played no special role in defining or redefining the design function of jewelry. Indeed, as the museum's respected former chief curator David McFadden admitted in a considered moment of curatorial candor, if presented with the possibility of acquiring the Hope Diamond now, he would likely reject it as not being up to the Smithsonian's standards!

THE HOPE DIAMOND AS A CULTURAL OBJECT

Objects—all objects that we know—are not merely creations of nature. They are invested with meanings made by humans. Sometimes these meanings are related to the physical attributes of the object, but often they are removed from such characteristics. We cannot find the stories that make the diamond part of human history under the microscope, for peer as we might, we will never glimpse meaning or social interactions in the diamond's molecular structure. Rather, we have ideas, fragments, and stories, factual and fictional, that reveal how diamonds have been conceived over space and time.

In Indian mythic texts, the diamond is known as *vajra,* the same term as that for the divine and powerful thunderbolt. In the Buddhist exegetical text *Questions of King Milinda,* the diamond is used as a metaphor for instructing initiates. Priests should be as pure in their livelihood as is a diamond, they should be as unalloyed as a diamond and not mix with wicked men.[8] Indian epics are also rich in descriptions of bejeweled cities, palaces, temples, and people, in which diamonds are mentioned along with other precious gems. Legends of quests into Indian diamond pits or valleys have long been known in the West. One legend has Alexander the Great venturing into a diamond pit, defeating serpents and recovering diamonds by cleverly employing slain sheep carcasses and vultures.[9] Pliny wrote that diamonds would melt in goat's blood, neutralize poison if eaten, dispel insanity if worn, and drive away worry.[10] Others in Roman times and throughout Europe's Middle Ages used gems as charm stones for rings and talismans. The idea was that such gems would either protect or impart their favorable characteristics to the wearer. Diamonds were also thought to aid women in childbirth and give strength to kings in battle. In medieval Europe, and in India, diamond dust was regarded as a poison.[11]

Another folk belief in Europe and the British Isles was that the diamond could signal and even foster the attraction of a man to his beloved. Queen Fastrada supposedly exhibited a compelling attraction to Charles the Great, even after her death, through a diamond.[12] And in an old English ballad collected by folklorist Francis Child, Hind Horn is given diamonds by Maid Rimnild, his beloved princess. He travels far to escape the wrath of her father, the king. But when he looks at the ring and sees "the diamond pale and wan," he knows he must return home to reclaim his beloved before she marries another, the implication being that as love fades so too does the luster of the diamond.[13]

Some of these "folk beliefs" have their own logic, whether factual or metaphorical. Others seem more arbitrary, and some may acquire an ex post facto rationale; for example, several commentators have explained the notion that ingested diamonds are poisonous as a ploy used by mine overseers to discourage workers from swallowing diamonds in an effort to steal them.

While the Hope Diamond shares some characteristics of the general category "diamond," just as the Wright Flyer shares some characteristics with other airplanes and the Star-Spangled Banner with other flags, it has acquired its own special importance. Construed ideas about it, what it stands for, what is historically significant about it have been articulated into stories—narratives about the object, biographies of sorts. As its curator, Jeffrey Post, profoundly says, "There is human history attached to the Hope Diamond." Human history is attached to objects through stories that become part of their identity and power. Stories about the Hope Diamond are rich and abundant and provide the basis of a current, contemporary, thoroughly modern folklore.

THE HOPE DIAMOND IN MODERN FOLKLORE

The Hope Diamond is an icon. An icon is not just an arbitrary symbol that stands for what is signified. An icon resembles, or in the root form re-assembles, that which is represented. Its status is thought to be beyond regular human making or control—that is, its condition is generally attributed to extraordinary natural, supernatural, divine, or superhuman circumstances.

For example, in India, a statue of Durga or Krishna is not just a statue made of metal that merely looks like the god or goddess. Rather, to be an icon the statue must be capable of being possessed—receiving or sharing in the actual stuff of the god or goddess. An icon is an image or likeness that is thought to have a substantial—as opposed to an arbitrary—relation to its referent. Hence when a devotee ingests yogurt or water that has been poured over the statue, he or she ingests the biomoral substance of the god dissolved therein, thus becoming more Durga-like or Krishna-like. Such acts are pretty common throughout the world in rituals surrounding sacred icons. The closer believers are to the icon, the more they participate with or engage it and the more they are touched by its power—which may be transformative. Muslim devotees of Sufis eat the flowers and may drink the bath water and even eat dirt from the graves of saints in order to partake literally of *barkat* or blessedness, conceived of as a kind of spiritual substance. In the Christian world, one finds special power attached to the remains of saints, and the sacraments of mass. African, Native American, Oceanic religious thought and ritual are full of such practices.

Stories about the Hope Diamond engender a logic like that of the sacred icon. The Hope Diamond has become an icon in that it is thought to be endowed with power, it is animated, it has *mana*. Some might view this power as the mysterious power of a curse; to others it is the power to draw a crowd. As an icon, the diamond affects those closest to it; some of it rubs off on them. Witness, for example, the Postal Museum's holding on to the packaging in which the gem was sent through the mail to the Smithsonian in 1958.

But of what is the Hope Diamond an icon? The supernatural? Regal splendor? Wealth? Love? Nature? Fame? The iconicity of the Hope Diamond is part of a history of values in society over the past two centuries. How the Hope Diamond is understood and valued reveals complex transformations and changing conceptual screens through which it is viewed.

Its initial earlier owners included several kings who possessed the Hope Diamond as part of their royal treasures. Diamonds, as crown jewels, indicate wealth and royal splendor. But kingship, among the Mughals and most certainly in France and England, was a troubled institution by the late eighteenth and early nineteenth centuries. The ability of kings to hold on to their wealth was challenged by upheavals in the monarchal order. Revolutions challenged the legitimacy of kingship. Several famed diamonds—the Moon of the Mountains, the Koh-i-Nur, the Regent, the Pigott—disappeared, only to emerge later with new owners. Some were supposedly lost in battle; others were stolen or sold without fanfare.

Kingship in Europe was also undercut by the rise of capitalism and the newfound power of the nonroyal wealthy. It was an interesting time. The issues of who could own things and what things could be owned motivated political movements and struggles throughout Europe, and even in the United States, by the mid-nineteenth century. Much debate went on over whether people were also things and could be sold—the basis of slavery and serfdom. Crown jewels came to be owned not so much by kings and queens as by the states that the monarchs served.

By the mid-nineteenth century, the Hope Diamond stood for the possession of wealth. It was an object of great value, as measured by purchase price. It could be used to pay off debts. To sell it was to lack wealth; to own it was to have wealth. In a world that was just warming up to the culture of acquisitive capitalism, possessing—that is, owning—the diamond, collecting jewels, were signs of success. Consider this description of Henry Hope: "He could easily afford to buy whatever he wanted. He was from a famous banking family. An enthusiastic collector of gemstones, he also liked to collect paintings."[14]

The importance of wealth and the status derived therefrom marked a transformation in European society. With the coming of factories and the Industrial Revolution, wealth could be generated through production and exchange. Objects of manufacture acquired a new sociality. Through labor, workers place parts of themselves in objects, which are then sold to consumers by owners. Hence people begin to relate to each other objectively—that is, through objects—and objects relate to each other sociologically—that is, through the social relations they embody. This investing of self in an object makes society possible in the form of gifts, social reciprocity, and exchange—a concept heralded by

Emile Durkheim but reviled by Karl Marx as alienation. The exchanged object becomes an icon or fetish of sociality. The sacred power in an object is that of society itself.

But what of the Hope Diamond? It is hardly an everyday object or a manufactured commodity. After Hope's death in 1839 the diamond rested with his descendants, idle, beyond and removed from exchange, until freed by a judge's order in 1902 in order to pay off the family's debts. The Hope Diamond is a symbol of the idle rich.

It is in this context that, at the beginning of the twentieth century, the Hope Diamond acquired a story: A string of owners and possessors over the next eight years meet untimely and tragic deaths. Jacques Celot commits suicide; Prince Kanitovski gives it to his lover, shoots her, and then is himself killed; Habib Bey drowns with his family; the Sultan Abdul Hamid II shoots his lover and has his palace attacked; Simon Monarides falls from a cliff to his death. The diamond, it is suggested, is cursed. This story became a modern folktale, and a cautionary one at that. The suggestion of such a tale may have been an invention of Cartier, in a lighthearted effort to entice the wealthy leisure class of the time—interested as they were in psychic phenomena, phrenology, numerology, seances, and the like—to buy the diamond. The story was elaborated, spread, and touted by Evalyn McLean, whose in-laws owned the *Washington Post*. But interestingly enough, it was a story that stuck and made some sense to a broad public. Public notoriety and the idea of the curse may have increased the salability and value of the diamond. But it also was a modern storyline that appealed to the larger public.

The Hope Diamond and the wealth it represented were far beyond the reach of the average citizen or common person. As a symbol of wealth, value, and the power to possess whatever one could buy, the gem became a vehicle of class revenge. Like other cautionary tales about greed and the acquisition of wealth, this one demonstrated that the unbounded desire to possess can get you killed.

If the curse of the Hope Diamond says that the wealthy cannot buy happiness, it also says they cannot buy love. The joining in diamonds of romantic love with capitalism in the West resulted from the discovery of diamonds in South Africa in 1866 and their subsequent large-scale mining. With the increased supply, the price of diamonds dropped dramatically. A one-carat diamond cost £529 in 1867 and only £110 in 1878. The prices of larger diamonds also fell to one-fifth or one-sixth their former value. While the South African diamonds were used in many different ways, it was not until early in this century that a new demand was invented. A hugely successful marketing campaign conducted by the DeBeers Mining Company and its Diamond Trading Cartel redefined diamonds as a material token of love that men in Europe and the United States gave to women upon engagement. Diamonds were made into an icon of "romantic permanence." "Diamonds are forever," advertised DeBeers. Indeed, Evalyn McLean received the Star of India diamond during her honeymoon in Paris in 1910.

Virtually indestructible, diamonds stood for the eternal character of romantic love and, presumably, marriage. Of course, if worth is measured in monetary terms, the bigger and more expensive the diamond, the greater the love. Rich people had money to buy big diamonds and thus could profess big love. Poor people could show their love only in more humble ways and thus had to settle for a diminished version.

The idea of a diamond as a refined replacement for low-class sexuality fit in with popular ideas about class and biology. For much of the nineteenth century, urbane and educated British, Americans, and Germans believed that all people had a limited amount of life force. This force could be employed in, say, intellectual, rational, or sexual and carnal pursuits. Whole groups of people could be so characterized—for example, in Immanuel Kant's 1796 *Anthropology* the Italians and French are hot, the British and Germans cold. But even within nations, classes would vary—the lower classes generally being regarded as hotter and the upper classes as colder. This idea emerges solidly in the theories of evolutionists and early eugenicists Herbert Spencer, Charles Darwin, Francis Galton, and Karl Pearson, who find intellectual prowess to be inversely proportional to human reproduction: The poor expend their energy in hot, sexual ways; the rich give their women elegant, refined, icy cold diamonds. Hence poor men are exceeded by the rich, and they and their wives have a reason to be jealous and envious—emotions that any folklorist knows lead to the evil eye, the black tongue, and other means of cursing.

The development of the curse as a vehicle of punishment for acquisitive and useless wealth is interesting. A curse is not a scientific phenomenon, a legal punishment, a rational judgment. Curses were used at the time by the "vulgar lower classes"; they represented the naiveté of children, the "superstitious spiritual life of pagans." That is, curses were weapons in the arsenal of the other, the marginalized, the lower-cultured peoples. They could be used by those conquered by British colonialism, scientific knowledge, and rational economism. Curses were for the underdogs, the defeated, the insulted.

During the period from 1890 to 1930, the American and European publics were intrigued with the idea of powers from vanquished, ancient, hidden societies. Indeed, it was at this time that James Frazier wrote *The Golden Bough,* Sigmund Freud produced *Totem and Taboo,* Emile Durkheim published *The Elementary Forms of the Religious Life,* and Andrew Lang, Robert Marret, and Bronislaw

Malinowski sought to define and delimit the boundaries of magic, religion, and science and their relationship to gender and sexuality.

The Tutankhamen curse intrigued people. In numerous short stories, detective stories, novels, and even early horror movies of the Egyptian mummy genre, audiences took delight and were entertained by seeing pretentious English or American or European gentlemen of science undone and humiliated by forces they refused to recognize. Indeed it is the power of the other, of the nonscientific and the nonrational, that stimulates audiences. The Hope Diamond curse offers, in a sense, a way for the public to root for the upending of those firmly held categories of modern life. Allowing themselves to entertain the possibility of the curse challenges and suspends the firmament; it allows for the expression of class resentment toward the wealthy by challenging the very rationality of the social order.

Curses work by enabling supernatural power to flow to the afflicted through contact with persons and objects. The curse may be verbal, but the words are often considered to be objective: They are thrown; they are not just arbitrary sounds that symbolize meaning but rather substantial, efficacious, and iconic speech. Their sounds and cadence enter the cursed. Curses may also be effected through other objects, icons, likenesses, or materials that serve as vehicles for their power. And, conversely, certain materials, words, and sounds can stop or neutralize a curse by impeding or resisting the power.

In South Asia, mothers draw black dots on the faces of their children. These dots imitate moles and make the child look uglier than he or she really is. The folk idea is that the dots will dissuade others from making nice compliments about the child, particularly ones that might be accompanied by jealousy or envy. Indeed, the dots are thought to absorb the power of the evil eye that might be directed toward the child. Diamonds, particularly uncut diamonds, may have operated the same way for kings, and even for the statues of the gods and goddesses. Given the uncut gem's ability to absorb and contain light but not reflect it, the diamond may have offered unique, powerful, and prolonged protection from many evil eyes—absorbing and containing the "negative energy." This usage is suggested even in Roman times by an anonymous second-century poet:

> The evil eye shall have no power to harm
> Him that shall wear the diamond as charm.
> No monarch shall attempt to thwart his will,
> And even the gods his wishes shall fulfill.[15]

The large Indian diamonds were owned by numerous kings. Several—for example, the Orloff and the Nassak—were purportedly eyes of deities that had been stolen from Hindu temples; they eventually came to rest in the collections of Catherine the Great and the Duke of Westminster, respectively. A similar, likely apocryphal, story was also circulated about the Hope Diamond. The point, however, is that the negative energies once contained in the Indian diamonds were released by the European cutting techniques. The desire to "open up the diamonds," for them to emit more "fire," "light," and "beauty" actually inadvertently opened up a Pandora's box of accumulated evil.

Evalyn McLean believed she was resistant to the curse: What was bad luck for others was good luck for her, she claimed, perhaps in an act of class bravado. An independent "character," McLean gained her entrée to wealth through her father, a poor miner from Colorado who struck gold. She had a priest bless the Hope Diamond to dissipate the curse. She reportedly also had her dog wear the diamond. But, as curse aficionados will emphasize, she eventually fell victim to it and endured the tragic deaths of her husband, son, daughter, and granddaughter.

After McLean's death in 1947, the Hope Diamond was purchased by Harry Winston, a rich and successful jeweler. The post–World War II years saw the return of American servicemen to their homes and a significant public and private investment in marriage and the family. Diamonds for engagement rings and as tokens of the successful realization of the American dream were in demand and strongly marketed. American materialism and consumerism flourished, as did internal critiques of such an emphasis. For example, diamonds as objects of false desire and counterfeit salvation provide the paradigm for the 1953 film *Gentlemen Prefer Blondes*. In the film, the gold-digging, husband-seeking Marilyn Monroe sings "Diamonds Are a Girl's Best Friend," a hymn to diamonds in general and the Hope Diamond in particular:

> Men grow cold as girls grow old
> And we all lose our charms in the end.
> But square-cut or pear-shaped
> Those rocks won't lose their shape.
> Diamonds are a girl's best friend.

And as Monroe pauses, she poses with lips moist, in her diamond-sparkly slinky tight red satin dress, and says seductively to the camera, "Talk to me, Harry Winston. Tell me all about it."

And what happens to the gold-digging Monroe, eager to marry a man just for his wealth and diamonds? Well, she falls in love with the poor guy, who turns out really to be the rich guy, love is reaffirmed—you don't have to be rich to be happy, but if you're happy you might get rich—and if your desires are natural, rather than unnatural (that is, extreme), you'll avoid the curse and get what you want.

In the 1950s, Harry Winston had another issue to deal with—not love but money. No curse threatened Winston's interests. But science did. Since the late 1800s several attempts had been made to create diamonds artificially in the laboratory through the application of great heat and pressure to carbon. J. Ballantine Hannay produced small stones in his laboratory in 1880, which were donated to the British Museum. The idea of man replicating in short order the almost unimaginable feats of nature was popularly known and even expressed in Superman comics, where the "Man of Steel" would squeeze a piece of coal into a glowing diamond. Still, this remained more myth than reality, as various scientific experiments were either unsuccessful or discredited. Indeed, Hannay's diamonds were not recognized as such until the 1940s. The atomic age wrought experiments in cyclotrons and atom smashers, with scientists from Harvard, the Argonne Laboratories, and the American Museum of Natural History finding that they could radioactively alter the colors of diamonds, at least temporarily. In 1953 the Atomic Energy Commission forbade the use of its equipment to radiate gemstones.[16] General Electric scientists, however, working to develop hard materials for industrial uses, made a breakthrough in 1955 and developed synthetic diamonds using a secretly patented process. These first synthetic diamonds were quite small (about 0.1 carat), but they led to larger creations in the years to follow. And in 1956 C. Guy Suits, General Electric's director of research, presented a 100-carat cluster of the synthetic, industrial diamonds to the Smithsonian Institution's National Museum of Natural History.

Harry Winston donated the Hope Diamond to the Smithsonian in 1958 and thereby endowed the Smithsonian's National Gem Collection with a value and standing that it would not otherwise have achieved. Indeed, the donation of the Hope Diamond, made in time for the opening of the Museum of Natural History's Gem Hall, brought the collection and the Smithsonian unprecedented publicity. And in the wake of the Hope Diamond donation, other gems came to the collection.

But if the Hope Diamond improved the position of the Smithsonian as a national treasure house, the reverse was also true. The Smithsonian aided in the legitimation of the worth of gems—as natural creations—juxtaposed with the earlier General Electric donation. While Winston's own motives may have been to enhance public education and his own immortality, his donation of the Hope Diamond affirmed the value of diamonds as both natural and historical/biographical objects, rather than synthetic and anonymous ones. The Hope

Diamond's celebrity and authenticity served as a symbol of other "real" diamonds, as opposed to the anonymity of artificial ones. Indeed, the Federal Trade
Commission soon ruled that man-made products could not be called diamonds.
As Marcus Baerwald notes, "The acceptance of natural diamonds is rooted in
centuries of history and tradition, world-wide romance, the approval of kings
and queens, and the blessing of fashion. Winning similar acceptance for syn-
thetics would be a long and incredibly difficult task. It is hard to image British
royalty being crowned with stones from a laboratory."[17]

THE HOPE DIAMOND AS MUSEUM ICON

The Hope Diamond was treated as an object of cultural attachment, craftsmanship, and social meaning, and so the most appropriate place to display it in the
Smithsonian would be not in a museum per se but at the Smithsonian's Folklife
Festival. Numerous presentations at the festival have looked at how Americans
and others from various countries and communities have regarded particular objects as part of their living cultural heritage. It could well fit into a comparative
program on charms, talismans, and ritual objects (for example, Zuni fetishes and
Hawaiian leis). The Hope Diamond could easily be a wonderful prop in presentations of the occupational folklife of diamond cutters, designers, and sellers.
It also could be used in narrative sessions concerning marital rituals, or it could
be used to discuss the folklife of objects, designs, and forms of adornment that
distinguish classes within a society (as has been done with Cape Verdean *pano*
making, African American hair braiding, and Pacific Island tattooing). Security
concerns aside, after the Hope Diamond was donated to the Smithsonian it became perhaps less appropriate for the festival, for it underwent yet another change
in meaning and significance. It became estranged from its former communities
of users and assumed a role as part of museum culture.

In the museum, the Hope Diamond, like other objects, is placed in a kind of
cultural formaldehyde. The old rules do not apply. The object is no longer possessed by an individual but rather by a faceless institution. It is no longer available for circulation and exchange. It is not so much an object of wealth now as
it is an object of history—natural and cultural. It is measured and scrutinized,
cataloged and historicized. It is surrounded by rationality, an institution, science
and systems. Indeed, it is in the heart of the decultured world. And it would
take truly wondrous power for the diamond to have its effect.

But it could. And imagine the reactions if, when the former director of the
National Museum of Natural History announced his retirement plans, he had

suggested that it was not just plain old museum dust, but diamond dust—Hope Diamond dust, to be exact—that led to his condition. Or, to play on the curse of wealth, imagine Secretary Heyman announcing that the Smithsonian is bankrupt and is selling the Hope Diamond in order to pay the bills. Or, imagine if you will—as horrible as it is—a tragedy striking visitors, guards, or others in the Gem Hall. What would the headline of the *Enquirer* read? "Hope Diamond Curse Strikes Again!" The lines for entry to the museum would be out the door and down the block. The suggestion that the power in the diamond somehow struck back against the rationality of such an antiseptic institution would tantalize, engage, and entertain millions. The Hope Diamond would become an instant folk hero, upending the order upon which the very edifice of our institution is built. "Hope Diamond Dazzles and Puzzles Smithsonian!" would read the *Star's* headline at every supermarket checkout counter in the country. Yes, the triumph of the underdog—magic over the scientists and bureaucrats. Imagine the talk shows, the scientific studies, the crazies coming out to debate the boundaries and relative power of the known and the unknown.

Of course, something like this could be arranged. We'd have to change the exhibitry of the Hope Diamond somewhat. But imagine a "Ripley's Believe It Or Not" kind of setup. See the diamond resting on black velvet under a spotlight at the center of a dimly lit rotunda, surrounded by columns suggesting the ancient, mysterious East. Around the diamond would be photographs of gruesome deaths caused by its curse. Text panels would include personal sworn testimony by people touched by its effects.

This is not beyond the realm of possibility. There is, for example, a National Park Service museum in Hawaii's Volcanoes National Park that has a similar display. Among the people of the big island is a belief that the island is alive, that the volcano is a part of life's cyclical rejuvenation caused by the goddess Pele. To take volcanic rock off the island of Hawaii is to take a piece of life from it. Removal violates the goddess and the natural process that she animates. In the Volcanoes National Park museum is an exhibit about the consequences suffered by those who took volcanic rock off of the big island—by either mistake or design. The museum displays a sample of letters from the cursed, attesting to a variety of woes. Also included are the offending bits of volcanic rock, dutifully and even sorrowfully returned. It is an impressive testament to the desire to believe in the unseen powers of the island—a critique, as it were, of modern life's inability to predict, know, and understand earth's ways.

But back to the Hope Diamond. In the exhibit there would be music playing—organ music of the Vincent Price variety. Visitors would have to file in one by one and sign a liability release form before entering. And when they came before the Hope Diamond they would, if they chose, be able to slip their index finger through a tiny hole in the Plexiglas case and actually touch the diamond, thus challenging the curse. If we charged admission, we'd make a fortune.

But if the power of the diamond operates on the principles of sacred icon and has stood for wealth and the resentment of it, for natural history and supernatural power, it now stands more as an icon of its own fame—not surprising in a world where fame carries its own value.

The Smithsonian advertises the Hope Diamond's fame. The famous have a name and enjoy name recognition. This idea could just as easily apply to objects. After all, we know that baskets and pots have ethnicity—Cherokee baskets, Zuni and Santa Clara pottery. The Hope Diamond has a unique, individuated name (though it has such cousins as the Hope Ruby and the Hope Sapphire). But more than a name, it has a biography—a chronological narrative, a genealogy, and most important, the power to engage other persons—humans—in relationships, albeit not necessarily nice ones.

There are not many other objects around the Smithsonian or elsewhere that have their own name and characteristics of personhood, that are famous in and of themselves. Directional and informational signs in the museum play this up; "and of course, the famous Hope Diamond," they read. Thus many people come to see the Hope Diamond because they have heard of it—it is famous—even if they don't quite know why. This seemed to be the case when I interviewed my daughter Jaclyn, then eight years old and an experienced museum visitor.

"Why do you want to see the Hope Diamond?"

"Because it's famous, Daddy."

"Why is it famous?"

"Because it's big."

"Would it be famous if it was a big paper clip?"

"No, Daddy."

"Why not?"

"Because it's rich—it's a lot of money. It's cursed. An actress died. A lot of people got killed. I don't know how the story goes."

Jaclyn had many things right. As a quick verbal survey by my research assistant revealed, most people do not know much about the Hope Diamond, save that it is famous. Most expect it to be much larger than it is—somewhere between the size of an egg and a baseball. And though people may even wait in line to see it, most are disappointed with its size—"I thought it would be much bigger." "It ain't so hot." "That's it?" are typical comments.

Nonetheless, everybody wants to tell their friends that they saw it, up close, and though in itself it wasn't much, viewing it was an experience to check off on a list, much like that of seeing a Hollywood star's house or filling up one's concert card. It is in this sense that we often speak of the Hope Diamond as an icon in American popular culture.

Indeed, Harry Winston understood how the Hope Diamond was famous in its own right and did a national Court of Jewels tour in the 1950s on which women could wear the Hope Diamond for an instant and get their picture taken with it. A chance to be close to the famous, to touch the famous, to be bathed in the famous—and then say, Oh, it was no big deal. To be close to fame, then either be transformed by it—become famous or pursue fame—or deny and resent it.

Such responses suggest something akin to worship. We in our own way worship stars—the famous, the glamorous, the recognizable, the popular. We want to touch, hold a piece of them, to absorb and even discard their stuff. Don't wash your hand after having shaken the president's, get an autograph, touch the glove, go backstage with the Grateful Dead. This fascination holds, even when the reason for the fame starts to be forgotten. Fame becomes a value in its own right—as actors, politicians, and sports figures know.

The tropes of the curse, of exaggerated wealth and resentment, exaggerated love and resentment, still play on the bigger-than-life—and bigger than it actually is—Hope Diamond. In this age of mass communications and public relations hype, the Hope Diamond is played for all it's worth. It is made ever more famous, and ever more worthy of worship and awe—in film, such as *The Curse of the Hope Diamond,* starring Diana Rigg, and in numerous stories in national publications. For example, a 1995 *Life* magazine story noted that:

> In all but the brightest light it smolders like a huge sullen eye. Yet when flooded with ultraviolet rays, it glows red-orange, an eerie echo of its bloody legend. The jewel, so the story goes, was once the eye of a Hindu idol Rama Sita. When it was stolen, Ram cursed everyone who would come to possess the stone. Indeed, fate has not been kind to those who have owned the eye of the god. . . . But the curse, says Ronald Winston, has increased the value of the big blue pebble. At auction, Winston says, the Hope could fetch as much as $200 million.[18]

As a famous object, powered by its biography, sustained by its venerable setting, with rich, powerful, and famous friends, the Hope Diamond does not now need to stand for anything except itself. It is its own symbol, its own icon. Its fame must merely be renewed, so that it stays in the public eye. Hence, photographs of the Hope Diamond sported by glamorous contemporary Hollywood actresses like Michelle Pfeiffer lend additional credence to its fame and promote it to another generation. After all, icons tend to get along famously with one another.

Where then within the Smithsonian should the Hope Diamond reside? My choice would be the National Museum of American History, for it is now, as an object of fame in a society that has placed such value on fame, that the Hope Diamond is most significant. If I were to put it next to any other object, it would probably be the famous ruby slippers worn by Judy Garland in *The Wizard of Oz*. Those slippers, it will be remembered, were also thought to be magical, to contain great power. The slippers were endowed by Hollywood writers—modern mythmakers—with telling a powerful tale about a child's, and indeed a nation's, quest to find "home." And with the passing of another generation of Americans, the slippers too have become less connected to a specific history and more an icon of the museum. Taken together, the Hope Diamond and the ruby slippers offer a nice structural parody on reality and illusion, mythmaking and history making, the valuing of museums and the museuming of value.

NOTES

1. This chapter is based on a presentation to the Smithsonian Forum on Material Culture, Twenty-fourth dinner meeting, "Gem, Jewel, and Icon: Looking at the Hope Diamond," December 2, 1993, at the National Museum of Natural History. I am indebted to the presentations of colleagues Jeffrey Post and David McFadden, the panel leadership of Adrienne Kaeppler, and the serious questions raised by Sally Hoffmann and Bill Sturtevant that led to the enrichment of this evolving interpretation. I also thank Diana Parker for her insights and Matt Hersh, a Smithsonian extern from the University of Virginia, and Linda Benner for their handy research help.

As a casual acquaintance of the Hope Diamond's, I have my own stories about the gem. In June 1985 Smithsonian secretary Robert McC. Adams and S. Dillon Ripley, secretary emeritus and chair of the Festival of India, invited the Indian prime minister, Rajiv Gandhi, to a luncheon in the Gem Hall to celebrate the opening of the Aditi exhibit in the National Museum of Natural History for the Festival of India. First Lady Nancy Reagan and numerous other dignitaries would also attend. The Smithsonian clearly wanted to impress the prime minister and the first lady and show off the Hope Diamond. I warned coordinator Jeffrey LaRiche and Assistant Secretary Ralph Rinzler that Rajiv Gandhi might be so impressed as to ask for it back—which, of course, he didn't.

My second experience was with an exact replica of the Hope Diamond. Giving the aforementioned talk about the Hope Diamond in the museum's Baird Auditorium, I conspired with copanelists, Smithsonian security guards, and the audiovisual technician to stage a mock theft of the replica in order to make a point about its value.

2. John Sampson White, *The Smithsonian Treasury: Minerals and Gems* (Washington: Smithsonian Institution Press, 1991).

3. Grahame Clark, *Symbols of Excellence* (London: Cambridge University Press, 1986), p. 10.

4. Max Bauer, *Precious Stones* (Rutland, Vt.: Charles E. Tuttle, 1969), pp. 76–77.

5. Marcus Baerwald, *The Story of Jewelry* (London: Abelard Schuman, 1960), p. 41.

6. Mary Winters and John Sampson White, "George IV's Blue Diamond," *Lapidary Journal,* December 1991, pp. 36–37.

7. Joan Younger Dickinson, *The Book of Diamonds* (New York: Crown, 1965), pp. 54–55.

8. George F. Kunz, *Curious Lore of Precious Stones* (London: Lippincott, 1913), p. 235.

9. Dickinson, *Book of Diamonds,* p. 2.

10. Samuel Tolansky, *The History and Use of Diamonds* (London: Methuen, 1962), p. 5.

11. Kunz, *Curious Lore,* 154.

12. Charles E. Brown, *Gems: Magic, Mysteries, and Myths of Precious Stones* (Madison, Wis.: State Historical Museum, 1932), p. 17.

13. Kunz, *Curious Lore,* p. 157.

14. Janet Hubbard Brown, History Mystery: The Curse of the Hope Diamond (New York: Avon Trade Books), 1991.

15. Ibid., p. 1.

16. Baerwald, *The Story of Jewelry,* p. 53.

17. Ibid., p. 55.

18. "The Legendary Hope Diamond," *Life,* March 1995, p. 72.

4

Herbert Ward's "Ethnographic Sculptures" of Africans

MARY JO ARNOLDI

Nineteen bronze sculptures by the English artist Herbert Ward are currently in the African collections of the National Museum of Natural History's Department of Anthropology (Figures 4.1 and 4.2).[1] Created between 1901 and 1911, eighteen of these bronzes depict Congolese peoples and were largely inspired by the artist's experiences in the Congo Free State (now Zaire) between 1884 and 1889.[2] The Ward bronzes are described by art historians as "ethnographic sculptures," a category of Western art that was especially popular in Europe and America from about the mid-nineteenth century through the early decades of the twentieth century. At the height of their popularity "ethnographic sculptures," which generally depicted peoples from Africa, the Americas, and Asia, were collected both by fine art museums and by the anthropology departments of natural history museums.[3] In 1922 the group of Ward's bronzes of Africans went on exhibit at the Smithsonian as part of a permanent installation of the Herbert Ward collection of African artifacts, and they remained on view for more than forty years.[4]

The Smithsonian's exhibition of the Ward collection and the Ward sculpture was part of the nineteenth-century Western invention of Africa, and its history brings into sharp focus the power that museum displays can wield in shaping our interpretations of cultures. By the mid-nineteenth century in both scientific and popular quarters, Africans had come to be classified as "savages" and their

Fig. 4.1. Sleeping Africa, by Herbert Ward. Bronze. 1902. Department of Anthropology, NMNH, Smithsonian Institution. E323,718. Reproduced with permission from Smithsonian Institution.

cultures as "primitive." Scientific and popular books on Africa, entertainments that featured African performers, ethnographic displays of African objects and works of art, like the Ward bronzes, all contributed to shaping Western attitudes about the African continent and to justifying its colonization.[5]

The politics of defining and representing Africans often has more to do with the interests of those with the power to represent African cultures than it does with understanding the groups being represented. In the case of the Ward bronzes, the sculptures clearly reflect dominant nineteenth-century Western attitudes toward Africans.[6] While these early definitions of Africans as primitive and savage have been thoroughly discredited in current anthropology, the inclusion of such artworks in any contemporary African exhibit in the National Museum of Natural History is wholly inappropriate. Herein lies the contemporary curatorial dilemma, which raises the following questions: What is the value of these eighteen sculptures to anthropology and to the Smithsonian collections at large? If these bronzes are no longer appropriate to exhibits on African cultures, do they have a place in art exhibits featuring European art? What is their research value for the history of either anthropology or art? In what Smithsonian museum, if any, should these sculptures be put back on public display in the late twentieth century?

Fig. 4.2. The Idol Maker, by Herbert Ward. Bronze. 1906. Department of Anthropology, NMNH, Smithsonian Institution. E323,735. Photograph reproduced with permission from the Menil Foundation.

THE 1922 WARD EXHIBITION AND SMITHSONIAN ANTHROPOLOGY

In 1912, following a visit to the Smithsonian, Herbert Ward wrote to Mr. Charles D. Walcott, secretary of the Smithsonian, stating his intention of bequeathing his African collection to the museum at his death. Ward's collection included nineteen bronzes: five heroic-size and four life-size bronzes and several table-size bronzes, busts, and studies for larger pieces. The collection also included a number of hunting trophies—an elephant head, various antelope heads, and gorilla skeletons. The largest part of the collection consisted of 2,700 objects from different African cultures, including carved figures and masks, raffia textiles, baskets, headrests, beaded and ivory jewelry, and ornaments, ceremonial staffs, knives, and spears.

Herbert Ward had collected a large number of African objects while working in the Congo Free State. Later, while living in Europe, he continued to augment his core collection. In 1927 Sarita Ward, his widow, enthusiastically wrote: "This collection to which he has added an appreciable amount from time to time as the occasion had arisen was by then [1906] a very important affair, numbering close upon three thousand objects, rivalling in value and interest the collection of the King of the Belgians."[7]

It was Ward's collection of 2,700 African objects, not the bronzes, that the museum's Department of Anthropology was eager to add to its ethnology collections. In 1912 the majority of the ethnology collections were Native American objects. The African holdings were small by comparison, and many were poorly documented. In a memo to William Henry Holmes, the head of anthropology, Walter Hough, curator in the Division of Ethnology, wrote: "Since I have read Mr. Ward's letter, I have become a hundred fold more interested in his specimens for the reason that he is competent to classify and give them their origin of locality, thus making the way of the museum man smooth and adding enormously to the scientific value of the material."[8]

Herbert Ward's name recognition must also have played a significant part in the museum's desire to acquire his collection.[9] In the late 1890s Ward had lectured extensively in America, and accounts of his lectures were syndicated in newspapers throughout the country. By 1913, when the Smithsonian publicly announced Ward's intentions of leaving the collection to the museum, he had already published three books about his experiences in the Congo Free State.[10] Ward's intended gift was given ample coverage by the press.[11] The *Washington (D.C.) Sunday Star* published an extended interview with Herbert Ward, along with photographs of several of his bronzes and of his studio museum in Paris.

Ward had conceived of his bronze sculptures as an essential part of his African collection, and he stipulated that the bronzes, the zoological specimens, and the 2,700 African objects be displayed together in a permanent exhibition. In a memo dated June 10, 1912, to the assistant secretary, Mr. Richard Rathbun, William Henry Holmes, the head of the Department of Anthropology, suggested that the museum should renegotiate with Ward. He wrote: "With respect to the sculptures, if they are included, it might be well to suggest that examples of these might be shown quite appropriately in the National Gallery of Art."[12] However, when the collection was finally transferred to the Smithsonian in 1921 following Herbert Ward's death, Mrs. Ward insisted that the museum keep faith with her husband's original conditions, and the museum agreed to do so.

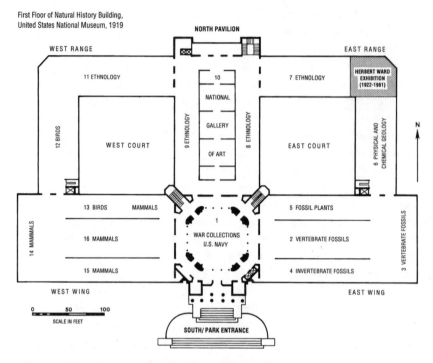

First Floor of Natural History Building,
United States National Museum, 1919

Fig. 4.3. Map of exhibit halls at the National Museum (now the National Museum of Natural History). Shaded area indicates the location of the Ward Gallery, opened in 1922.

In 1921 Mrs. Ward was invited to Washington to consult with the museum curators on the plans for the Ward exhibition. The National Museum, as it was known at that time, included not only ethnological, archaeological, and natural history exhibits but also the National Gallery of Art (this museum building now houses only natural history and anthropology exhibits).[13] The Smithsonian's fine arts collection was prominently displayed in the large axial hall of the north wing, which opened off the museum's spacious rotunda. Flanking the art gallery were two Native American ethnology halls, while the exhibition halls dedicated to Africa, Asia, and Oceania intersected the fine arts gallery at its northernmost end. In a 1920 planning memo, Walter Hough suggested that if the Ward bronzes were to be exhibited, they should be installed at the intersection of the art gallery and the ethnology halls in order to visually connect the Ward bronzes to other Western art collections on display. Hough's proposed plan, however,

Fig. 4.4. Herbert Ward's Paris studio museum prior to 1911. Smithsonian Institution photo no. 75-5893. Reproduced with permission from the Smithsonian Institution.

would have necessitated removing and reinstalling a large number of the existing ethnology exhibits. Because of financial and space constraints, the idea to link the Ward bronzes with the art gallery was never realized. Instead, some of the existing African exhibits at the far east end of northernmost ethnology hall were dismantled and the Ward collection installed there (Figure 4.3).

In planning for the exhibit, Mrs. Ward suggested that the Smithsonian re-create her husband's studio museum in Paris (Figure 4.4), which had been housed in a large second-story room above the artist's studio. By painting the walls a gray-green color and installing an elaborately carved wooden "harem" screen across the bank of exterior windows, Ward had created a dramatic atmosphere, somber and subdued. On the three interior walls he had arranged his African objects, including arrows, ivory tusks, spears, bracelets, knives, headrests, whistles, and spoons in decorative displays. The smaller bronze sculptures were set in niches and on tables, and the larger works were placed throughout

Fig. 4.5. View of the Ward Gallery, National Museum Building, circa 1922. Smithsonian Institution photo no. 26914-A. Reproduced with permission from the Smithsonian Institution.

the room. The visual effect of this space was overwhelmingly decorative, with patterned Turkish kilims on the floors, African raffia textiles wrapped around the bases of the bronzes, a carved screen, and dense displays of weapons and other African objects on the walls.

The Smithsonian installation clearly intended to re-create some of the drama that marked Ward's Paris exhibit. Curtains were hung over the exterior windows of the gallery to subdue the light, and the walls were painted a dusky greenish color. In almost every review of the opening of the exhibit, critics made a point of remarking upon the effect of the muted lighting and likened the ambience of the gallery to that of a jungle (Figure 4.5).

Mrs. Ward also recommended that the museum create a distinct exhibition space for the Ward collection by separating it from the other African exhibits by an ornamental railing. The museum created a sectional wooden railing and decorated each end of the three sections with a reproduction of one of a pair of

African figures that were in the Ward collection. Reproductions of these figures (a male and female pair) also appeared as decorative motifs on a sculptural base that Ward himself had created for his bronze *The Tribal Chief*. The original African sculptures that were the inspiration for these decorative elements were installed in a case with other examples of African figurative carvings.

Echoing Ward's Paris installation, the Smithsonian curators mounted the elephant head and various antelope heads on the walls and surrounded them with African weapons arranged in symmetrical decorative patterns. This "trophy style" of display with its self-consciously and painstakingly designed walls of weapons was not peculiar to the Ward Paris museum but was fashionable throughout this period in both private homes and public displays of ethnographic materials. While this display technique drew attention to the decorative potential of the ethnographic objects, its primary function was to "glorify" the trophy collectors themselves.[14] At the Smithsonian, the glorification of the collector was amplified by the inclusion of a label about Herbert Ward in the gallery. This label read:

> The Herbert Ward African Collection
>   formed by Herbert Ward 1863–1919
> Herbert Ward was born in London, England, in 1863. At the age of fifteen he set out on travels which took him over many of the unexplored lands of the World, and at twenty-one he began his work in Africa. While in the Congo in the employ of the Belgian Government he rendered important aid to Stanley in his explorations. For more than five years Mr. Ward lived among the natives of Central Africa and during that time he developed the idea of preserving an epitome of the primitive life with which he was surrounded and which would be an index of the primitive life of all men. The African Negro that Mr. Ward studied impressed him as possessing fine qualities of simple dignity and loyalty. Mr Ward was by instinct and training a lover of art and constantly recorded his impressions of the natives at first hand. The records which he made on the spot were used in his subsequent famous works of sculpture which portray the soul of Africa.
>   Mr. Ward in his collection has contributed a noble effort for the benefit of art, science, and humanity.
>   This collection, in accordance with Mr. Ward's wishes, on his death was placed in the Smithsonian Institution, in 1921, by his widow, Mrs. Sarita Ward.[15]

During this period it was a standard practice for the museum to acknowledge specific collectors on case labels in the ethnology exhibits. Yet the Ward text was far more extensive and went far beyond merely naming the collector. It validated Ward as an adventurer, a collector of African artifacts, and the artist-interpreter of Africa through his bronze sculptures.

Despite the similarities between Ward's Paris museum and the Ward gallery at the Smithsonian, there were several important differences in the two exhibits. These differences advanced the museum's philosophy of ethnographic display and asserted its scientific voice in the exhibit as the dominant voice. In 1916 in a paper delivered to the American Association of Museums, Walter Hough laid out the Smithsonian's principles for ethnographic displays:

> It was decided to display the collections geographically by ethnic units, but with open arrangement. . . . The unit of exhibit comprises a family group case showing the physical characteristics of the race, costume, domestic arts, etc.; and cases exhibiting textiles, pottery, and other products of material culture. Single figures are also used as illustrations of races, and accompanying the exhibit are transparencies and other pictorial material. . . . Cases containing synoptic series showing the development of invention form an attractive and educational section of the exhibit.[16]

In Paris Ward had mounted all types of African objects—weapons, ornaments, spoons, masks, figures, etc.—in decorative patterns on the walls or placed them randomly together in showcases. In Washington the curators set about sorting and organizing the African materials by object type and by material. They installed their groupings in separate cases that ran around the perimeter of the gallery. Carved masks and figures were put together in a single case. Knives, sheaths, staffs, and other weapons were displayed together. Textiles and ornaments and musical instruments each merited their own case. Short text labels were placed in each of the object cases, and these labels reinforced the scientific lessons that the curators sought to teach through these objects (Figure 4.6). For example, the label for the costume and ornament case read:

> This case contains textiles native to the Congo and costumes made up in whole or part from them. This primitive industry offers instructive phases of aboriginal handicraft with filaments and some examples of the work show progress in taste and skill. Notable are the tufted and tie-and-dye fabrics. Personal ornaments, such as necklaces, pendants, carved combs, etc., show the striving for esthetic effects in a savage state of culture. The primitive loom is for making raffia cloth. The basketry shows appreciation of form and decoration. On the floor of the case are neck ornaments and fetters of metal.[17]

The visual force of this typing, ordering, and classifying of objects tempered the original lushness, exuberance, and decorative splendor of Ward's Paris exhibit, and in its new organization the Smithsonian exhibit acquired the imprimatur of science.

The curators installed the small bronzes around the perimeter of the gallery

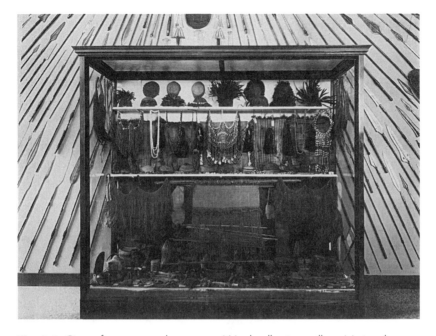

Fig. 4.6. Case of costume and ornament. Ward collection gallery. National Museum Building, circa 1922. Smithsonian Institution photo no. 26819-B. Reproduced with permission from the Smithsonian Institution.

and then pulled the larger bronzes forward toward the open center of the gallery space. These large bronzes dominated the display, and, in effect, their central placement mimicked the positioning of the "family life group" cases that dominated the ethnology exhibits elsewhere in the museum. Although the staff recognized that the bronzes were self-consciously "fine art" and clearly not family life group mannikins, the bronzes do share with these mannikins an arresting realism. The life-group cases generally presented families engaged in various lifeways activities. Ward's bronzes, including *The Idol Maker* (Figure 4.1) and *The Charm Doctor* (Figure 4.7), could have been seen as visually analogous to the family life group cases, even though they were single-figure compositions. In rationalizing how the Ward exhibition, which included the Ward bronzes and African objects, fit in with the museum's philosophy of ethnographic display, Secretary Walcott noted:

> His [Ward's] museum idea was to tell the story of man in the best way possible, and to illustrate the dead specimens with works of high artistic lines. This idea

Fig. 4.7. The Charm Doctor, by Herbert Ward. Bronze. 1902. Department of Anthropology, NMNH, Smithsonian Institution. E323,732. Reproduced with permission from the Smithsonian Institution.

[is] pursued in the National Museum by [William Henry] Holmes with cases of specimens, dwelling groups, family groups, technical groups, transparencies and paintings, creating an atmosphere. Museum art employes [the] dramatic art of suggesting environment. Ward accomplished this. No loss to art in his method. An isolated statue by Ward in an art gallery would impress one as a good piece of work, and no further. 17 [19] statues on a phase of human culture surrounded by examples of handicraft, is an education.[18]

For museum anthropologists William Henry Holmes and Walter Hough, the proximity of the Ward bronzes to the African carved figures, masks, staffs, and decorated weapons in the cases and on the gallery walls read as a visually powerful developmental sequence in the evolution of art. William Henry Holmes had devoted much of his professional career to the study of art, and he held strong views about the progressive evolution of art. In his discussion of Holmes, Curtis Hinsley noted that Holmes believed that art had progressed "from geometric, nonideographic to delineative forms; from motives of religious superstition to refined sense of beauty, from imitation to spontaneity."[19] No lover of the new abstract art of Picasso, Braque, and others, Holmes must have seen Ward's naturalistic and hyper-realistic renderings of Congolese people as examples of the highest achievement in art. Echoing similar sentiments, Walter Hough stated: "The maker of an African sword and Praxiteles were one in the effort to express themselves in terms of art. The steps from the aboriginal craftsman to the sculptures of Mr. Ward are plain to those who study the development of art."[20]

The correspondence between Ward's personal invention of the Congo and the Department of Anthropology's scientific one is complex and subtle. Ward's Congolese as he invented them in his bronze statuary were romantic, anecdotal, and impressionistic, in contrast to the museum's vision, which invoked the authority of science to depersonalize, order, type, and classify peoples. Through the combination of different, and sometimes competing, exhibition strategies Ward's and the museum's voices did converge in this exhibit. These voices created an image of Africans that did not question the accepted "verities" of Victorian categories of race and evolution but intentionally and powerfully reconfirmed them. That they were successful in communicating their message is borne out in the following review of the exhibition, which appeared in a Dearborn, Michigan, newspaper in 1922:

> Primitive life is mirrored in a remarkably interesting collection of African weapons and original sculptures left to the Smithsonian Institution in Washington by the sculptor, Herbert Ward. . . . The collection includes a splendid assembly of relics—knives and spears, musical instruments, ivory carvings, a huge elephant's head and several hundred wooden idols. More important, however, are bronzes that Herbert Ward made when he returned from the Congo. Theodore Roosevelt, who visited his studio in Paris, said: "In his figures the Negro of the Congo is seen on his native soil, child-like and cruel, friendly and brutal, age-old man who lived in Europe several thousand years ago, and yet a man with eternal youth in his soul that has preserved him in his stalwart strength to the present."[21]

THE WARD BRONZES AS "ETHNOGRAPHIC SCULPTURES": AN ANALYSIS

Both the museum staff and the public shared a definition of the bronzes as works of Western fine art. It is not surprising, then, that Gertrude Brigham, the reviewer from the *Christian Science Monitor,* described the Ward exhibition as an art exhibition rather than an ethnological display.[22] "Ethnographic sculptures," like the Ward bronzes, had many admirers, and many, like the Ward bronzes, were collected by both art museums and the anthropology departments of natural history museums. For some of the admirers, these sculptures were seen as bridging the gap between arts and sciences. With their attention to the realistic rendering of the physical features of their subjects, ethnographic sculptures resonated with the new science of anthropology, which in the mid-nineteenth century was engaged in describing and classifying the universe of racial types. In certain artistic circles, the admirers of ethnographic sculptures also promoted them as challenging the accepted academic ideal of beauty, which was based on classical Greek sculptures and had held sway in European art since the Renaissance.[23]

Ward was among a number of European artists who in the late nineteenth century had actually traveled and worked in Africa. While in the Congo Free State he kept journals, made numerous drawings of the different peoples he encountered, and took photographs of his surroundings. His large collection of African objects also provided him with a rich body of source material, which he regularly incorporated into his sculptures. Ward's personal experiences in Africa lent an air of empirical accuracy to his Congo figures, a point that the Smithsonian exhibition label emphasized. Yet, a closer study of these images shows that Ward's representations vacillate between empirical accuracy and allegory, with most images falling squarely in between these two poles.

Two of Ward's earliest works, *The Bakongo Girl* (1901) (Figure 4.8, left) and *The Aruimi Man* (1900) (Figure 4.8, right), with their carefully wrought details of coiffure and scarification and their expressionless faces, most closely resemble the busts produced for anthropology museums during this period to serve as empirical records of different racial types. The ethnic affiliation of Ward's two figures was carefully identified in his titles, something he never did in any of his later works. *The Bakongo Girl* is clearly based on a drawing of a young woman that Ward made in the Congo and that he published in his 1890 book. The details of her coiffure, costume, and accoutrements faithfully reproduce his original drawing (Figure 4.9).[24] Although the figure *The Aruimi Man* is not modeled after any surviving drawing by Ward, the man's distinctive facial scarification would also seem to have been based on firsthand observation (Figure 4.10). In a photograph published in Frederick Starr's 1912 book, *Congo Natives,* the facial scarification of an unidentified man from Yambuya (a town on the Aruimi River where Ward had been stationed in 1887) closely approximates the rendering on the Ward bust.[25]

His 1902 sculpture *The Charm Doctor* departs from the overt emphasis on

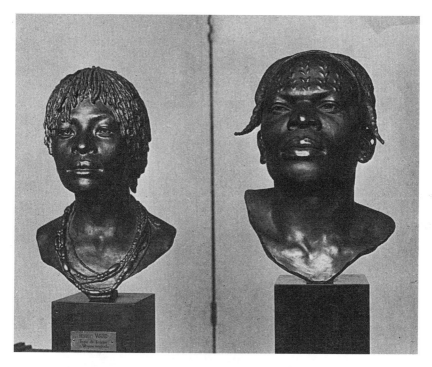

Fig. 4.8. The Bakongo Girl and The Aruimi Man, by Herbert Ward. Bronze. 1901 and 1900. Department of Anthropology, NMNH, Smithsonian Institution. E323,713 and E323,712. Reproduced with permission from the Smithsonian Institution.

racial typing in the busts and serves more as a visual anecdote (Figure 4.7). The bronze is based on a series of drawings and written accounts that Ward had published from his encounters with *ngang'a nkisi*, Bakongo ritual experts. The sculpture closely resembles an engraving that was published in his 1890 book. It shows a dancing male figure holding a small carved wooden figure high in the air (Figure 4.11).[26] In this account Ward devoted several pages to his encounters with these ritual experts. Although Ward's drawings always showed a *ngang'a nikisi* wearing a feather headdress, he chose not to represent this significant costume element in his sculpture. The figure, however, does hold a small carved image aloft in his hand; the image is modeled after one of the Bakongo *minkisi* statues that were in Ward's collection of African objects (Figure 4.12). While the dramatic pose of the figure, balancing on one foot with his arm raised in the air, demonstrated Ward's formal skill as a sculptor, the dancing and gesticulating

Fig. 4.9. An engraving by
W. B. Davis after an
original drawing by Herbert
Ward, "A Bakongo Girl,"
published in Ward's book
*Five Years with the Congo
Cannibals* (New York:
Robert Bonner's Sons,
1890), p. 88.

figure also reinforced the popular stereotype of the exotic dancing African, as surely as the tone of his books had done. Of one encounter with the *ngang'a nkisi* he wrote:

> Dead silence ranged as the *nganga* leapt into their midst, rattling in his hands images, leopard claws and calabash-tops, and chanted a weird song. . . . After reciting the facts of the case with a drawling intonation, he executed a dance, the like of which I had never seen before. The wild, leaping figure, with its dress of leopard skins and charms, presented a weird picture.[27]

Unlike the other early works, *Sleeping Africa,* which was completed in 1902, is clearly allegorical with its image of a semi-nude African woman lying asleep on the continent of Africa (Figure 4.2). While Ward used certain ethnographic

Fig. 4.10. An engraving after an original drawing by Herbert Ward, "An Aruimi Type," published in Ward's book *Five Years with the Congo Cannibals* (New York: Robert Bonner's Sons, 1890), p. 159.

details of scarification, coiffure, and costume (probably Ngala) to impart a feeling of veracity and realism to this figure, he drew upon the centuries-old European artistic convention of representing the continents as females.[28] The representation of a sleeping figure in Ward's allegory also has a long history in Western art. A late-sixteenth-century print, *Vespucci Landing in America,* for example, depicts a sleeping woman (America) being awakened by Vespucci, an allegory for the European conquest of America. Ward's *Sleeping Africa* is one in a long line of such allegorical images of "civilized" Europe awakening the sleeping "primitive," with the slumbering figure symbolizing a state of barbarism and ignorance.[29]

Most of Ward's bronzes are more correctly described as ethnographic pastiches. Ward's *Idol Maker* from 1906 is a good example. In this work Ward's primary concern for expressing "the soul of Africa" overrode any need to create an empirically accurate representation (Figure 4.1). Even ignoring the obvious problems with the title of the bronze and Ward's inaccurate rendering of the local carving technique, the piece still jars. While the scarification on the forehead of the carver resembles that of *The Aruimi Man* (Figure 4.8) and shows him to be

Fig. 4.11. An engraving by W. B. Davis entitled "Nganka Nkisi," published in Ward's book *Five Years with the Congo Cannibals* (New York: Robert Bonner's Sons, 1890), p. 41.

a member of one of several groups living on the upper Congo River, the wooden figure that he is carving is in a Teke style, from a group that lived along the lower Congo River. This mixture of ethnographic details from different areas and peoples was clearly a conscious choice by Ward. He had not only cataloged similar African carvings in his collection as Teke, but he was also familiar with Teke patterns of facial scarification, which he described in his 1890 book: "The Bateke, who I have already mentioned as inhabiting the shores of Stanley Pool . . . score their cheeks and temples with long, thin incisions."[30]

A similar deconstruction of Ward's other bronzes would reveal many of the same inconsistencies. Ward himself always intended to create "something symbolical," although he did so in the guise of an arresting realism. He said of his own work that he did not intend to create "an absolute realistic thing like wax works in an anatomical museum—but to make something which demands two different requirements: the thing must have the spirit of Africa in its broad sense, and at the same time fill the requirements of the art of sculpture."[31]

Despite the artist's intent to capture "the spirit of Africa in a broad sense," the bronzes' inclusion in the anthropology exhibits at the Smithsonian, with their emphasis on scientific empiricism, made it almost inevitable that over the forty

Fig. 4.12. A Kongo figure, minkisi, from the Ward collection, Smithsonian Institution. E323,278. Photograph by Diane Nordeck. Reproduced with permission from the Smithsonian Institution.

years that the sculptures remained on view, they would come to be understood by the public to be accurate depictions of particular African groups and a part of the ethnographic record of Africa. Because they are ethnographic pastiches, however, they hold little documentary value for the anthropological study of the rich history and cultures of Zaire, and they have no place on exhibit in the National Museum of Natural History.

Should the Ward bronzes be transferred to one of the Smithsonian's art museums and displayed as examples of turn-of-the-century European "ethnographic sculpture"? If they were included in such an exhibition, would reinstalling them in an art museum be a sufficient shift in their context of display to successfully historicize the images and simultaneously to communicate to the viewer that the artist's sculptures of Africans do not represent either philosophical or empirical "truths"? That would be a difficult task, and I am not optimistic that it could yet be accomplished.[32] The insidious racism toward Africans that dominated the nineteenth-century European and American popular imagination still persists in many quarters today, and these same false and oppressive stereotypes are pernicious even in the late twentieth century. Until such time as these negative stereotypes are finally overturned and rendered powerless, our museum publics might be better served if the Ward bronzes remained in the anthropology reserves as part of the Smithsonian's research collections, rather than being put once again on public display.

NOTES

1. Some of the descriptive materials relating to the Ward exhibition at the Smithsonian have appeared in Mary Jo Arnoldi, "A Distorted Mirror: The Exhibition of the Herbert Ward Collection of Africana," in *Museums and Communities:The Politics of Public Display,* ed. Ivan Karp and Steven D. Lavine (Washington, D.C.: Smithsonian Institution Press, 1992), pp. 428–57. They are used here with the kind permission of the Smithsonian Institution Press.

2. Herbert Ward was born in 1863 and died in 1919 at the age of fifty-six. He worked in the Congo Free State from 1884 to 1889. Once back in England, Ward began a career as a popular writer and lecturer, drawing his material from his Congo experiences. In the late 1890s he began his career as an artist, first as a painter and later as a sculptor. His sculptures were exhibited at the Royal Academy in London and regularly at the Paris Salon. During his lifetime, individual bronzes were collected by the Musée Luxembourg (now the Musée d'Orsay) in Paris, by the Musée National in Nantes, by the National Museum, Cardiff, Wales, and by the Johannesburg Art Gallery, South Africa. The Musée Royal de l'Afrique Centrale in Tervuren, Belgium, has a group of his large plaster sculptures and more recently has acquired a table-size bronze for the fine arts collection.

Only one of Ward's nineteen bronzes does not depict a Congolese. This bronze represents a head of a gorilla. It is one of his last pieces (1912) and is the only animal sculpture he ever executed.

3. The French art critic Gérard de Rialle used the term *la sculpture ethnographique* (ethnographic sculpture) to describe these sculptures in a review of the Salon des Artistes Français in Paris in 1863. Cited in Antoinette Le Normand-Romain et al., *La sculpture ethnographique de la Vénus hottentote à la Téhura de Gauguin* (Paris: Réunion des Musées Nationaux, 1994), p. 42.

4. The Ward exhibit was dismantled in the early 1960s. With the consent of Ward's descendants, a U.S. court ruled that the conditions of the will were null and void. Ward's African objects were integrated with other African collections in new exhibits.

The zoological specimens were transferred to the appropriate departments. A few of the bronzes were reinstalled in corridors and stairwells throughout the museum, but most were placed in museum storage.

5. Throughout this period Africans were the subject of publications of anthropological societies and were regularly featured in popular travelers' accounts. Articles in the mass-circulation press and public lectures by both self-styled adventurers and missionaries also contributed to the popular image of Africans as savages. Impresarios brought Africans to world's fairs and other expositions, and these living "African" villages with their daily dramatic reenactment of dances, ceremonies, and battles proved to be extremely popular with European audiences, as did the more conventional exhibits of African objects in museums. For a discussion of this period, see Patrick Brantlinger, "Victorians and Africans: The Genealogy of the Myth of the Dark Continent," in *Race, Writing, and Difference*, ed. Henry Louis Gates Jr. (Chicago: University of Chicago Press, 1986), pp. 185–222; and Annie E. Coombes, *Reinventing Africa: Museums, Material Culture, and Popular Imagination* (New Haven and London: Yale University Press, 1994).

6. Hugh Honour recently wrote of the Ward bronzes: "His [Ward's] choice of subjects, the ways in which he posed the figures, and the facial expressions he gave them, reflect his belief that the Congolese were in a state of arrested development. . . . They are not images of 'savages' so much as of 'savagery' as understood in his time—of scientific, technological, social, artistic and religious 'backwardness' " (Hugh Honour, *Image of Blacks in Western Civilization*, vol. 4, *From the American Revolution to World War I*, pt. 2, *Black Models and White Myths* [Houston: Menil Foundation, 1989], pp. 220–22).

7. Sarita Ward, *A Valiant Gentleman* (London: Chapman and Hall, 1927), p. 165. She is referring to Belgian King Leopold II's large collection of arts and material culture from Zaire, which forms the core of the collection of the Musée Royal de l'Afrique Centrale at Tervuren, outside of Brussels.

8. Walter Hough Papers, National Anthropological Archives, Smithsonian Institution. Later, Hough wrote of the collection: "More than that [Ward] had prescience almost to gather from the Congo natives abundant examples of their weapons and other objects of their arts and industries at a time when such specimens would be of the utmost value to science" (Walter Hough, "An Appreciation of the Scientific Value of the Herbert Ward African Collection," *The Herbert Ward African Collection* [Washington, D.C.: United States National Museum, 1924], pp. 37–38).

9. From the mid-nineteenth century, travel literature about Africa stirred the public imagination and contributed to shaping popular attitudes and opinions about the continent. Livingstone's *Missionary Travels* (1857) and Stanley's *In Darkest Africa* (1890), both describing the Congo, sold 70,000 and 150,000 copies, respectively, in English alone (Brantlinger, "Victorians and Africans," p. 195). Americans began to be increasingly aware of the Congo during this period through lectures and publications by various missionary societies. King Leopold II's commercial agents also worked at promoting American investment in the Congo. In 1910 King Leopold gave a collection of Congo materials to the American Museum of Natural History in New York, on whose board were many important bankers and businessmen. At the turn of the century the Congo Free State was increasingly in the news in Europe and America as labor atrocities committed against Africans in the Congo were revealed by missionaries, diplomats, and various benevolent associations. Prominent Americans, such as George Washington

Williams and Mark Twain, responded by publishing searing criticisms of King Leopold's Congo administration and of its labor practices.

10. Herbert Ward's books included *Five Years with the Congo Cannibals* (New York: Robert Bonner's Sons, 1890); *My Life with Stanley's Rear Guard* (New York: C. L. Webster, 1891); and *A Voice from the Congo* (New York: Charles Scribner's Sons, 1910).

11. Gertrude Brigham, "Smithsonian Institution Receives Herbert Ward Statues of African Jungle People," *Christian Science Monitor,* March 15, 1922, pp. 8–9; D. Jay Culver, "Herbert Ward—An Artist and Adventurer," *Dearborn Independent,* May 27, 1922, p. 11; Sterling Helig, "Unique Gift for the Smithsonian," *Washington (D.C.) Sunday Star,* March 16, 1913, pp. 2–3.

12. Records of the Anthropology Department, National Anthropological Archives, Smithsonian Institution.

13. The current museum known as the National Gallery of Art was established only in the 1930s and is not part of the Smithsonian museum system. At the beginning of the twentieth century, the Smithsonian created a National Gallery of Art. In 1920 Congress officially recognized it as a Smithsonian bureau. It was later renamed the National Collection of Fine Arts and is now called the National Museum of American Art.

14. For an analysis of the trophy-style display, see Coombes, *Reinventing Africa,* pp. 71–72.

15. Records of the Anthropology Department, National Anthropological Archives, Smithsonian Institution.

16. Walter Hough, "Installation of Ethnological Material," in *Proceedings of the American Association of Museums,* 10:118 (Pittsburgh: [Association], 1916), p. 118.

17. Records of the Anthropology Department, National Anthropological Archives, Smithsonian Institution.

18. Draft manuscript, Walter Hough Papers, National Anthropological Archives, Smithsonian Institution.

19. Curtis M. Hinsley, Jr., *Savages and Scientists: The Smithsonian Institution and the Development of American Anthropology, 1846–1910* (Washington, D.C.: Smithsonian Institution Press, 1981), p. 105.

20. Walter Hough Papers, National Anthropological Archives, Smithsonian Institution.

21. Culver, "Herbert Ward," p. 2.

22. Brigham, "Herbert Ward Statues," p. 8. Brigham wrote of the Ward exhibition: "African ethnology in a leading art exhibition is a novelty, not merely in Washington, but the world. . . . Guests were received in the apartment specially designed to accommodate the immense collection. . . . The walls were bedecked with the fantastic array of knives and other weapons. . . . [B]elow them, in cases were exhibited other trophies—a huge elephant's head, a giant python, ivory carvings, a variety of textiles and garments, musical instruments, drums—the whole forming a setting for the magnificent sculptural compositions in bronze."

23. Le Normand-Romain et al., *La sculpture ethnographique,* pp. 33–50.

24. Ward, *Five Years with the Congo Cannibals,* p. 88.

25. See plate 103 in Frederick Starr, *Congo Natives* (Chicago: Lakeside Press, 1912), for the photograph of the man from Yambuya. It is interesting to note that Aruimi is a river name and not the name of any specific ethnic group living in this area. During

the 1880s many of the groups living along the upper Congo River and its tributaries were identified by Europeans only by the names of these rivers.

26. Ward, *Five Years with the Congo Cannibals,* p. 41.

27. Ibid., pp. 43–44. For an informed discussion of the complex role that *ngang'a nkisi* play in Kongo culture, see Wyatt MacGaffey, "The Eyes of Understanding: Kongo Minkisi," in *Astonishment and Power: Kongo Minkisi and the Art of Renee Stout* (Washington, D.C.: National Museum of African Art, Smithsonian Institution, 1993), pp. 20–103.

28. A well-known series of "ethnographic sculptures" representing the continents from the late nineteenth century was commissioned for the Universelle Exposition of 1878. This grouping remained on display in Paris, on the terrace of the Palais du Trocadéro, until 1935. It is currently on display on the terrace of the Musée d'Orsay in Paris. See A. Pingeot and A. Le Normand-Romain, *Musée d'Orsay: Catalogue sommaire illustré des sculptures* (Paris: Editions de la Réunion des Musées Nationaux, 1986).

29. Frances Susan Connelly, *The Sleep of Reason: Primitivism in Mod9ern European Art and Aesthetics, 1725–1907* (University Park: Pennsylvania State University. 1995), pp. 17–18.

30. Ward, *Five Years with the Congo Cannibals,* pp. 136–38.

31. Helig, "Unique Gift for the Smithsonian," pp. 2–3.

32. A recent attempt by the curator of the exhibition "Into the Heart of Africa" (Royal Ontario Museum, 1989) and the curators of "The West as America" (National Museum of American Art, 1991) to reinterpret nineteenth-century images of Africa and of the West in America roused vociferous criticism by different publics. Both exhibits attempted to show how nineteenth-century artistic and textual constructions of Africa and of the American West were far from neutral—indeed, were highly problematic. The sometimes willful misunderstandings of the exhibitions' intentions and messages underscores the political dimensions of museum representation and the difficulty of historicizing and reinterpreting artistic images that have been invested with an aura of "truth."

5

Capable of Flight
The Saga of the 1903 Wright Airplane

TOM D. CROUCH

Those who doubt the power of historic objects to inspire awe and wonder should spend some time in the National Air and Space Museum's Milestones of Flight Gallery. This is the spot where visitors to the world's most popular museum encounter the icons of the aerospace age: Charles Lindbergh's *Spirit of St. Louis;* the Bell X-1, first aircraft to fly faster than sound; the *Friendship 7* spacecraft, in which the first American orbited the globe; the *Apollo XI* command module that carried the first human beings to the Moon; the *Pioneer* and *Voyager* spacecraft that have traveled beyond the limits of the solar system.

The ultimate in winged icons, the world's first airplane, hangs in the place of honor at the very center of the Milestones Gallery. The 1903 Wright Flyer is *the real thing,* the actual assemblage of wood and wire that took to the skies for the very first time. "It is," a British ambassador to the United States once remarked, "a little as if we had before us the original wheel."[1]

Small wonder that this gallery has such an enormous impact on visitors. Flight is one of our oldest dreams and most potent symbols. To fly is to achieve mastery over the environment, to taste ultimate freedom, to escape earthly restraint. From the beginning, we placed our gods in the sky and made flight the universal attribute of divinity. As Plato explained: "The natural function of the wing is to carry that which is heavy up to the place where dwells the race of gods."

The gods did not give us wings, so we made them for ourselves. The historic airplanes and spacecraft on display in the Milestones Gallery are proof of our success. Here are the machines that have carried us from the sands of Kitty Hawk to the edge of the solar system in less than a century. The psychological impact of the achievement is stunning. If human beings can fly, is there anything they cannot accomplish?

Ironically, the symbolic power of the craft that first took to the air in powered flight was not immediately apparent to Wilbur and Orville Wright. During the critical years 1900–1905, they gave little thought to preserving the historic aircraft that had served as their stepping-stones on the road to the invention of the airplane.

The brothers simply abandoned their earliest machines to the elements once they had served their intended purpose. The wind, sun, and sand of the Outer Banks of North Carolina made quick work of the 1900, 1901, and 1902 Wright gliders. The brothers burned their 1904 machine, the world's second powered airplane, to create hangar space for its successor. True to form, they abandoned their 1905 aircraft, the world's first practical airplane, immediately after it had flown the world's first aircraft passenger. Wilbur and Orville reasoned that it had served its purpose.

Fortunately, the Wrights made an exception in the case of their 1903 airplane. The craft had been badly damaged in an accident on the ground following its four successful flights on the morning of December 17, 1903, but the brothers took the time and trouble to pack and ship the broken bits of wood, wire, and fabric home to Ohio. The sad remains of the world's first airplane went through the 1913 Dayton flood in the original packing crates, which had sat unopened for more than a decade.[2]

At the urging of others, Orville Wright finally unpacked and restored the historic machine in 1916. As the full extent of public interest in the craft became apparent, he realized that the world's first airplane could be employed as a crucial bargaining chip in resolving his bitter and long-running battle with officials of the Smithsonian Institution.

The dispute between the Wrights and the Smithsonian was rooted in the crash of a rival flying machine into the icy waters of the Potomac River on December 8, 1903. Officially known as the Langley Aerodrome, the craft had been dubbed *"Mud Duck"* and the *"Buzzard"* by Washington journalists. It was the brainchild of Samuel Pierpont Langley, a self-trained astronomer who had become secretary of the Smithsonian, and the nation's unofficial chief scientist, in 1887.

Langley had become interested in flight after attending a lecture on the subject at the annual meeting of the American Association for the Advancement of

Fig. 5.1. The 1903 Wright airplane and camp buildings, Kill Devil Hills, North Carolina, November 24, 1903. Photograph from the collection of the National Air and Space Museum, Smithsonian Institution.

Science in 1886. After ten years of aeronautical experimentation, Langley and his Smithsonian engineers had produced a series of steam-powered model aircraft with wingspans of up to fifteen feet. The program culminated in May and November 1896, when two of these aircraft successfully covered distances of up to 4,200 feet through the air.

The age of flight seemed suddenly close at hand, and Langley was the most likely candidate to inaugurate it. In 1898, with the help of his influential friend Charles Doolittle Walcott, of the U.S. Geological Survey, Langley received a fifty-thousand-dollar grant from the War Department for the development of a full-scale, man-carrying flying machine. Completed in 1903, the Langley Aerodrome sported tandem wings spreading fifty feet from tip to tip. With a 52-horsepower radial engine spinning the twin propellers at 575 rpm, it looked and sounded like a gigantic dragonfly.

But there were problems. The control system was so primitive that Charles Matthews Manly, Langley's chief aeronautical assistant and volunteer "pilot," would be little more than a helpless passenger. The takeoff and landing arrangements were even more frightening. Like the models that had preceded it, the Aerodrome was designed to be launched into the air by a catapult mounted on the roof of a houseboat anchored in the Potomac. The untried structure would encounter maximum stress at the very moment of takeoff. If all went well, the machine would simply settle into the river at the end of its flight. Under ideal conditions, the pilot, housed in a fabric-sided cockpit on the underside of the craft, would finish his great adventure sunk up to his eyebrows in the muddy water, with the airplane resting on top of him. If something went awry—if, say, the airplane strayed over land—well, it was better not to think of that.

Manly made his first trip down the launch rail on October 7, 1903, and fell straight into the water. One reporter quipped that the Great Aerodrome had the flying qualities of "a handful of mortar." Two months later, on December 8, Manly climbed back into the cockpit for a second try. This time the rear wings began to fold up even before the machine reached the end of the rail. Seconds later, the Great Aerodrome, Samuel Pierpont Langley's pride and joy, was a tangle of wood, wire, fabric, and bent tubing floating in the river.

Langley was reviled on the floor of Congress and in the nation's newspapers. The disaster also cast a pall over those who had hoped for a quick solution to the problems of heavier-than-air flight. In his final report on the Langley project, Maj. N. W. Macomb, a U.S. Army observer, commented, "We are still far from the ultimate goal, and it would seem as if years of constant work and study by experts, together with the expenditure of thousands of dollars, would still be necessary before we can hope to produce an apparatus of practical utility on these lines."[3]

Nine days after the Langley crash, on December 17, 1903, Wilbur and Orville Wright made four flights over an isolated stretch of North Carolina beach. For the first time, a heavier-than-air flying machine had left the ground under its own power, moved forward through the air a distance sufficient to demonstrate that it was capable of sustained flight, and landed safely, all under the control of the pilot.

The Wrights knew that they had not achieved their final goal at Kitty Hawk. The flights of December 17 had been only one more step, although a rather large one, on the road to the development of a practical flying machine. Even their best flight of the day, during which Wilbur had covered 852 feet through the air in 59 seconds, would not sound terribly exciting to a world that had waited millennia for flight. The attitude of the *Dayton Journal*'s Frank Tunison was typical. When informed of the events at Kitty Hawk, he remarked: "Fifty-

Fig. 5.2. The 1903 Wright airplane took to the air for the first time at 10:35 on the morning of December 17, 1903. Prior to takeoff, Orville Wright pointed the tripod and camera at the spot where he thought the airplane would leave the launch rail. John Daniels, an observer from the nearby U.S. Lifesaving Service Station, was asked to trip the shutter at the appropriate moment. The result is a great moment in history, frozen forever on a glass photographic plate. Photograph from the collection of the National Air and Space Museum, Smithsonian Institution.

seven seconds [*sic*], hey? If it had been fifty-seven minutes then it might have been a news item."

The brothers returned home to Dayton, where they located a suitable pasture/flying field eight miles east of town. Here they would fly two new powered machines in relative secrecy during 1904 and 1905. By the fall of 1905, the practical airplane was a reality.

Wilbur and Orville Wright's work stood in marked contrast to that of Samuel Langley. Between 1899 and 1905, working far from the glare of publicity that surrounded the Smithsonian project, they had moved steadily through an evolutionary sequence of seven machines: one kite (1899), three manned gliders (1900, 1901, 1902), and three powered aircraft (1903, 1904, 1905). Each successive machine was a distillation of the lessons learned and the experience gained with its predecessors. The aircraft were the result of a careful process of design, which incorporated not only flight-test experience but the results of ground-based research conducted with a wind tunnel that they had constructed themselves in the fall of 1901. The process itself, quite as much as the final product, marked Wilbur and Orville Wright as engineers of genius.

The Wright brothers spent the next three years on the ground, unwilling to risk exposing their machine until their ideas had received patent protection and they had negotiated contracts for the sale of their technology. With their first public flights in Europe and America in the summer and fall of 1908, they emerged as the first genuinely heroic figures of the twentieth century.

But trouble lay ahead. The Wrights had been granted a patent so broad that it was virtually impossible to build a successful airplane without infringing on it. The brothers were more than willing to let any honest experimenter use their patent free of charge, but they put those who sought to make a profit in a different category. They let it be known that any aviator who sold tickets to a flying exhibition, or who built airplanes for sale, would have to pay a royalty to the patent holders—or face a suit for infringement.

In January 1910 the Wrights obtained an injunction against their principal American rival, Glenn Hammond Curtiss, a onetime motorcycle racer and manufacturer turned flying-machine builder. The resulting case was fought out in the courts over the next four years. The leaders of the budding American aviation community were forced to take sides; the contest was bitterly fought, and feelings ran high in both camps.

Wilbur Wright died of typhoid fever in the spring of 1912. His brother, convinced that the strain of the patent suit had been a major factor in weakening Wilbur, resolved to push on to a final resolution of the dispute. That came on January 13, 1914, when the U.S. Circuit Court of Appeals handed down a final decision in favor of the Wright Company.[4]

That decision set the stage for the Wright-Smithsonian dispute. Samuel Langley had died in 1906. The new secretary of the Smithsonian, Charles D. Walcott, had played an influential role in funding the 1903 Aerodrome and was eager to redeem the reputation of his old friend. He installed a Langley memorial tablet on the wall of the Smithsonian Castle, established the Langley Medal to be awarded for contributions to aeronautics, and created the Langley Aerodynamical Laboratory, which he hoped would grow into a great national facility for the conduct of aeronautical research. May 6, the day on which Langley had flown the first of his successful steam-powered unmanned models, became an unofficial holiday, Langley Day, at the Smithsonian.

On January 21, 1914, Lincoln Beachey, the best-known American stunt pilot of the day, wired the Smithsonian with a request to rebuild and test the 1903 Langley Aerodrome. Beachey had a clear interest in the recent court decision. He had learned to fly at the Curtiss school, had been the star aerial performer on the Curtiss exhibition team, and was a Curtiss stockholder. Smithsonian administrator Richard Rathbun may have had this in mind when he passed the telegram on to Walcott with a recommendation: "I do not think you will want to grant Mr. Beachey's request."[5]

Alexander Graham Bell, a Smithsonian regent and a friend of both Langley and Walcott, agreed. Bell suggested that the Langley machine was too valuable an artifact to be tampered with or risked in flight, although he did suggest that an exact replica might be constructed. Walcott refused Beachey's request, but a seed had been planted. It was obvious that the ultimate step in redeeming Langley's reputation would be to fly the Aerodrome, demonstrating that, had conditions been slightly different, the honors heaped on Wilbur and Orville Wright would have gone to Samuel Pierpont Langley instead.

When invited to bring one of his float planes to Washington to participate in the 1914 Langley Day celebration, Glenn Curtiss remarked that he "would like to put the Langley aeroplane itself in the air." This time Walcott jumped at the chance. Without informing Bell or any of the other regents, he authorized Albert F. Zahm, who had been a key witness for Curtiss in the patent trial and was now the man in charge of the Langley Aerodynamical Laboratory, to turn over all the surviving parts of the old machine to Curtiss.[6]

"The main objects of these renewed trials," Zahm remarked, "were first to show whether the original Langley machine was capable of sustained free flight with a pilot, and secondly, to determine more fully the advantages of the tandem-wing type of aeroplane."[7] There obviously are better ways to test the flying qualities of tandem-wing airplanes than to rebuild the shattered remnant of an eleven-year-old machine that never flew. It was clear that the only real purpose of the tests was to demonstrate that the Langley machine had been "capable" of flight in 1903. Both Curtiss and the Smithsonian stood to benefit from proof that the old machine was airworthy. Curtiss could return to court, arguing that the pioneer status granted the Wright patent was unwarranted. Walcott would have demonstrated that his old friend Langley had not really failed at all.

Curtiss and Zahm announced that they would return the craft to its condition at the time of the 1903 tests. If that was their goal, they failed to achieve it. The wings constructed for the machine in the Curtiss plant differed from the originals in chord (the straight-line distance from the leading edge to the trailing edge), camber (distance from the peak of the arch of the wing to the imaginary chord line), and aspect ratio (the ratio of span to chord). The trussing system that linked the wings to the fuselage was much different as well. The king posts had been relocated, and the wires were trussed to different spars at different points. This was particularly important, for most authorities believed that the failure of the wing structure, not a catapult defect, had been responsible for the 1903 disaster.[8]

There were other changes as well. Curtiss fitted the craft with his own yoke-and-wheel flight control system. After the first trial, he altered the tail to serve as both rudder and elevator. Finally, he rejected the old catapult launch system, mounting the machine on floats. This change can be excused in the name of simple self-preservation. It does not seem to have occurred to anyone at the time, however, that Curtiss had come up with a way to land the machine safely, which had been impossible with the original craft.

On the morning on May 28, 1914, the rebuilt Aerodrome, with Curtiss himself at the controls, sped across the surface of Lake Keuka, near the site of the Curtiss factory at Hammondsport, New York, and lifted into the air for a flight of 150 feet. After a few additional hops of similar length, the craft was taken back into the shop, where the 1903 Langley engine was replaced with a modern Curtiss power plant.

Walcott and Zahm were overjoyed. In an account of the tests published in the 1914 Smithsonian *Annual Report,* Zahm claimed that the Aerodrome "has demonstrated that with its original structure and power, it is capable of flying with a pilot and several hundred pounds of useful load. It is the first aeroplane in the history of the world of which this can truthfully be said." Rather than providing a list of alterations, Zahm reported that the old Aerodrome had been flown "without modifications." "With a thrust of 450 pounds," he concluded, "the Langley aeroplane, without floats, restored to its original condition and provided with stronger bearings, should be able to carry a man and sufficient supplies for a voyage lasting practically the whole day."[9]

This was only the beginning. The 1915 *Annual Report* repeated the claim: "The tests thus far made have shown that former Secretary Langley had succeeded in building the first aeroplane capable of sustained free flight with a man." Similar statements would appear in various Smithsonian publications in years to come.[10]

Then there was the label. When the Aerodrome was shipped back from Hammondsport, Walcott ordered that it be returned to its original 1903 condition. It was then exhibited in the Arts and Industries Building with a label explaining that it was the "first man-carrying aeroplane in the history of the world capable of sustained free flight."

Orville Wright was justifiably outraged. At the outset of their careers, he and his brother had written to the Smithsonian for advice on useful readings in the field of aeronautics. They had always been careful to mention that the involvement of the world-renowned Samuel Langley in aeronautics had been an important factor in convincing them that the problem of flight could be solved. At the same time, they owed no technical debt to Langley, nor had they ever believed that his machine could fly.

The Wright brothers' relationship with the Smithsonian had begun to sour soon after Langley's death in 1906. Walcott, at Bell's suggestion, had awarded the first Langley Medal to the Wrights. In preparing the text of their remarks for publication, however, the secretary quoted an earlier Wright letter that, in the words of one observer, "helped to create a false impression . . . that the Wrights had acknowledged indebtedness to Langley's scientific work."[11]

The brothers had also become suspicious when, in 1910, Secretary Walcott all but refused their offer to donate the 1903 Wright airplane to the Smithsonian. Walcott had written in March 1910 requesting "one of your machines, or a model thereof, for exhibition purposes." The Wrights agreed to have a model of any of their craft constructed for the museum. "Or," they wrote, "we can reconstruct the 1903 machine with which the first flights were made at Kitty Hawk. Most of the parts are still in existence."

The brothers were stunned when the secretary replied that the Smithsonian would prefer the 1909 military flyer. In addition, Walcott requested a series of models of Wright aircraft and several full-scale engines to display in conjunction with specimens from the Langley collection, "making the exhibit illustrate two very important steps in the history of the aeronautical art." The Smithsonian planned to exhibit the 16-horsepower Wright engine of 1903 next to the 52-horsepower Langley engine; a 1909 Wright aircraft with parts of the Langley machine; and scale models of manned Wright aircraft with the unmanned Langley steam models of 1896. Small wonder that the Wright brothers' suspicions were aroused.[12]

Now the Smithsonian had sponsored the reconstruction and testing of the Langley machine by a man with whom the Wrights were locked in a bitter patent fight. Orville asked his brother Lorin to visit Hammondsport during the tests to see for himself what was going on. Curtiss workmen seized his camera and confiscated the film.[13]

Fortunately, many of the changes that had been made in the Aerodrome were visible in the photographs released by the Smithsonian. Some additional detective work by Orville's English friend and patent agent, Griffith Brewer, who offered a lecture on the episode at the Royal Society of the Arts in 1921, resulted in a complete catalog of the changes made to the 1903 Aerodrome during the first and second episodes of rebuilding at Hammondsport. The evidence seemed overwhelming to most unbiased readers: The 1914 test had not demonstrated that the 1903 Langley Aerodrome was "capable" of flight.

Orville Wright remained aloof from the controversy until 1921. "A denial of these [Smithsonian] statements by me might have been looked upon by the public as a jealous attack upon the work of a man who was dead," he later remarked. "It was not until 1921 that I became convinced that the officials of the Smithsonian, at least Dr. Walcott, were fully acquainted with the character of the tests at Hammondsport. I had thought up to that time that they might have been ignorant of the fundamental changes which had been incorporated in the machine . . . and that when these changes were pointed out to them they would hasten to correct their erroneous reports. They did not do this, but have continued to repeat their earlier statements."[14]

Leaders of the world aviation community had been impressed by the revelations of Brewer's 1921 report. The English aeronautical engineer Leonard Bairstow spoke for many when he remarked the following year that "the Hammondsport trails were not part of the work of Langley, and in the opinion of many of us were ill-advised."[15]

In spite of such support, Orville began to feel like David battling Goliath. His letters to officials of the Smithsonian, including Chief Justice William Howard Taft, had little effect. Nor could he interest the press in an argument over events that had occurred twenty years earlier.

Then, in the spring of 1925, he played his trump card, announcing that the 1903 Wright airplane would be sent to the Science Museum of London. The idea had been suggested by Griffith Brewer, who had been involved in planning aeronautical exhibits for the museum, which was moving into new quarters in South Kensington. Orville Wright's decision to act on his friend's advice created a furor. In response to those who asked that he reconsider, Orville replied: "I believe my course in sending our Kitty Hawk machine to a foreign museum is the only way of correcting the history of the flying-machine, which by false and misleading statements has been perverted by the Smithsonian Institution."[16]

It was a stroke of political genius. The announcement that this priceless national treasure was being sent abroad galvanized public attention.

Orville himself had scarcely given the old machine a thought prior to 1916, when he received a request to display the reassembled craft at ceremonies dedicating a series of new buildings at the Massachusetts Institute of Technology. During the first week of June 1916, he ordered the crates brought to the Wright factory from the barn where they had been stored. Company workmen then laid out the material so that Orville could assess the situation and decide how to proceed.

The crankcase of the original engine had been broken in the accident of December 17, 1903. The crankshaft and flywheel had disappeared following a 1906 New York exhibition. For that reason, Orville decided to outfit the 1903 machine with the very similar engine that had powered the 1904 and 1905 airplanes. Most of the wooden members of the elevator and rudder, and the main wingspars of the central bay, would have to be replaced. New fabric would also be required for the central wing bay. Beyond that, most of the original parts of the machine could be refurbished and retained.

The restored aircraft was unveiled at the MIT dedication and subsequently displayed at various aviation events in New York and Dayton between 1916 and 1924. Beginning in December 1926, Orville, his secretary Mabel Beck, and Jim Jacobs, a trusted workman, performed some additional restoration work on the woodwork and completely re-covered the machine with new fabric. Following a visit to Dayton in February 1926, Brewer informed M. J. B. Davy of the Science Museum: "All the original parts of the Machine are being preserved. Those which are complete [are] being utilized, and those which are broken or missing being replaced by obviously new parts."

Brewer suggested to Davy, and to museum director Sir Henry Lyons, that the craft might be ready for unveiling when King George V opened the final section of the new Science Museum building in 1927. In fact, the crates containing the restored 1903 Wright aircraft, complete with instructions for assembly, were finally loaded aboard the Atlantic Transport Line vessel *Minnewaska,* which sailed for England on February 11, 1928.[17]

Orville Wright's decision to send the world's first airplane to an English museum took Secretary Walcott by surprise. For the first time he found himself on the defensive. Recognizing that he could no longer base his claim that the Langley Aerodrome had been "capable" of flight solely on the Hammondsport tests, he invited Joseph Ames and David W. Taylor, both recognized aviation authorities and distinguished members of the National Advisory Committee for Aeronautics (NACA), to look into the case and offer a judgment as to the airworthiness to the old machine.

Ames and Taylor apparently were not provided with a complete list of the changes made to the Aerodrome in 1914. While the two men admitted that the 1914 machine had been much stronger than the 1903 craft, they concluded that "structurally the original Langley machine was capable of level and controlled flight." They argued that, while the Wrights "were the first to navigate the air," Langley, "after years of effort, following a different road, was in sight of the same goal." Orville Wright disagreed, as did most of the rest of the American aeronautical community and the qualified engineers who have examined the craft since that time. But Secretary Walcott, resting his case on the report, refused to budge.[18]

Charles D. Walcott died in 1927. His successor, Charles Greeley Abbot, reduced the label on the Aerodrome to read: "Langley Aerodrome—The Original Langley Flying Machine of 1903, Restored." Moreover, in 1928, the year the Wright plane was shipped to London, the Smithsonian Board of Regents passed a resolution declaring that "to the Wrights belongs the credit of making the first successful flight with a power-propelled heavier-than-air machine carrying a man." The resolution was meaningless. No one, not even Secretary Walcott, had questioned the Wrights' priority in having made the first flight. The controversy was over which plane had been the first "capable of flight."

Secretary Abbot and Orville Wright met and corresponded, seeking a solution that would satisfy Orville without unduly embarrassing the Smithsonian. Speaking in Washington on December 17, 1933, Abbot suggested the creation of a committee to mediate the differences between Wright and the Smithsonian and proposed that Charles Lindbergh head the group. Orville accepted and spelled out his understanding of the arrangement.

He suggested that the work of the committee be limited to a study of the specific problem, that is, the Smithsonian claim that the 1914 Hammondsport tests had demonstrated the capability of the 1903 Aerodrome for flight. If the committee judged that the Langley machine was so capable, Orville would bring the 1903 Wright airplane home. If Wright was vindicated, however, he would expect the Smithsonian to "rectify the offenses committed by it in the past in its own publications by printing full corrections in these same publications. These corrections shall be unequivocal, and shall be given a prominence and circulation equal to that given to the former statements of which they are a correction, so that in the future the matters involved can not be misunderstood."[19]

Lindbergh, who wanted to help in any way he could, met with Abbot and Wright independently in January 1934. He told both men that he believed the first step should be to establish the basic facts in the case. He asked Orville Wright to begin the process by preparing a statement of the important differences between the 1903 Aerodrome and the machine flown at Hammondsport in 1914.

Lindbergh met with Abbot again in late January. In a letter describing that meeting to Orville Wright, Abbot said that Lindbergh feared he would not be able to devote enough time to the study of the questions involved. Abbot therefore suggested that the secretaries of War, Navy, and Commerce each be asked to name an individual to serve on a committee that would weigh the evidence. He proposed that this committee be asked to address five specific questions:

1. In what ways was the 1914 machine similar to the 1903 Aerodrome?
2. In what ways were they different?
3. What bearing do the 1914 tests have on a determination of the capacity of the 1903 machine to fly?
4. What bearing do the flights of Langley's models in 1896 and 1903 have on the determination of the capacity of the full-scale 1903 Aerodrome to fly?
5. What other facts, if any, would assist in determining the capacity of the 1903 Aerodrome to fly?

Orville was unwilling to accept such a committee. Each of the members had some official connection to the Smithsonian. He left unspoken the obvious fact that, as a courtesy and in the interest of fair play, he should have been offered an opportunity to participate in selecting the members of the committee. Moreover, he believed that Abbot's proposed charge to the group was much too broad. Orville was really interested in only two things: a published list of the differences between the 1903 Aerodrome and the 1914 Hammondsport machine and an admission by the Smithsonian that the craft had in fact been heavily modified.

Orville proceeded as if the committee idea had never been raised. He sent Lindbergh a list of alterations to the Langley craft based on Griffith Brewer's 1921 paper, with specific dimensions of the 1903 Aerodrome on one side of the pages and those of the 1914 machine on the other. It was his feeling that with such data in hand, any reader could see the difference between the two craft at a glance.

Lindbergh passed the list on to Abbot, who, finding no substantial errors, returned it to Orville with a proposal that it be published as part of a long article that would include:

1. An account of Langley's work up to 1903
2. A history of the Aerodrome from 1903 to 1914
3. Republication of Zahm's original article of 1914
4. Orville's comparison of the 1903 and 1914 machines
5. Zahm's notes on Orville's list of changes
6. The facts relating to the subsequent exhibition of the 1903 machine since 1914

Once again, Orville was outraged. Abbot was suggesting that the simple comparison of the 1903 and 1914 machines be buried in a mass of extraneous material, including the offending article that had launched the controversy in the first place. He wrote to Abbot on March 15, 1935, outlining in clear and precise terms that sort of article that might lead to the return of the 1903 Wright Flyer:

> Instead of a paper such as you have proposed may I offer the following sugges-
> tions: That the Smithsonian publish a paper presenting a list of specifications in
> parallel columns of those features of the Langley machine of 1903 and the
> Hammondsport machine of 1914, in which there were differences, with an
> introduction stating that the Smithsonian now finds that it was misled by the
> Zahm report of 1914; that through the Zahm paper the Institution was led to
> believe that the aeroplane tested at Hammondsport was "as nearly as possible in
> its original condition"; that as a result of this misinformation the Smithsonian
> had published erroneous statements from time to time alleging that the original
> Langley machine, without modification, or with only such modifications as were
> necessary for the addition of floats, had been successfully flown at Hammonds-
> port in 1914; that it ask its readers to disregard all of its former statements and
> expressions of opinion regarding the flights at Hammondsport in 1914, because
> these were based on misinformation as the list to follow will show. The list and
> specifications are to be agreed upon by the Smithsonian, Colonel Lindbergh
> and myself.

This was Orville Wright's final word on the subject. He would not require the Smithsonian to admit that the 1903 Aerodrome was incapable of flight. He would be satisfied with a simple admission that the Smithsonian statements re-lating to the 1914 tests were untrue. Secretary Abbot did not respond to the proposal.

Lindbergh, both fascinated and puzzled by the controversy, offered a thought-ful assessment of the situation in a 1939 diary entry. "The fault," he believed, "lies primarily with the Smithsonian people. But Orville Wright is not an easy man to deal with [on] the matter. I don't blame him much, though, when I think of the way he was treated for a period of years. He has encountered the narrow-mindedness of science and the dishonesty of commerce."[20]

The tide of public opinion was clearly flowing in Orville Wright's favor. Over the next eight years Abbot was bombarded with requests that the Smith-sonian take the steps required to obtain the return of the 1903 Wright airplane. Bills were introduced in Congress calling for an investigation and the creation of a committee to resolve the dispute. A new organization, Men with Wings, was established to support the return of the 1903 airplane from England. Private cit-izens and aviation leaders offered to mediate a solution.

Liberty, Collier's, and other national magazines took up the cry with articles titled "Bring Home the Wright Plane," "The Road to Justice," and "Bring Back Our Winged Exile." With the exception of the acerbic English editor C. G. Grey, the aviation trade press was almost exclusively pro-Wright.[21]

It was an extraordinarily difficult time for Abbot. By the mid-thirties the feud threatened irreparable damage to the Smithsonian's reputation. Orville was widely portrayed as an oppressed citizen beset by a powerful government bureaucracy that was blind to justice. Occasionally Abbot's patience wore a bit thin. In 1930 the Macmillan Company sent the Smithsonian an advance copy of John Goldstrum's *Narrative History of Aviation,* which contained an account of the controversy to date, favorable to Orville Wright. The secretary, against the best legal advice, threatened to sue for defamation of Secretary Walcott's character.[22]

By 1937, both Orville Wright and C. G. Abbot had, in truth, given up any hope of reaching an agreement. In response to a letter from the president of the National Cash Register Corporation asking that he make one more attempt to negotiate a solution, Abbot remarked: "I regret that the Institution's experience on this subject during the past ten years, when it has made many efforts to compose these differences, has been so unpleasant and discouraging that without trustworthy assurances of success, the Institution would now hesitate to move at all . . . lest it should only arouse renewed misrepresentation."[23]

Orville Wright was just as discouraged. In a last will and testament prepared in 1937, he included a stipulation that the 1903 airplane should remain in London after his death, unless the will was amended by a subsequent letter from him indicating a change of heart.

Then, early in 1942, Fred C. Kelly stepped forward. Kelly, a writer who was working on an authorized biography of the brothers, had begun to fear that his book might never be completed. Orville seemed convinced that Kelly was not getting the story on paper with the clarity and precision he required. Kelly, eager to put the inventor in his debt, quietly wrote to Abbot, suggesting that he would be willing to assist in preparing a statement that would satisfy Orville Wright.

Kelly knew precisely what would work—the publication of the differences between the 1903 Aerodrome and the 1914 machine flown at Hammondsport, plus a disavowal of the 1914 Zahm report. With great difficulty and considerable finesse, he moved Abbot toward just such a publication. It finally appeared a paper published by the Smithsonian on October 24, 1942, preceded by a note: "This paper has been submitted to Dr. Orville Wright, and under date of October 8, 1942, he states that the paper as now prepared will be acceptable to him if given adequate publication."[24]

Was the long feud over? Charles Abbot was by no means certain. Orville Wright did not respond to the long-awaited publication. Rumors that the aircraft would return to the United States appeared in the press during the months immediately following World War II, then disappeared. Orville Wright died on January 30, 1948, without having informed the Smithsonian of the ultimate fate of the 1903 Wright airplane.

At the time of the inventor's death, Secretary Abbot had recently retired. His successor, Alexander Wetmore, when informed of the stipulation regarding the airplane in the 1937 will, remarked to Gen. H. H. "Hap" Arnold: "So far as I know, no such letter calling the machine back to the States was ever issued." Believing that the plane would stay in England, Wetmore planned to have a full-scale replica constructed for the museum.

As the executors of the Wright estate were to discover, however, Orville had decided that the publication of Abbot's 1942 article *was* satisfactory. He had written on December 8, 1943, to inform the director of the Science Museum that he would be asking for the return of the machine once the war was over and the craft could be safely transported. This letter, which had not been made public by either Orville Wright or the Science Museum, fulfilled the condition of the 1937 will for the return of the aircraft.

Further evidence of intent was found in a stipulation contained in an unsigned will on which Orville Wright and his lawyer had been at work at the time of his death: "I give and bequeath to the U.S. National Museum of Washington, D.C., for exhibition in the National Capital only, the Wright aeroplane (now in Science Museum, London, England) which flew at Kitty Hawk, North Carolina, on the 17th of December, 1903."[25]

As the situation became clearer during the weeks following Orville's death, Smithsonian officials immediately began discussions with the executors of the Wright estate, and with the English government, to arrange the expeditious return of the world's first airplane. A great many problems still had to be resolved. The executors and their lawyer insisted on steps to ensure that the Wright heirs would not be liable for an enormous inheritance tax on the priceless relic. Moreover, they were anxious to obtain guarantees that the Smithsonian would not return to its old ways.

The final arrangement, approved by the Internal Revenue Service, called for the executors to sue the heirs for possession of the machine. This was required to ensure that no heir could claim that he or she had been cheated out of money that might have been made from the sale of the airplane. The executors stated in open court that since the aircraft was beyond price, it would be sold to the United States National Museum for the sum of one dollar, thus freeing the estate of any potential tax obligation. The people of the United States were the ultimate beneficiaries.

The contract for the sale of the world's first airplane to the museum would include other provisions as well, safeguards against a reopening of the feud. The airplane, for example, was never to be exhibited outside the Washington area. A specified label, approved by a committee of Orville Wright's old friends, was always to appear with the machine. Finally, if the Smithsonian ever again recognized any other aircraft as having been capable of powered, sustained, and controlled flight with a pilot on board before December 17, 1903, the executors of the estate would have the right to take possession of the machine once again. The Smithsonian signed.

The twenty-year exile of the world's first airplane was coming to an end. An estimated ten million people had seen the machine since its unveiling at the Science Museum on March 23, 1928. Museum officials had always recognized that the aircraft was an international treasure on loan to them and deserving of the greatest care. They had disassembled and moved it to the basement of the museum for safekeeping during the Munich Crisis. Back on display a month later, it remained suspended, protected by curtains and bomb pads, during the early months of World War II. Finally, two weeks after the fall of France, it was sent back to the safety of the basement.

On April 8, 1942, the aircraft was inspected, treated with preservatives, repacked in the crates in which it had crossed the Atlantic, and transferred to a storage chamber maintained by the Royal Army Ordnance Corps 100 feet beneath a quarry at Corsham, near Hawthorn, Wiltshire. It was moved to Corsham 2B, a nearby Admiralty storage chamber with improved climate control, on February 17, 1943.

Not long after Orville Wright had expressed his desire to bring the aircraft back to the United States following the war, Science Museum officials requested permission to keep the machine long enough to construct a replica to replace the original. Orville agreed. The aircraft apparently went back on display in South Kensington in the spring of 1946, and remained in place through the fall of 1948, while detailed drawings were prepared and a replica constructed.

The 1903 Wright airplane was lowered to the floor of the Science Museum for the last time on October 18, 1948. Captain J. L. Pritchard, secretary of the Royal Aeronautical Society and a leading historian of flight, had arranged a small ceremony to mark the occasion. Mr. George Tomlinson, minister of education, made a few appropriate remarks before symbolically turning the aircraft over to Mr. L. Satterthwaite of the U.S. Embassy. Some of the biggest names in

British flight research were in attendance, along with a handful of British aeronautical pioneers who had known the Wrights.

The machine was trucked to Southampton and carefully stowed aboard the Cunard–White Star liner *Mauretania*. Dr. Shaw, director of the Science Museum, would accompany the airplane on its voyage across the Atlantic. Originally scheduled to arrive in New York on November 10, 1948, the *Mauretania* was diverted to Halifax, Nova Scotia, by a longshoremen's strike. Paul E. Garber, who had served as the Smithsonian's chief aeronautical expert since 1920, rushed north from New York and was waiting in Halifax to greet his distinguished guest and accept responsibility for the airplane when the ship docked on November 11.

Garber, a lieutenant commander in the U.S. Navy during World War II, had arranged for a Navy truck to transport the precious cargo from the New York to Washington. Stuck with the crates on a dock at Halifax, he called Admiral Melville Pride with an additional request. "This is Commander Garber," he said. "I'm in Halifax with the Wright brothers' Kitty Hawk Flyer and I don't even have a wheelbarrow. Could you have someone come and get me?" "Good God, Garber," came the reply. "You think of the damnedest things."

The aircraft carrier USS *Palau* docked at Halifax on November 17. Two days later, Garber, his English guests, and the world's first airplane disembarked at the New York Naval Shipyard Annex, Bayonne, New Jersey. A U.S. Navy honor guard stood watch as the crates were loaded aboard a Navy tractor-trailer, the sides of which were outfitted with a pair of huge banners that read:

The Original Wright Brothers Aeroplane

The Kitty Hawk, 1903

Enroute From London, England

to Washington, D.C. for Permanent Exhibition

in the U.S. National Museum

"Operation Homecoming"

To complete the picture, both the tractor trailer and the accompanying staff car sported U.S. flags and an admiral's ensign on their fenders.

The little procession drove south from Bayonne through New York City; Woodridge, Patterson, Newark, Elizabeth, and Trenton, New Jersey; Philadelphia, Pennsylvania; Wilmington, Delaware; and Baltimore, Maryland. The story was being widely reported in the press, and small crowds and honking horns greeted the Operation Homecoming caravan along the way. The mayor of

Fig. 5.3. The USS Palau transported the crates containing the world's first airplane from Halifax, Nova Scotia, to New York City. Photograph from the collection of the National Air and Space Museum, Smithsonian Institution.

Patterson went so far as to proclaim November 20, 1948, Kitty Hawk Day, urging his fellow citizens to "display the flag of our nation as a tribute to this famous plane and its honored inventors."[26]

The Wright-Smithsonian feud officially came to an end on the morning of December 17, 1948. Eight hundred fifty people attended the ceremony in the North Hall of the Smithsonian's Arts and Industries Building. They sat in chairs facing a temporary speaker's platform—and the great tattered flag that Francis Scott Key had seen still flying over Fort McHenry in the dawn's early light of September 14, 1814. The Star-Spangled Banner was but one of the American icons in this building. George Washington's uniform, Thomas Jefferson's writing desk, Benjamin Franklin's stove, gowns worn by every First Lady since Martha Washington, and other precious reminders of two hundred years of American life were stuffed into every corner of the National Museum.

Visitors entered this cluttered treasure house through the North Hall, which housed the most popular single object in the Smithsonian—the *Spirit of St.*

Fig. 5.4. The caravan arrives at the east door of the Arts and Industries Building. Photograph from the collection of the National Air and Space Museum, Smithsonian Institution.

Louis. The silver Ryan monoplane had held the place of honor, suspended high above the central entrance doors, since its arrival at the Smithsonian in 1928. A month before the ceremony, workmen had carefully moved the *Spirit* toward the rear of the hall to make room for a new centerpiece. Charles Lindbergh had not complained. When the curator, Paul Garber, informed him of the impending move, Lindbergh remarked that he was honored to know that his machine would be sharing the hall with the world's first airplane, the 1903 Wright Flyer.

The ceremony began promptly at 10:00 A.M., for timing was a matter of some importance. Precisely forty-five years before, just after ten o'clock on the morning of December 17, 1903, the Wright Flyer had rolled down a sixty-foot takeoff rail laid out on the sand flats some four miles south of the fishing village of Kitty Hawk, North Carolina, and had climbed into the air.

Secretary Wetmore opened the proceedings with a short welcoming speech, then introduced the Honorable Frederick Vinson, chief justice of the United

Fig. 5.5. The 1903 Wright airplane suspended in the rotunda of the Arts and Industries Building. Photograph from the collection of the National Air and Space Museum, Smithsonian Institution.

States and chancellor of the Smithsonian Institution. Vinson, in turn, welcomed the guests and called Maj. Gen. Luther D. Miller, chief of chaplains of the U.S. Army, to the podium to offer the invocation. Col. Robert Landry, President Truman's Air Force aide, read a message from the President, after which Sir Oliver Franks, British ambassador to the United States, offered a few remarks.

With the preliminaries out of the way, Milton Wright, a nephew of the Wright brothers, came forward to present the world's first airplane to the National Museum. Vice President Alben W. Barkley accepted the machine on behalf of the people of the United States. The U.S. Air Force closed the event with a spectacular flyover that brought two huge B-36 bombers, twelve B-29s, and "a score" of jet-propelled F-80 fighters thundering down the Mall to welcome the Wright Flyer home.

Many of the guests who filed out of the historic North Hall of the Arts and Industries Building to enjoy the flyover would also be attending a special black-tie dinner that evening. The occasion would be the award of the prestigious Collier Trophy to Capt. Charles Yeager, John Stack, Lawrence Bell, and other members of the NACA/Air Force/industry team that had conducted the first supersonic-flight research program. A few of the guests, it is to be hoped, paused to read the label on the world's first airplane, hanging at long last where it had always belonged. It may have led them to wonder at the progress wrought in the forty-four short years that separated Kitty Hawk from the sound barrier.[27] The label read:

The Original Wright Brothers Aeroplane

The World's First Power-Driven

Heavier-Than-Air Machine

in Which Man Made Free, Controlled, and

Sustained Flight

Invented and Built by Wilbur and Orville Wright

Flown by Them at Kitty Hawk,

North Carolina

December 17, 1903

By Original Scientific Research the

Wright Brothers Discovered

the Principles of Human Flight

As Inventors, Builders, and Flyers

They Further Developed the Aeroplane

Taught Man to Fly

and Opened the Era of

Aviation

NOTES

1. Sir Oliver Franks, "Britain and the Wright Brothers," remarks in Wright biographical file, "Operation Homecoming," Archive, National Air and Space Museum, hereafter, NASM Archive.

2. For additional information on the postflight history of the early Wright aircraft, see Tom D. Crouch, "A Machine of Practical Utility: The 1905 Wright Flyer," *Timeline* 2, no. 4 (August–September 1985): 25–37; Mabel Beck, "The First Airplane After 1903," *U.S. Air Services* (December 1954): 9–10.

3. For quotation, see S. P. Langley and Charles Manly, *Memoir on Mechanical Flight* (Washington, D.C.: Smithsonian Institution, 1911), p. 278. For a more complete

treatment of the Langley project, see Tom D. Crouch, *A Dream of Wings: Americans and the Airplane, 1875–1905* (New York: W. W. Norton, 1981); Langley and Manly, *Memoir on Mechanical Flight;* J. Gordon Vaeth, *Langley: Man of Science and Flight* (New York: Roland Press, 1966).

4. For additional information on the Wright patent suits, see Tom D. Crouch, *The Bishop's Boys: A Life of Wilbur and Orville Wright* (New York: W. W. Norton, 1989); C. W. Hayward, *Practical Aeronautics* (Chicago: American Technical Society, 1917); Arthur G. Renstrom, *Wilbur and Orville Wright: A Bibliography* (Washington, D.C.: Library of Congress, 1968), pp. 100–122.

5. Lincoln Beachey to Smithsonian, January 21, 1914; Richard Rathbun to Charles Walcott, January 21, 1914, RU 45, Smithsonian Institution Archives, hereafter SIA.

6. A. F. Zahm, "The First Man-Carrying Aeroplane . . . ," *Annual Report of the Smithsonian Institution,* 1914 (Washington, D.C.: U.S. Government Printing Office, 1915, p. 218.

7. Ibid.

8. See, for example, Raymond A. Bisplinghoff, *Aeroelasticity* (Cambridge, Mass.: Addison-Wesley, 1955), p. 3.

9. Zahm, "Man-Carrying Aeroplane," p. 222.

10. *Annual Report of the Smithsonian Institution,* 1914 (Washington, D.C.: U.S. Government Printing Office, 1915), p. 122.

11. Fred C. Kelly, *The Wright Brothers* (New York: Harcourt, Brace, 1943), p. 185.

12. C. Walcott to W. Wright, March 7, 1910; W. Wright to C. Walcott, March 26 and April 11, 1910, Papers of Wilbur and Orville Wright, Manuscript Division, Library of Congress, hereafter, Wright Papers, LC.

13. Lorin Wright, "Memorandum," July 15, 1915, in *The Papers of Wilbur and Orville Wright,* ed. Marvin W. McFarland (New York: McGraw-Hill, 1953), p. 1090.

14. O. Wright to William Howard Taft, May 14, 1925, in "Smithsonian Controversy" file, Wright Papers, LC.

15. Leonard Bairstow, "The Work of Samuel P. Langley," manuscript in Langley Papers, SIA.

16. Kelly, *Wright Brothers,* p. 194.

17. Beck, "The First Airplane After 1903"; for shipping information see Mabel Beck to Director, Science Museum, February 10, 1928, Science Museum Correspondence files, Sc.M. 1883/1/27, copy in NASM curatorial files, Wright 1903 airplane.

18. J. Ames and D. W. Taylor, "A Report on the Langley Machine," box 111, folder 3, RU 45, SIA.

19. O. Wright, mimeographed press statement, July 1937, Wright Papers, LC.

20. Lindbergh, Wright, Abbot correspondence, Wright Controversy files, SIA. See also C. A. Lindbergh, *The Wartime Diaries of Charles Lindbergh* (New York: Harcourt, Brace, Jovanovich, 1970), p. 188.

21. Sample articles in files on the Wright Controversy, RU 46, SIA.

22. Letters and memoranda on Macmillan and Goldstrum in Abbot Papers, box 111, RU 46, SIA.

23. C. Abbot to John Ahlers, August 20, 1940, Wright Papers, LC.

24. C. G. Abbot, "The 1914 Test of the Langley Aerodrome," *Smithsonian Miscellaneous Collections* 103, no. 48 (October 24, 1942).

25. Assorted legal notes and typed copy, O. Wright Will and Probate Petition, Probate Court of Montgomery County, Ohio, August 6, 1948, box 107, folder 6; box 108, RU 46, SIA.

26. Materials relating to the history of the 1903 airplane at the Science Museum, its transfer back to the United States, and "Operation Homecoming" are to be found in the office of the registrar, National Air and Space Museum, and in the Wright aircraft and biographical files, NASM Archive.

27. Descriptions of the ceremony, articles, invitations, memoranda, and related items are to be found in box 107, RU 46, SIA.

6

Crystal Skulls and Other Problems
Or, "Don't Look It in the Eye"

JANE MACLAREN WALSH

A larger-than-life, masterfully carved rock crystal skull arrived at the National Museum of American History in July 1992. It had been sent through the U.S. mail by an anonymous donor.[1] The skull is quite large: Its sitting height is 22.5 cm. (about 9 in.), erect height 25.5 cm. (10 in.), and maximal cranial breadth 22.8 cm. (8.25 in.).[2] It weighs 14 kilos, or nearly 31 pounds. A handwritten, unsigned note accompanying the object said, in part, "This Aztec crystal skull, purported to be part of the Porfirio Díaz collection, was purchased in Mexico City in 1960. . . . I am offering it to the Smithsonian without any consideration. Naturally, I wish to remain anonymous. I hope you enjoy it as much as I have."[3]

Crystal skulls form a rare and controversial category of object. Traditionally they have been believed to be pre-Columbian Mexican in origin, possibly Aztec or Mixtec. Recently there has been speculation that they may be sixteenth-century European, perhaps examples of Spanish ecclesiastical art. Some people believe the skulls to be of more recent manufacture—that they are fraudulent creations intended to deceive. The controversial nature of the object presents a classic curatorial dilemma: Should we accession, catalog, and exhibit an object of such admittedly problematic authenticity? Is it possible to determine whether or not it is genuine? How does one go about such a task? Supposing it is proven to be fraudulent, is there room in the national collections for a fake, even a spectacular fake?

Fig. 6.1. Smithsonian Institution crystal skull, two views. Photo by Gulezian/ QuickSilver.

This crystal skull, then, embodies the essence of the museum object in that it presents us with an inherent mystery. Requiring that a number of questions be answered, it also poses the problem of exactly how one is to go about finding these answers. What is this thing? Who made it? When was it made? Why was it made? For what purpose was it made? Representing a sort of museological catechism, these are questions that museum people are somehow compelled to answer. In the process of seeking the answers, I discovered that looking at some other crystal skulls and examining more than a century of acquisition and development of expertise in this particular area provided some interesting clues and directions. I will present my research as a series of problems.

THE PROBLEM OF THE SKULLS

There are about a dozen large rock crystal skulls extant in the world, and perhaps several dozen smaller ones.[4] The larger category encompasses a height range of 10 to 22 cm., with the Smithsonian skull being the largest; most of the smaller skulls are between 2 and 6 cm. in height. Nearly all of these skulls, including the two exhibited in the National Museum of Anthropology and History in Mexico City, are considered to be pre-Columbian, created by Aztec or Mixtec lapidaries. Only three of the large variety are in museums: one is in France, another in England, and the third, as we know, is in Washington's Smithsonian Institution.

The French crystal skull, which is not quite life-size, is in the collection of the Musée de l'Homme. This skull is considerably smaller and, in style and manufacture, cruder than the Smithsonian specimen. A recent request for information about the history of its acquisition and any scientific testing yielded no substantive answer other than its intrinsic value to the museum. Daniel Levine, curator of the American collections, believes that the skull is perhaps the most important pre-Columbian object in the collection. According to a copy of the catalog data, the skull was a gift of Alphonse Pinart and was exhibited at the Exposition universelle in 1878.[5] While it is accurate to list M. Pinart as the donor, the collector of the crystal skull was Eugène Boban, a French antiquarian and dealer who had shops in Paris and Mexico City.[6] He lent a number of pre-Columbian Mexican objects from his collection for an exhibition in Paris in 1867–68. His Mexican artifacts were part of a display of scientific collections gathered by the Commission Scientifique during the French occupation of Mexico and reign of Maximilian.[7] M. Boban also exhibited another group of his Mexican pre-Columbian artifacts—casts and originals—during the first meeting of the International Congress of Americanists at Nancy in 1875.[8] These Mexican artifacts and the crystal skull were shown at the Exposition universelle in Paris in 1878, where Alphonse Pinart apparently purchased it from Boban, along with a number of other objects,[9] and gave it to the museum.[10] The skull, which now bears the catalog number 78. I. 57., weighs 2 kilos, 75 grams (6 lbs.), is 11 cm. (4⅜ in.) high and 15 cm. (5⅞ in.) long.[11] It has appeared in a

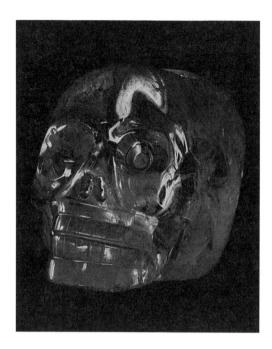

Fig. 6.2. Musée de l'Homme skull. Donated by Alphonse Pinart, 1878; purchased from Eugène Boban.

number of publications; perhaps the earliest was written by Professor E. T. Hamy, then director of the Trocadéro, and published in *Galerie Americaine de Musée d'Ethnographie du Trocadéro* in 1897.[12] Another, much smaller, crystal skull (1–1.5 in.) in the Pinart collection was also purchased from Eugène Boban.

The British Museum recently exhibited its large crystal skull in an exhibition titled "Fake? The Art of Deception." The skull was featured in a section called "The Limits of Expertise,"[13] i.e., Is it a fake, or isn't it? This life-size rock crystal skull measures 21 cm. (8 3/16 in.) in length, 13.6 cm. (5 3/8 in.) in width, and 14.8 cm. (5 11/16 in.) in height and weighs 175.25 Troy ounces.[14] The museum originally acquired the skull from Tiffany and Company, Union Square, New York. It was entered into the British Museum catalog as number 98-1 on January 3, 1898.[15] According to a notation in the catalog, the purchase was effected through a Mr. G. F. Kunz.

The discussion of the crystal skull in the "Fake" exhibition catalog offers a number of possibilities for the skull's origins, all of which are intriguing, although inconclusive. A recent inquiry into the collection history of the skull, however, produced a wonderful letter filled with fascinating data, descriptions of a series of scientific tests, and a variety of opinions regarding its origin, Brazil

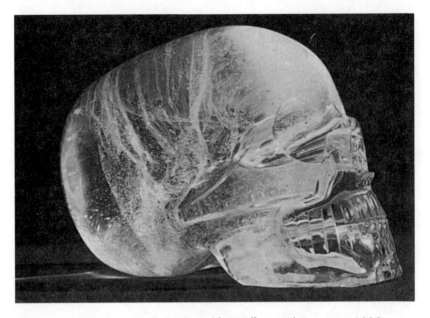

Fig. 6.3. British Museum skull. Purchased from Tiffany and Company, 1898. Tiffany purchased from Eugène Boban, 1886.

being now the most widely accepted.[16] In addition to this, Elizabeth Carmichael recently forwarded a just-completed report concluding that the quartz from which the skull is carved "is more likely to come from rocks of the Brazilian Shield than those within the Aztec domains of Central America and Mexico."[17] Carmichael, assistant keeper in the Museum of Mankind, noted that an examination of the skull carried out in the 1960s under high magnification uncovered an engraved line, within the incised lines used to indicate the teeth, which had a noticeably irregular mark. "This was thought more like the kind of mark that might be made by a jeweller's wheel than any other form of tool, such as those which might have been employed by pre-Hispanic Mexican lapidaries."[18] The assumption was, therefore, that the British Museum specimen—this life-size crystal skull—was most likely fashioned out of imported Brazilian rock crystal, with the assistance of European tools. If that were the case, it would stretch to the breaking point the credibility of the skull's earlier attribution to pre-Columbian Mexico, although the possibility of its being just post-contact would still be feasible, albeit improbable.

An interesting footnote to my inquiry into the acquisition history of the skull was provided by the same person who assisted in the original British Museum purchase, Mr. G. F. Kunz. George Frederick Kunz was a mineralogist and occasional Smithsonian collaborator. He was also the author of *Precious Stones of Mexico*.[19] In this standard reference work, there is a section about Mexican quartz, in which Kunz notes that rock crystal was used by ancient Mexicans, who fashioned the material into ornaments and skulls. "Examples of these rock-crystal skulls are to be seen in the Blake collection in the U.S. National Museum at Washington; the collection of the late A. E. Douglas, in the American Museum of Natural History in New York City; and the Trocadéro Museum in Paris. The largest one, however, is now in the Archaeological Department of the British Museum, for which it was secured by Sir John Evans, during his visit to the United States in 1897, by purchase from Messrs. Tiffany & Co."[20] After expressing his opinion that the skull was very characteristic of Mexican work, Kunz offers a short review of his knowledge of the skull's provenance. "Little is known of its history and nothing of its origin. It was brought from Mexico by a Spanish officer, some time before the French occupation of Mexico, and was sold to an English collector, at whose death it passed into the hands of E. Boban, of Paris, and then became the property of Tiffany & Co."[21]

This is the very same Eugène Boban, who acquired and sold the rock crystal skull to Alphonse Pinart, who in turn donated it to the Musée de l'Homme (then the Trocadéro), where it was exhibited in 1878. Twenty years later the British Museum would catalog a similar work. Neither catalog mentions the earlier collector and actual purveyor of the artifact.

THE PROBLEM OF M. BOBAN

Eugène Boban also attempted to sell pre-Columbian Mexican artifacts to the Smithsonian Institution, including, I believe, the very same crystal skull that Tiffany's, and eventually the British Museum, bought. This attempt, however, took place in 1886, some twelve years before the Tiffany sale, when he first contacted William Henry Holmes and carried on a somewhat protracted correspondence.

What I have been able to discover about Eugène Boban is that he was a French citizen, who spent more than two decades of his life in Mexico. He arrived in the early 1860s, when he was in his late twenties,[22] and departed, I believe for good, in 1886. He was a member of the Société Americaine and the Société d'Ethnographie de France as early as 1864, and he was awarded a bronze

Fig. 6.4. M. Eugène Boban. Inscribed "to Mr. Thomas Wilson with fond regards—New York, 27 July, E. Boban." Smithsonian Institution, National Anthropological NPC 028770.00, Photo Lot 70.

medal by that society in 1874.[23] Boban was associated with the French Scientific Commission chartered by Napoleon III and was responsible for providing the commission with much of his collection of pre-Columbian artifacts for exhibition in Paris in 1867–68. He also exhibited portions of his Mexican collection at the first International Congress of Americanists in Nancy in 1875[24] and later at the Exposition universelle in 1878 at the Trocadéro in Paris. He published a number of papers on things pre-Columbian, small descriptive notes about particular pieces in which, I believe, he had a financial interest.[25]

In Mexico City he operated an establishment called the Museo Científico, which doubled as a rare-book, antiques, and antiquities shop.[26] In 1867, while the French still occupied Mexico, he advertised himself as "the antiquarian to His Majesty the Emperor." [27] In the early 1880s he became acquainted with Gumercindo Mendoza, then director of Mexico's National Museum, and occasionally purchased artifacts from Sr. Sanchez, director of the museum's physical anthropology collections.[28] He was an acquaintance of Leopoldo Batres, Mexico's inspector of monuments, who had been appointed to that post by Porfirio Díaz, then president of Mexico. In the mid-1880s Batres began excavations at the archaeological site of Teotihuacán and the reconstruction of the Pyramid of the Sun.

Eugène Boban was also a dealer in rare books and manuscripts. Some of his sales catalogs indicate that he had parts of numerous libraries, the collections of

Brasseur de Bourbourg, Joseph M. A. Aubin, and Alphonse Pinart, among others. In the late 1880s he became the agent in the sale of the largest and most important collection of early Mexican manuscripts, the J. M. A. Aubin collection, which was bought by Eugène Goupil. Goupil arranged for the elaborate publication of a catalogue raisonné of his newly acquired collection, to be compiled and written by Boban. The three-volume tour de force, *Documents pour servir à l'histoire du Mexique,* published in 1891, has since become a standard source and is considered "a work of major importance."[29]

Boban was the consummate collector, with broad interests and a knowledge and familiarity with historical documents and pre-Columbian objects from a large variety of Mexican sites. He was also interested in pre-Columbian Mexican fakes. In an 1881 sales catalog from Boban's Paris establishment titled *Catalogue d'ouvrages scientifiques,* Boban presented a detailed discussion of his collection of counterfeit Mexican antiquities, in addition to lists of a number of casts, some from the Cristy collection in London, a variety of prehistoric European artifacts, and several obsidian pieces from Mexico. Nearly all the forgeries, he noted, were made in the suburbs of Mexico by the Indians of Santiago (Tlatelolco) and Los Angeles (a nineteenth-century suburb west of Tlatelolco). "These objects are neither molded from casts nor copies of ancient monuments of the country, they are pure fantasy, they are a type of bizarre caricature, whose inspiration evades us but whose principal purpose is to delude the public. Of course, these objects do not have any archaeological value, to the contrary, they come to cast disfavor on the beautiful monuments . . . and unfortunately, as they are very easy to obtain and very cheap in the country, . . . many of these monsters strut about in the beautiful glass cases of our museums in Europe."[30]

"It was with the intention of unmasking them," Boban continued, referring to the fakes, "to point them out to amateurs and above all to museum directors, that we exhibited a series at the Exposition universelle of 1878 in the Anthropology section."[31] M. Boban, the "honest merchant,"[32] appears to be taking the high ground here, but I believe the actual cause of this caveat emptor was the embarrassment caused him by an earlier exhibit in 1867–68. That exposition displayed the fruits of the Commission scientifique to Mexico and featured much of Boban's collections of Mexican antiquities. Paul Eudel recounts in *Le Truquage* a French national embarrassment with the display of some artifacts collected by the Mexican commission. He describes in some detail a large and impressive vessel from Texcoco, which was covered with the visages of the Aztec gods and became the center of much attention and admiration: "One beautiful, bright, sunny day, under the influence of the humidity, the divinities began subtly to detach themselves."[33] French antiquarians and archeologists were acquainted with the fairly widespread manufacture of fraudulent antiquities very early on, although this awareness apparently did not deter them from continuing to collect dubious objects of problematic authenticity.

In 1885 Désiré Charnay, an archeologist associated with the Commission scientifique, candidly admitted that he also had been fooled, when he had ordered several hundred casts to be made of objects prominently displayed in the National Museum of Mexico. This collection he "placed in the Trocadéro during the Paris Exhibition; but on an expert in such matters seeing them, he at once detected and exposed the fraud."[34] Charnay continued with a rather chauvinistic description of the state of European science: "It is a curious circumstance, that Mexicans, even the best informed among them, as well as foreigners, should so often be victimised by vulgar forgers of antiquities, who trade on the passions of the collector and the gullibility of the public; and that such things cannot be done in Europe without immediate detection, can only arise from the superior knowledge of our savants."[35] Charnay was not the only Frenchman to be fooled by Mexican forgeries: there were others like Biart, Pinart, Hamy, and Boban. The last name may also have been among those doing the fooling, however.

Returning to Eugène Boban's 1881 Paris sales catalog with its discussion of fakes, following the lists of Old World artifacts, European casts, pre-Columbian Mexican obsidian objects, and the modern ceramic fakes, which are priced between 5 and 50 francs, there is a separate section titled "objets divers." This group of objets d'art includes a marble sculpture from the time of Louis XIV priced at 250 francs, a Japanese warrior costume for 125 francs, and the "representation of a human skull in rock crystal of natural human size, a masterpiece of lapidary art." This singular piece, the most expensive in the book, is listed at 3,500 francs.[36] Three years after he had presumably sold one rock crystal skull with a Mexican and pre-Columbian provenance to Alphonse Pinart, M. Boban has yet another skull. This one is larger than the Musée de l'Homme skull, i.e., life-size, has no provenance attached, and is listed in a completely separate category from the pre-Columbian Mexican objects he sells, fake or otherwise. The skull, apparently, was not sold during the 1881 auction; Boban, as events indicate, brought it with him when he returned to Mexico.

In the early 1880s several events caused Eugène Boban to cross paths with the Smithsonian Institution in the person of William Henry Holmes. Holmes, who had been the official artist on the Hayden Survey for the U.S. Geological Survey in the 1870s, had spent a year studying art in Europe between 1879 and 1880. During part of that time he was in Paris, where he may have seen the Exposition universelle and most certainly visited the Trocadéro. In April 1884 Holmes was invited to join a photographic expedition to Mexico with a Mr.

and Mrs. Chain, artists, and William Henry Jackson, photographer, at the behest of the Santa Fe Railroad.[37] He spent some of his two-month trip in the National Museum in Mexico City conferring with department directors Jesus Sanchez and Gumercindo Mendoza, examining their extensive collections and photographing a number of their exhibits; Holmes was particularly interested in so-called Aztec pottery, which he had become convinced were modern fakes.

William Henry Holmes published two articles on the subject of bogus antiquities, one in *Science* called "The Trade in Spurious Mexican Antiquities"[38] and an extended version of this in the Smithsonian *Annual Report* for 1886.[39] In them he argued that many of the so-called pre-Columbian ceramic collections in both national museums of the United States and Mexico, then presumed to be Aztec, were, in fact, recent and intentional forgeries. Drawing on the research for his articles and his knowledge of Smithsonian collections, Holmes was shocked to see numerous examples of what he considered obvious fakes on prominent display in Mexico.[40] The photographs taken by Holmes, or perhaps by Jackson, document the exhibit of the questionable objects.[41] The museum's director, Mendoza, had concluded that the ceramics, what Holmes called "eccentric black-ware excrescences," were to be classed as ordinary domestic Aztec pottery. He had speculated that this utilitarian ware had continued from pre-Columbian times to the present day. "It was not all that science demanded," Holmes wrote, so "I undertook to examine into the subject more closely."[42] I will return to Holmes's inquiry into the subject a bit further on.

In 1884, the year Holmes was visiting Mexico, the inspector of monuments, Leopoldo Batres, began his excavations at Teotihuacán.[43] Batres became a powerful personality in Mexican archeology, but his science was limited. As a self-taught archaeologist, he accomplished his explorations "without the benefit of any technical skill and without making a serious study of the subject."[44] Holmes's 1884 photograph collection includes a number of photographs of Teotihuacán, and the beginnings of the excavations. He presumably met with the inspector of monuments at that time. He was at least indirectly acquainted with Batres through infrequent correspondence and occasional exchanges of publications.[45]

Another visitor to the pyramids at Teotihuacán was Eugène Boban. In 1885 a local Mexico City newspaper reported that he was touring the site with Batres.[46] In 1886, Holmes received up-to-date reports about the Teotihuacán excavations from a friend in Mexico City: "Sr. Batres, the inspector of museums, proposed to employ a regiment of soldiers in exploring the ruins about the pyramids of San Juan Teotihuacan believing that he will unearth a buried Pompei. His proposition strikes me as absurd."[47] This blunt assessment comes from

Figs. 6.5 and 6.6. William Henry Holmes/William Henry Jackson photographs of exhibits in the National Museum of Mexico in 1884, which include a large number of nineteenth-century fakes. Smithsonian Institution, National Anthropological Archives, Photo Lot 93.

Wilson Wilberforce Blake, yet another Mexico City book, manuscript, and antiquities dealer, who published an English-language guide to the National Museum.[48] Blake had also acquired in the mid-1880s a collection of pre-Columbian artifacts made by a Father Fischer, who had been "spiritual adviser to Maximilian and a member of his Cabinet during the second empire," according to a catalog Blake published in the *American Antiquarian*.[49] The collection of some 663 pre-Columbian Mexican objects, which included a small (1½ × 1¼ × 1 in.) crystal skull, was sold to the Smithsonian in 1886.

Apparently, sometime between January and March of 1886, Holmes was contacted by Eugène Boban, who offered to sell him all or part of his pre-Columbian Mexican collection, including one crystal skull.[50] The last week in March, Blake wrote again to thank Holmes for the copy of his *Science* article and to give yet another report on the Teotihuacán excavations. "I was out to the pyramids last week, to see what Batres is doing. He is a fraud—has done nothing but manage to get himself interviewed about twice a week. He is not only a fraud but a swindler."[51] In answer to questions posed by Holmes, presumably about crystal skulls and Eugène Boban, Blake continued, "The only rock crystal skull of any value is the one I got in the Fischer collection."[52] Then Blake goes on to appraise another antiquities dealer with a description of a recent and apparently well-publicized scandal:

> Well, Frenchman named Boban—who has a private museum here—and is a member of various French societies and seems to be very intelligent, although not honest, brought from Germany a glass skull made to imitate rock crystal. Batres persuaded him into a partnership to defraud the National Museum, by selling it as genuine rock crystal from Orizaba for $3,000. Sanchez was on the point of buying it but first had Dr. Kaska examine it who at once pronounced it glass and the two busy B's are under a cloud.

Although it should be kept in mind that Mr. Blake is negotiating to sell his own collection to the Smithsonian Institution, he is obviously completely distrustful of both the Mexican archeologist and the French antiquarian and attempts to caution his friend Holmes further: "Boban has closed his museum and will remove to New York, soon. Look out for him. He hopes to sell a great many things to the Smithsonian. He has some valuable antiquities, but his ownership of them gives them a suspicious character."[53]

While one might be correct in assuming that Blake is reporting this scandal to Holmes because he wishes to discredit Boban and thereby seal his own deal with the Smithsonian, his information does not contradict much of what I have learned about Boban. He was certainly correct about Eugène Boban's imminent move northward and his attempt to sell his collection to the Smithsonian Institution. By the end of 1886, M. Boban had moved to New York City and had placed his "Extensive Archaeological Collection . . . comprising antiquities of Mexico, Guatemala, Central and South America, Egypt, Greece, Rome and Gaul" up for sale at George A. Leavitt and Company, an auction house on Broadway. Annotated copies of the first and second[54] sales catalogs were found with some of Holmes's papers in the Smithsonian Archives,[55] along with a more than a dozen letters from Boban, all dated between January and April 1887, and a very curious poster with the title "Cuadro Arqueologico y Etnografico de la Republica Mexicana" and a date of 1885.[56]

The foreword to the first annotated sales catalog describes the "extensive and remarkable Collection" as being mainly pieces "discovered by Monsieur Eugène Boban, or purchased directly from other explorers, he drew largely from the following sources: The Mexican Section of Antiquities, at the Paris Exposition of 1868; the Zapotecas series of Funereal Vases, obtained from the heirs of Monsieur Martin, formerly Consul In Mexico; the Collection, gathered on the Gulf Coast, of the late Dr. Fuzier, Chief of the Polytechnic School, Paris; the Collection of Señor Don Jose M. Melgar, Mexican Archaeologist: the remainder of the collection made by Count de Waldeck."[57]

The Mexican Section of Antiquities at the 1867–68 Paris exposition actually already belonged to Boban and was not acquired from that exhibition, as the catalog intimates.[58] Fuzier was also associated with the commission, as, apparently, was Jose Melgar of Mexico. The items from Count J. F. de Waldeck, whose reputation as competent scientist and truthful person has been in doubt for a number of years, were a few of his drawings.[59]

Presumably, in the nineteenth century as well as the twentieth century, objects belonging to dealers gained in monetary value by virtue of their having been exhibited in a reputable museum or gallery or by their having belonged to important and, therefore, presumably discerning people. Numerous pieces in Boban's collection, including many listed in the 1886 catalog, were said to have been in the cabinet of Maximilian. Boban, as a member of the Société d'Ethnographie, frequently published short articles describing individual pieces or discrete collections that interested him.[60] In addition, Dr. Ernest T. Hamy, director of the Trocadéro, published a number of pieces from the Boban-Pinart collection in the Revue d'ethnographie in 1883 and 1887, and in the Journal de la Société des Américanistes de Paris in 1898. Nearly all of the objects depicted in the above-cited journal articles, and a large proportion of the Boban collection offered to the Smithsonian Institution, which Holmes had photographed and sketched, appear to be fairly obvious nineteenth-century fakes.[61]

In Holmes's annotated version of the catalog, where he noted the price and the name of the buyer, I came across an interesting item in the geology, mineralogy, and gems section, rather than in the pre-Columbian Mexican section: on page 84, item number 1491, in all likelihood what had been offered for 3,500 francs five years earlier with no provenance attached, a "Human skull, natural size, dolicephalous in shape, deep eye-sockets, nose cavity, uper [sic] and lower jaws, cut from a large and solid block of hyaline rock-crystal. Smooth, polished surface. A magnificent, perfect and unique specimen. Length 20, height 14¼, width 13 centimeters."[62] In this catalog, however, it is endowed with a provenance: Mexico. The basic description of this item is followed by a paragraph indicating its originality: "The human skull played an important part in the religious ceremonial of the Ancient Mexicans, and small specimens in terra-cotta, green stone and rock crystal are not infrequently found in museums and private collections, but the Boban specimen is by far the largest and finest one known, and is considered by him one of the most curious and important, as well as one of the most valuable objects in his collection."[63] According to Holmes's annotation, the skull sold for $950.00 to someone named Ellis, a fact that is supported by a *New York Times* notice, listing "a Mr. Ellis" as the purchaser of the highest-priced object in the "largest sale ever held in this country." The one-paragraph *Times* notice was headlined "Antiquities Sold Cheap" and stated that such a collection would have brought $20,000 to $40,000 in Paris, but the New York total was $10,500, a "disappointment to the collector."[64] Mr. Ellis, I believe, was a partner at Tiffany and Company, which apparently had a number of buyers, including a Mr. Savage, mentioned in another article and present at the sale.[65]

THE PROBLEM OF NINETEENTH-CENTURY FAKES

The final years of the nineteenth century were a "museum-making era," according to William Henry Holmes, who imagined that "future generations are perhaps to be congratulated that such is the case."[66] The drawback to this collection building, however, was the "wide-spread fancy for hunting and hoarding relics," giving "a considerable money value to antiquities." Holmes believed that this led to attempts "on the part of dishonest persons, to supply the market by fraudulent means."[67] Despite his conviction that most of the spurious pieces would eventually be detected and thrown out, he feared that "in the mean time they will have made an impression upon literature, and upon the receptive mind of the public, that is most difficult to eradicate." It was, therefore, the "duty of interested persons to publish, at the earliest opportunity, all reliable information tending to expose frauds."[68]

Holmes wanted to establish scientific criteria for determining the authenticity of Mexican pre-Columbian objects. To do this, he believed, archeologists would need to understand the "fundamental principles of art growth."[69] In speaking about pottery, he noted:

> Every proper product of the shaping arts is intended for some normal use. In indigenous work, vessels made for use in the domestic arts are suitable to that end; those made for ceremonial purposes are adapted to that end, and are embellished with symbols suitable to their office. They are in all cases exactly what a natural indigenous growth makes them. Forms are not interchangeable and embellishments, especially those of an ideographic character are not used indiscriminately as long as the art is in a normal condition.[70]

Today, more than a century later, while fraudulent objects in museum collections are exposed by interested persons on a regular basis, the problem persists— not with Holmes's eccentric black pottery, long since removed from display in both the Smithsonian and the National Museum in Mexico, but with a variety of other artifacts of problematic authenticity. In 1978 Professor Esther Pasztory, in the tradition of Holmes, examined three Aztec masks, depicting the god Xipe Totec, which are housed in two different European museums and were all collected during the last century or early in this one. Though they are works of exceedingly sophisticated craftsmanship, Pasztory believes them to be forgeries. Her criteria in this regard are based almost entirely upon a thorough understanding of Aztec iconography, since the deities depicted on the inside of the masks were represented as no Aztec artisan, certainly not one as accomplished as this, would have crafted them.[71]

Artifacts from Mexico collected in the mid- to late nineteenth century, when interest in pre-Columbian art was at a peak, were gathered by two major groups of collectors: "ordinary travelers looking for inexpensive souvenirs and well-to-do collectors willing to pay high prices for unusual antiquities."[72] Consequently, in the case of forgeries, according to Pasztory, two kinds of artisans attempted to supply these two markets. The blackware specialists, whose factories at San Juan Teotihuacán had been exposed by Holmes and Batres,[73] sold unknown quantities of figurines and impressively large fanciful vases and urns to visitors at the great pyramids.[74] The practice, as any tourist knows, continues to this day at every major pre-Columbian site in Mexico. The wealthier travelers, on the other hand, who were interested in forming important collections, demanded finer objects, not only of finer craftsmanship but also of rare and valuable materials. Holmes noted in a supplement to his article that "fraudulent specimens reached the U.S. in two ways, through the agency of travelers who purchased them in Mexico, and through traders who ship them to New York in large lots."[75] Clearly Eugène Boban fits neatly in this second category as an important supplier of artifacts for institutions bent on collection building and the wealthier collecting class. These practices also have survived the passage of time.

Important museum objects acquired during the last century throughout Europe and the United States have often subsequently become a source of consternation and embarrassment. Among the well-known works that Pasztory considers, at best, dubious are the gold statuette of Tizoc, which found its way to the Heye Foundation,[76] the stone masks at the British Museum and the Musée de l'Homme (the latter piece collected by none other than M. Boban), and perhaps even the famous rock crystal skulls in the Musée de l'Homme and the British Museum, to name but a few. Pasztory notes that all of the above "present a similar problem of well-made objects in precious media of problematic authenticity."[77]

THE PROBLEM OF THE SMITHSONIAN SKULL

Knowing what we now know about the busiest of B's in this saga, M. Eugène Boban, what are we to make of the skull delivered to us through the mail? It is the largest of all of the known examples,[78] twice the size of the Musée de l'Homme's skull and considerably larger than the British specimen. In style and carving it resembles more the British Museum skull, although it has been hollowed out, leaving a oval-shaped hole 14.4 × 11.5 cm. The cranial wall at the base is approximately 5 cm. thick. Notwithstanding the removal of such a proportion of quartz, it still weighs 14 kilos.

From the little information provided by the donor, we know only that he was told when he purchased it in the 1960s that it had once belonged to President Porfirio Díaz. Although this story has a familiar ring to it, like those told for so many of Boban's pieces, which he claimed had come from the collection of Maximilian, it might, in fact, be the case. If so, it would place the Smithsonian skull in the same approximate time period as the other two large skulls. Don Porfirio, who was first elected in 1876 to a four-year term on the slogan "No Reelection," returned to the office in 1884 and didn't leave again until a revolution removed him in 1910. Díaz had a close associate and friend in Leopoldo Batres, appointing him to the inspector of monuments position. Batres also had a close association with Eugène Boban. The French antiquarian edited and published Batres's *Cuadro Arqueológico,* and each was content to attach his own name to the writing of the other. Wilson W. Blake's report of Boban and Batres's attempt to sell a crystal skull to the Mexican National Museum coincides nicely with the skull's appearance in New York six months later, when Boban was apparently forced to leave Mexico City with his entire collection after twenty-five years of residence.

Blake also told Holmes that Boban had brought the skull from Germany and that it was glass. While he was mistaken about the last part, he may have had something with the German attribution. In southern Germany there is a town called Idar-Oberstein[79] that has been an important lapidary center since the fifteenth century. According to William Foshag, the late Smithsonian geologist, the industry in Idar-Oberstein was "devoted entirely to cutting the agate mined from local deposits" and carving, polishing, and engraving a variety of beautiful objects.[80] Unfortunately, the town saw a decline in the early nineteenth century, when the local agate supply was exhausted, but "industry managed to continue in reduced activity through the use of Swiss rock crystal and smoky quartz." At about the same time, German immigrants from the region of Idar-Oberstein went to Brazil and initiated the shipment of large quantities of Brazilian agate and rock crystal home.[81] The crystal of the British Museum's skull, tested in the 1960s and 1990s, is thought to be most likely Brazilian in origin.[82]

CAN WE LOOK IT IN THE EYE?

Returning, at long last, to my museological catechism:

What is this thing? I can say that it is a beautifully carved rock crystal skull, the largest known example of its type. It is related, I believe, to at least two other large rock crystal skulls in museum collections.

Who made it? I do not know who, in particular, made it. Tradition and the wisdom of nineteenth-century expertise has it that such skulls are Aztec or Mixtec. Some people, who have crystal skulls in private collections, believe that they are Mayan,[83] but all are thought to be of Mexican or Central American manufacture. Then, of course, there is the possibility that they may have been made by nineteenth-century German craftsmen.

When was it made? Although not one of the rock crystal skulls, large or small, now in museum collections was found in any sort of archaeological context, since the late 1870s they have been thought to belong to a period just before or just after first contact—that is, sometime in the early sixteenth century. This may, in fact, be the case for the smaller skulls, those that measure between 2 and 6 cm. in diameter. It is also possible that the three large skulls presently under discussion were all made between 1867 and 1886, the approximate time span of Eugène Boban's sojourn in Mexico.

Why or for what purpose was it made? Nearly all of the small skulls (2–6 cm. high) are drilled through from top to bottom, although at least one small skull I have seen is carved from a green stone and drilled horizontally through the temples. This latter case would indicate to me an almost certain pre-Columbian provenance, since this is exactly the way the skull of a sacrificial victim would have been attached to an Aztec *tzompantli* (skull rack).[84] All the smaller skulls have been called pendants, presumably for necklaces. Recently some museum people have theorized that they were used as bases for post-contact crucifixes. During the Renaissance artists frequently depicted the Crucifixion as taking place on a hilltop, representing Golgotha. The Hebrew word *gulgoleth* means "skull." Artistic visions of the event often show a cave at the base of the hill, and within the cave lies a single skull, said to be that of Adam. If in fact the smaller skulls are pre-Columbian pendants, perhaps representing the god of death, Mictlantecutli, it would seem an easy accommodation for Spanish priests to use the conquered pagan symbol, convert it to their own religious iconography, and reuse it as the base for the holy cross. A beautiful example of this iconographic conflation was exhibited in the "Mexico, Splendors of Thirty Centuries" show at the Metropolitan Museum of Art in 1990. The object is a reliquary cross said to have been made in Mexico City between 1575 and 1578. Of all the larger crystal skulls, only the Musée de l'Homme example has been drilled through vertically, perhaps to accommodate a more imposing crucifix. The other possibility, of course, is that they were all made by Europeans for exactly that purpose, as bases for crucifixes, and have no relationship to pre-Columbian Mexico at all.

The larger skulls might have been set atop some tenoned base, since some of them have been hollowed out. Perhaps they were used as the visage of some wooden figure or held secure to some altar in pre-Columbian times. They do not appear, otherwise, to fulfill Holmes's criterion for having some normal use, at least none that is obvious to us at this particular time. An alternative explanation is that they were made during the last half of the nineteenth century to deceive, or as Eugène Boban put it, their "principal purpose" was "to delude the public."[85]

Is there room in the national collections for an object of such problematic authenticity? Despite the fact that I am reasonably convinced that the Smithsonian skull is a nineteenth-century fake, I believe it is important to give such artifacts space in our collections. William Henry Holmes debunked the fraudulent pre-Columbian Mexican pottery a century ago, but we still have a number of examples in storage. As this essay, I hope, conveys, there is much to be learned from these objects, fake or otherwise.

Another reason for keeping the skull in the Smithsonian collection is that I may, of course, be entirely wrong about this. Six months after the anonymous crystal skull reached my office, yet another found its way to the Smithsonian. A smaller, exquisitely carved rock crystal skull was brought to me by a George Washington University student, who sought my opinion about the authenticity of the piece, which had been acquired by his father, an antiques dealer! This skull, about 10 cm. high, has a somewhat simian look to its appearance, with a rather prognathous aspect. It also has circles, like goggles, around the eye sockets, a detail that is always associated with the Mesoamerican rain god, Tlaloc. The most interesting feature of this crystal skull is a prominent and deeply carved glyph on the top of the cranium. Two Mexican archeologists to whom I showed the glyph instantly recognized it as Xochicalco in style. When shown the crystal skull whose cranium it decorated, both exhibited the very same wary, questioning smile. A Xochicalco-style glyph, if authentic, would date this particular artifact to somewhere between 800 and 950 A.D., predating by several centuries the work of Aztec and Mixtec lapidaries.

Clearly all of this is not what science or William Henry Holmes would seem to demand, but as the British Museum's "Fake" catalog noted in its chapter "Limits of Expertise": "It would be misleading to end with the comforting impression that scientific advance and scholarly expertise can solve all problems."[86]

While my own expertise in this realm has expanded considerably, I have only recently begun to examine the possibilities of a group scientific examination of five large skulls and at least twice that number of smaller ones. I hope to obtain permission from museums and private collectors in order to borrow a variety of skulls for examination and eventually exhibit these extraordinary objects and the results of our study. I have already received some encouragement from the British, particularly Elizabeth Carmichael, in this endeavor, and the National Museum of Anthropology and History in Mexico City. Several private collectors have also expressed interest in submitting their prized possessions to whatever battery of tests Smithsonian mineralogists and scientists at the conservation and analytical lab can devise. In the brief time the skull has been with us, it has accomplished what all museum artifacts are intended to accomplish—the stimulation of curiosity and scientific inquiry. The Smithsonian's crystal skull is yet a work in progress.

NOTES

1. Richard Ahlborn, who had initially received the skull addressed to the "Mezo-American Museum" [sic], called to ask if I thought the Department of Anthropology might be interested in taking it. Unaware of the pitfalls ahead, I volunteered to come

right over and pick it up. He assured me that it was much too heavy to carry between museums but that he would arrange for it to be delivered. When I requested a cart to move the rather cumbersome skull, I received a warning from museum technician Neil Hauck: "Don't look it the eye," he said. "I read somewhere that they're cursed."

2. Cranial measurements were taken by David Hunt of the Division of Physical Anthropology. Other measure notations include GOL index 270, OBH 55, ORB 57, DKB 24, GOG 169, NRB 55.

3. Smithsonian Institution acc. file, 6/22/92.

4. Since the arrival of the Smithsonian skull I have been visited by and have corresponded with a number of collectors of crystal skulls. This communication has allowed me to gain a broad perspective on size, quality of material, and stylistic differences, in addition to some understanding of the variety of anecdotal histories associated with such artifacts.

5. Daniel Levine, letter to author, May 5, 1995.

6. Esther Pasztory, "Three Aztec Masks of the God Xipe," in *Falsifications and Misreconstructions of Pre-Columbian Art*, ed. Elizabeth H. Boone (Washington, D.C.: Dumbarton Oaks, 1989), p. 94; Paul Eudel, *Le Truquage, Altérations, Fraudes et Contrefaçon dévoilées* (Paris: Edouard Rouveyre, 1900), p. 11. Ministère de l'Instruction Publique, *Archives de la Commission Scientifique du Mexique*, vols. 1–3 (Paris: Imprimerie Impériale, 1867).

7. Maximilian von Hapsburg was installed briefly as emperor of Mexico by Napoleon III and an invading French army. Following the army was the French Scientific Expedition, which secured a variety of scientific data and important collections of pre-Hispanic codices and objects (Ministère de l'Instruction Publique, *Archives*).

8. "Exposition D'Antiquités Américaines," *Congrés International des Américanistes, 1. Session, Nancy* (Paris: Maisonneuve, 1875), pp. 21–26.

9. Ross Parmenter, *Explorer, Linguist, and Ethnologist: A Descriptive Bibliography of the Published Works of Alphonse Louis Pinart, with Notes on His Life* (Los Angeles: Southwest Museum, 1966), p. 21. E. T. Hamy, "Note sur une figurine Yucatèque de la collection Boban-Pinart au Musée d'Ethnographie du Trocadéro," *Journal de la Société des Américanistes de Paris* 2 (1897–98): 105–8; E. T. Hamy, "Note sur une inscription chronographique," *Revue d'ethnographie* 2 (1883): 192–202; Eugène Boban, *Catalogue d'Ouvrages Scientifique* (Paris: Imprimerie de Madame Veuve Bouchard-Huzard, 1881).

10. Dr. Hamy also published several short articles about objects from the Boban collection, including one in the *Journal de la Société des Américanistes de Paris* 2 (1897–98): 105–8, which describes a Yucatec ceramic figurine (an apparent fake) as being part of the "collection Boban-Pinart" (p. 105).

11. The Musée de l'Homme's typed inventory, which gives the skull number as 78.I.57, dates to the early 1930s, when the catalog was redone. An earlier Trocadéro ledger lists the skull as catalog number 7621. The earliest reference to the skull is in the 1897 work of E. T. Hamy, *Galerie Americaine de Musée d'Ethnographie du Trocadéro* (Paris: Ernest Leroux Editeurs, 1897); it does not give any number for the large skull but does list the smaller crystal skull as catalog number 25189. These three numbers may represent three different systems, since 7621 would appear to precede 25189, but in fact the lower number seems to have been entered some time after 1900 and the higher number dates at least to 1897 (Dr. Sally McLendon, personal communication to author, April 1996). Dimensions from Hamy, *Galerie Americaine*, p. 31; Levine, letter to author.

12. Eduard Seler published an earlier piece, "L'orfeverie des Anciens Mexicains," in *Gesammelte Abhandlungen zur Amerikanischen Sprach- und Alterthumskunde* 2 (1890). See pp. 635 and 637, in which he writes about the use of crystal in pre-Columbian Mexico; although he discusses rock crystal lip plugs, he does not mention the skull in the Trocadéro collection.

13. Mark Jones, ed., *Fake? The Art of Deception* (Berkeley: University of California Press, 1993), pp. 296–97.

14. George F. Kunz, *Precious Stones of Mexico* (Mexico: Imprenta y Fototipia de la Secretaría de Fomento, 1907), p. 11.

15. Elizabeth Carmichael, letter to author, May 4, 1995.

16. Ibid.

17. A. H. Rankin, "Preliminary Studies of Fluid Inclusion and Solid Inclusions in a Crystal Skull from the Museum of Mankind, London (BM 1891.1), and Their Bearing on the Reported Aztec Origin of the Skull" (unpublished open file report, 1995), p. 1.

18. Jones, *Fake?* p. 2.

19. Kunz, *Precious Stones of Mexico.*

20. Ibid., p. 11.

21. Ibid.

22. Boban's obituary appeared in 1908, in M. Boule, ed., *L'Anthropologie* (Paris: Masson et Cie. Editeurs). It said that he died at the age of seventy-four.

23. *Annuaire de la Société d'Ethnographie 1886* (Paris: Bureau de la Société d'Ethnographie, 1889).

24. The photograph of M. Boban was located in the National Anthropological Archives, photo lot number 70, inv. number 02877000. It was inscribed to Thomas Wilson, who was an archeologist working for the Bureau of American Ethnology. Wilson had been U.S. consul at Nancy in the 1870s, where he presumably became acquainted with Boban, who was a member of the Americanist group in France at that time.

25. Eugène Boban, "Antiquités Mexicaines: Terres cuites reproduisant des déformations craniennes," *Musée Archéologique* 1, bk. 1 (Paris: Leroux, 1875): 45–51; "Antiquités Mexicaines: Grelots d'or trouvés dans un tombeau Zapoteco," *Musée Archéologique* 1, bk. 1 (Paris: Leroux, 1876): 143–54; "Le Vase en obsidienne de Tezcoco," *Revue d'ethnographie* 3 (1885): 70–71.

26. Perhaps one of the many establishments Holmes had described as the "relic shops in the City of Mexico" (William Henry Holmes, "The Trade in Spurious Mexican Antiquities," *Science* 7, no. 159 [1886]: 323).

27. *Diccionario Porrua de Historia Biografia y Geografia de Mexico* (1970), p. 271.

28. *The Boban Collection,* Part 1, *Antiquities, Curios, and Coins* (New York: Geo. A. Leavitt & Co., 1886), p. 34, item 303.

29. John B. Glass, "A Survey of Native Middle American Pictorial Manuscripts," in *Handbook of Middle American Indians: Guide to Ethnohistorical Sources,* pt. 3, ed. Howard F. Cline (Austin: University of Texas Press, 1975), p. 564.

30. Boban, *Catalogue D'Ouvrages Scientifique,* pp. 47–48. I am indebted to Randall Dean for locating a number of Boban items, including this one, and for his and Robert Kaupp's assistance with the French translations.

31. Ibid.

32. Paul Eudel, *Le Truquage, Altérations, Fraudes et Contrefaçon dévoilées* (Paris: Edouard Rouveyre, 1900), p. 50.

33. Eudel, *Truquage,* p. 51.

34. Désiré Charnay, *The Ancient Cities of the New World* (New York: Harper Bros., 1887), p. 55.

35. Ibid.

36. Boban, *Catalogue D'Ouvrages Scientifique,* pp. 48–49.

37. William Henry Holmes, Random Papers of a Lifetime, W. H. Holmes Papers, Archives of American Art, NAA Microfilm, vol. 5.

38. Holmes, "The Trade in Spurious Mexican Antiquities," pp. 170–72.

39. William Henry Holmes, "On Some Spurious Mexican Antiquities and Their Relation to Ancient Art," in *Annual Report of the Board of Regents of the Smithsonian Institution for 1886* (Washington, D.C.: Government Printing Office, 1889).

40. Holmes, ibid., p. 320.

41. NAA, no. 93, box 8, Latin American Archaeological sites and artifacts.

42. Holmes, "Spurious Mexican Antiquities," pp. 320–21.

43. Sonia Lombardo Ruíz, *El Pasado Prehispánico en la Cultura Nacional. Antologías, Serie Historia* (Mexico: Instituto Nacional de Antropología e Historia, 1994), pp. 38–39.

44. Ignacio Bernal, *A History of Mexican Archaeology* (London: Thames and Hudson, 1980), p. 149.

45. Record Unit 7084, W. H. Holmes Papers, Smithsonian Institution Archives (hereafter SIA).

46. Lombardo Ruíz, *El Pasado Prehispánico,* p. 118.

47. Wilson Wilberforce Blake to Spencer Baird, February 24, 1886, Baird Correspondence, corres. #17619, SIA.

48. W. W. Blake, *The Toltec Teocallis and Aztec Antiquities of Mexico—As Illustrated by the Archaeological Collections in Its National Museum* (New York: C. G. Crawford, 1891).

49. W. W. Blake, "Mexican Relics," *American Antiquarian and Oriental Journal* 8 (January–November 1886): 239.

50. I have not found this letter from Boban, nor have I located Holmes's letter to Blake, but I have reconstructed their contents from Blake's reply.

51. W. W. Blake to W. H. Holmes, March 29, 1886, Accessions USNM, no. 17619, 1886, SIA.

52. In a letter to Spencer Baird in the fall of 1886, Blake wrote: "I received a note from Dr. Holmes stating that the crystal skull had been tested with chemicals and found genuine" (corres. #17619, SIA). A footnote to this footnote must be entered here: We have apparently misplaced Blake's crystal skull, since I can find no crystal skull with the catalog number assigned it in 1887. There are four small carved skulls, one or two of which could be the Blake skull, but over the last century they have been assigned other catalog numbers. The most likely piece is found in the Foshag collection. Dr. Foshag, a Smithsonian mineralogist, had a strong interest in pre-Columbian lapidaries and changed the identifications of many of our pre-Columbian objects fashioned from materials such as jade, obsidian, and rock crystal.

53. March 29, 1886, Holmes Random Records, vol. 5, National Anthropological Archives, microfilm.

54. The second catalog is dated October 11, 1887, *The Boban Collection, Part 2, Antiquities, Curiosities, Manuscripts, Etc.* (New York: Geo. A. Leavitt & Co.), and includes a number of books and manuscripts, some apparently belonging to the Aubin and Pinart collections, and objects that hadn't sold in the first auction.

55. Record Unit 7084, SIA.

56. This particular poster adds weight to Blake's appraisal of Boban's character, i.e., that he is "not honest." The poster has a number of engravings depicting various pre-Hispanic monuments and objects, along with explanatory text. Some of the objects are from the collection of the National Museum of Mexico, and others, I have since discovered, belonged to Boban, whose name appears under the title as author. After the passage of a century, however, the label, with Boban's name and then-current address in New York City, has faded considerably and reveals beneath it the name of the poster's actual author, Leopoldo Batres (Holmes Papers, Record Unit 7084, SIA).

57. *The Boban Collection,* Part 1, p. 5.

58. *Archives de la Commission Scientifique,* vols. 2–3.

59. Howard F. Cline, in an article about Waldeck, noted that the historian W. H. Prescott questioned his "fanciful" stories, and John L. Stevens, who followed Waldeck into the Maya region, acknowledged him as a pioneer but thought that he was somewhat of a charlatan ("The Apochryphal Early Career of J. F. de Waldeck, Pioneer Americanist," *Acta Americana* 5, no. 4 (1947): 278–300).

60. E.g., *Musée archéologique* (1875) and *Revue d'ethnographie* (1885).

61. This is my own opinion and that of a number of my colleagues in Washington and Mexico City to whom I have shown the photographs.

62. *The Boban Collection,* part 1, p. 84.

63. Ibid.

64. *New York Times,* December 19, 1886, p. 3.

65. Ibid.

66. Holmes, "The Trade in Spurious Mexican Antiquities," p. 170.

67. Ibid.

68. Ibid.

69. Holmes, "On Some Spurious Mexican Antiquities," p. 321.

70. Ibid.

71. Esther Pasztory, "Three Aztec Masks," pp. 77–105. On the inside of the mask the god type is shown with four arms rather than two, with two dangling hands of the flayed victim.

72. Ibid., p. 93.

73. There is an interesting sequence of publications on this matter. Eugène Boban, the dealer, seems to have published his ideas about Mexican fake antiquities first, in 1881. W. H. Holmes followed with his two articles, which bear some similarity to Boban's writing. Paul Eudel, who published *Le Truquage* in 1900, mentions Boban and quotes extensively from his sales catalog. The last in the series is Leopoldo Batres, with *Antigüedades Mejicanas Falsificadas—Falsificación y Falsificadores* (Mexico: F. S. Soria) in 1907, who cites Eudel and proceeds to quote the entire passage of Boban without any attribution, but he may have only been returning the plagiaristic favor.

74. Holmes, "The Trade in Spurious Mexican Antiquities"; Holmes, "On Some Spurious Mexican Antiquities"; Batres, *Antigüedades Mejicanas Falsificadas.*

75. Holmes, "The Trade in Spurious Mexican Antiquities," p. 264.

76. Marshall H. Saville, *Tizoc: Great Lord of the Aztecs* (New York: Museum of the American Indian, Heye Foundation, 1929); Dudley T. Easby and Frederick J. Dockstader, "Requiem for Tizoc," *Archaeology* 17, no. 2 (Summer 1964): 85–90.

77. Pasztory, "Three Aztec Masks," p. 94.

78. Since first embarking upon this research I have personally examined three other large crystal skulls that were brought to my office, and I have seen photographs of seven others, all in private collections (one in Canada, the rest in the United States). There is another in Mexico in a private collection, but it is of the smaller variety.

79. I am indebted here to Linda Welzenbach, a researcher for the new Gem and Mineral Hall in the National Museum of Natural History.

80. William F. Foshag, "A Visit to Idar-Oberstein," *Gems and Gemology* 7, no. 11 (Fall 1953): 339.

81. Ibid.; Kay Swindler, "In Idar-Oberstein Gemology Rises Again," *Gems and Gemology* 6, no. 6 (Summer 1949): 191–93; Michael O'Donoghue, *Quartz,* Butterworths Gem Books (London: Butterworths).

82. Carmichael, letter to author; Rankin, "Preliminary Studies."

83. The famous Mitchell-Hedges skull in Canada was purportedly found at the Mayan site of Lubantun, and a smaller skull in the Parks collection in the U.S. was the gift of a Tibetan lama, who had received it from the hands of a Guatemalan Mayan shaman.

84. In the center of the capital city of the Aztecs, Tenochtitlán, there was an enormous skull rack, which, according to the chroniclers of the time, contained more than a hundred thousand skulls of sacrificial victims.

85. Boban, *Catalogue d'Ouvrages Scientifique,* pp. 47–48.

86. Jones, *Fake?* p. 291.

DILEMMAS OF CURATORSHIP

7

Curating the Recent Past
The Woolworth Lunch Counter, Greensboro, North Carolina

WILLIAM YEINGST AND LONNIE G. BUNCH

The only reason that I do history is to make America better.
—Carter G. Woodson, Founder,
Association for Study of
African American Life and Culture

In a very real sense, the Museum guards our national memory.
—Roger Kennedy, Former Director,
National Museum of American History

In February 1995, while on a research trip to Raleigh, North Carolina, a curator at the National Museum of American History (NMAH) was stopped in the hallway of the county courthouse by a man who pointed and exclaimed quite loudly, "I saw you on television talking about that lunch counter." After a few minutes of conversation that was heard throughout the building, the man ended the encounter by saying, "I hadn't really thought about how important that counter is, but I am glad that it is in the Smithsonian."

In a way, that conversation culminated a yearlong effort to acquire and exhibit portions of the lunch counter from the F. W. Woolworth store in Greensboro, North Carolina, the site of one of the most important episodes of the post–World War II Civil Rights movement. In 1993, William Yeingst of the NMAH began his efforts to obtain a section of this lunch counter for the museum's collections. After more than a year of negotiation, cajoling, research, and trips on little planes to Greensboro, the museum opened a small exhibit that sought to introduce museum visitors to that aspect of the struggle for racial equality in recent American history.

This essay uses the acquisition and exhibition of the Woolworth lunch counter as a prism to analyze the challenges and demands of exploring and interpreting contemporary history and to examine how crafting this history has changed and expanded the roles and obligations of curators in American museums. We would argue that despite the difficulties and uncertainties that accompany work in the field of contemporary history, presenting these often difficult and murky issues to the public *is* one of a museum's most important obligations—especially if museums are to be, as they so often claim, effective and contributing educational institutions.

The need to understand and embrace the ambiguity and complexity of America's past, especially the more recent past, is one of the most difficult concepts for the museumgoing public to grasp. The ambiguity is reflective of the legitimacy of multiple perspectives of the past and the fluidity of historical interpretation. And the complexity raises as many questions as it answers and explores difficult issues of change, conflict, achievement, power, possibility, and disappointment. By exploring the distant past, curators often avoid many of the more contested aspects of historical interpretation because of the public's lack of a direct or personal connection to that history. The decision by many curators and museums to examine contemporary history—events that transpired within the memories of museum visitors—forces both curators and visitors into an uncomfortable, and often unacknowledged, confrontation over the meaning, ownership, complexity, and interpretation of the recent past.

The presence of contemporary history in American museums, though still underrepresented, is not new. The ascendancy of the "new social history" with its focus on history "from the bottom up" and its desire to give voice to those who were traditionally outside the narratives of history, spurred new research, collecting, and exhibition opportunities in American cultural institutions. Those curators trained in or influenced by this "more democratic" history also found that traditional strictures against analyzing the more recent past were loosened, if not eradicated. Yet those early efforts tended to be sporadic and driven by the passions of individual curators, not by institutional initiatives.

Thus the historic efforts of curators like Keith Melder of the National Museum of American History, with his collecting of Civil Rights–era material, or Tom Frye, with his documentation of contemporary California culture at the Oakland Museum, were stellar but singular. Even calls like the pleas from the Association for the Study of State and Local History during the 1980s for the museum profession to "collect the twentieth century" failed to raise all the issues and ambiguities that make exploring contemporary history in museums so contested, so difficult, so dangerous, and ultimately so important to museums and to the publics they serve. If curators and museum scholars are to explore history that is still alive for many Americans in a manner that is effective, useful, and meaningful, then we must wrestle, both internally and publicly, with many legitimate concerns that question the nature of contemporary cultural interpretation, the role of museums in American society, and the relationship between authorship and ownership of the past.

To be more effective interpreters of the past, museum professionals must have answers to such questions as: How do museums negotiate the tension between academic history and popular memory? Who has the authority to interpret the past to the public, and what are the limits of that authority? Are museums simply places of confirmation, validation, and tradition? How do history museums balance public expectation with scholarly inquiry? What truly is the best role for the public in public history? Are they sources of inspiration and information, collaborators, cultural critics, or "students" to be educated? Who has the right to shape and revise museum interpretations or presentations? How do you balance curatorial and institutional prerogatives? How do museums candidly explore questions of race, class, and gender without falling into the interpretive trap of simple affirmation or perpetual victimization? What is the role of objects in idea-driven interpretations? Should museums explore questions in which the public has seemingly little interest, and if so, how?

Finding answers to these questions is problematic even in the best of times, but today, in an age of uncertainty, in the politicized era of the *"Enola Gay,"* it is difficult to find the civil discourse and institutional support needed to grapple with these issues. As museums are drawn into the current "culture wars," the debates over the role of museums in our society and, more specifically, over how recent history should best be remembered, preserved, and interpreted become less academic and more acrimonious. There is a tendency, from some political and public quarters, to think that museums have raised the wrong questions or pushed too hard or too fast to examine the rough edges of history. Yet if curators are to explore these issues—and we think that it is essential that they do—exhibits and collections must challenge as well as celebrate, educate as well as entertain, and stimulate thought as well as sustain tradition.

The acquisition and exhibition of the Woolworth lunch counter at the National Museum of American History is an instructive case study. It illuminates many of the challenges and opportunities inherent in exploring contemporary history in American museums, from addressing thorny questions of race in America, to ensuring the participation of various communities in the acquisition and interpretation, to presenting debates involving voice, multiplicity of meanings, and the role of the artifact.

As Martin Luther King Jr. wrote from the Birmingham city jail on April 16, 1963:

> Perhaps it is easy for those who have never felt the stinging darts of segregation to say, "wait." But when you have seen vicious mobs lynch your mothers and fathers at will and drown your brothers and sisters at whim; when you have seen hate-filled policemen curse, kick and even kill your black sisters and brothers . . . then you will understand why we find it difficult to wait. There comes a time when the cup of endurance runs over, and men are no longer willing to be plunged into the abyss of despair.

To understand why the Woolworth lunch counter, it is important to know the history, symbolic value, and significance of this object, as well as its place in the struggle for racial equality in America. During the 1950s and 1960s, the Civil Rights movement challenged the country to live up to its ideals of racial equality, citizenship, and democracy. It dared America to become a nation with equal justice for all. The Civil Rights movement struggled to end discrimination and segregation and to gain equal access to voting rights, education, and public facilities. Led by African Americans, thousands sustained the movement through individual acts of moral and physical courage and collective acts of defiance. It was this atmosphere that inspired four African American students from North Carolina Agricultural and Technical College to confront the F. W. Woolworth store in Greensboro, North Carolina, in 1960.

By 1960, the F. W. Woolworth Company possessed over two thousand stores and accumulated nearly $2 billion in annual sales. While most Woolworth stores treated their African American customers as equals, the company allowed their southern stores to abide by local custom. What this meant in practice was that in the South, including the Greensboro store, African Americans were not allowed to sit down at the lunch counter. Blacks could purchase food, but only from the seatless takeout area. The lunch counter in the Greensboro store was more than just a place to eat while shopping; it symbolized to both white and black southerners the segregated world that existed throughout large portions of the United States. For whites, the segregated lunch counter reinforced notions of power and racial superiority. For African Americans, the counter was a constant reminder of their second-class status and their vulnerability.

Fig. 7.1. On the second day of the Greensboro sit-in, Joseph McNeil and Franklin McCain are joined by William Smith and Clarence Henderson. Courtesy of the Greensboro News and Record.

On February 1, 1960, four black college students—Ezell Blair Jr. (now Jibreel Khazan), Franklin E. McCain, Joseph A. McNeil, and David L. Richmond, after weeks of planning, struck a blow against segregation in Greensboro (Figure 7.1). The four sat down at the "whites only" lunch counter and asked to be served. Their request was refused. When asked to leave, they remained seated. Over the next six months, hundreds of students, local and national civil rights organizations, churches, and community residents fueled this "sit-in." For nearly half a year, media from throughout the nation chronicled the exploits of the sit-in and the ensuing economic boycott of Woolworth. Finally, on July 25, 1960, the lunch counter was desegregated. The Civil Rights movement had won a significant struggle.

The Greensboro campaign was not the first time that the sit-in strategy was used. In fact, sit-ins and economic boycotts were staples of African American protest in the early twentieth century. What made this event significant was that it was a sustained and visible student protest that allowed the media to disseminate this story to the nation. Also, the success of this direct-action campaign garnered more support for the Civil Rights movement as more Americans saw that it was possible to achieve change. But the sit-in's most important accomplishment was that it ignited a youth-led movement to challenge injustice and racial prejudice. Black and white college students now realized that they had a role to play in this struggle. Soon thousands of young Americans became part of this movement for social change, as marchers, in voter registration, as freedom riders, and as participants in sit-down strikes throughout the South.

Recognizing the historical importance of the Greensboro sit-in was an essential element in piquing the museum's interest in the lunch counter. The collaborative process that brings a new acquisition, such as the objects from the luncheonette of the F. W. Woolworth store in Greensboro, to the Smithsonian Institution is a combination of interrelated theoretical, historical, and practical considerations, with a modicum of luck added in. In October 1993, while listening to the evening business report, William Yeingst was struck by the announcement that the Woolworth Corporation was closing more than nine hundred stores nationwide. Because of his interest in increasing the museum's holdings in the area of youth culture and his knowledge of the museum's desire to rectify the paucity of African American material culture, Yeingst decided to alert the museum and to see if the Greensboro store was part of Woolworth's corporate restructuring. The next morning, a call to the manager of the Greensboro store confirmed that the store was to close in three days and that the lunch counter was, for the most part, unchanged from the time of the sit-in. The request for additional information was referred to Woolworth corporate officials in New York City.

With that preliminary information, we began the "negotiation phase" of this acquisition. After calling the public relations office of the Woolworth Corporation, we were directed to Aubrey Lewis, the vice president for corporate relations. Discussions with Mr. Lewis revolved around the historical significance of the sit-in and the way that the Woolworth Corporation would be portrayed. Ultimately, the museum's request for artifacts from the store clearly delineated the importance of the sit-in of February through July 1960 and argued that any materials donated would be held in trust for the American people, forming a lasting record of one of the most significant events in recent American history.

Our interest was cast in broad terms that suggested the power of the objects as symbols that would help the museum interpret not only the history of the Civil Rights movement but also aspects of recent southern history, Woolworth's role in American business history, and the process of urbanization in the South.

We also argued that the NMAH could assure the long-term care and preservation of the objects. And though we could not promise that these artifacts would be exhibited, we felt that eventually the nearly six million visitors who come to the museum each year would have the opportunity to view this material. After several lengthy discussions, Lewis made it clear that while the corporation supported this donation, he would not act without the joint approval of the community of Greensboro.

We then flew to Greensboro, outfitted with video and still cameras, tape measures and business cards, to meet with members of the Greensboro City Council, employees of Woolworth, and representatives of the African American community. At all of our meetings with various segments of the Greensboro community we hammered home the notion that the story of the sit-in was an episode of national significance that should be celebrated and preserved both in Greensboro and in Washington, D.C.—and that the changes wrought by the Civil Rights movement, though costly, painful, and incomplete, made America a better, more democratic nation. This approach seemed to appease all the interested parties.

The final hurdle involved negotiations with Sit-in Movement, Inc., a small local organization that some African American residents of Greensboro had formed to purchase and preserve the Woolworth store and to turn the site into a national Civil Rights museum. We were concerned that the members of this organization might want to retain all the artifacts for their exhibits. Additionally, we did not want it to seem as if the National Museum of American History stormed into Greensboro and took what it wanted, with little regard for the community it left behind. We spent much time discussing with Sit-in Movement, Inc., their plans for the site. We reviewed with them the funding, exhibition, interpretive, staffing, and collections challenges that any new museum faces. We made suggestions about sources of information and support, such as the Association for State and Local History, the American Association of Museums, and the North Carolina Humanities Council. And most important, we echoed their enthusiasm for the creation of their museum.

After reviewing their plans, we then discussed our needs. We requested four stools, a corresponding eight-foot section of counter, mirrors, a soda fountain, and a section of cornice, all as close to the original sit-in site as we could determine using historic photographs. Recognizing the national attention that would come with this donation, Sit-in Movement, Inc., agreed to our request. The Woolworth Corporation, now comfortable with the reaction of the local community, also supported the donation and agreed to dismantle and crate the objects, with the assistance of a Greensboro carpenters union whose members would donate their labor. After we shook hands with all parties and solicited their support for any future public programming about the sit-in, the deal was done. We walked away elated. During a follow-up trip to Greensboro, members of the Smithsonian staff oversaw the dismantling, crating, and transport of the artifacts to the museum. Now part of the collections of NMAH, the lunch counter had acquired another layer of meaning—it became a museum document that would help shape our understanding of the American past.

Almost immediately, there were discussions about how to exhibit the lunch counter. Unfortunately there were no major exhibitions close to fruition that could make use of these artifacts. Nor were there pots of money available to dramatically redo existing exhibits, such as the Political History Hall, which explored the struggle over voting rights. There seemed only two choices: Either keep the newly obtained collections in storage for an undetermined period of time or exhibit the collections in a very modest manner that would allow only limited contextualization. Along with many others in the museum, we felt that the importance of these artifacts warranted exposure, even in a temporary setting.

The decision to place the lunch counter in the second-floor hallway, within viewing distance of the Star-Spangled Banner, was not without its problems (Figure 7.2). Because the hall space is better suited for viewing icons than exhibitions, there was the real risk of exhibiting these artifacts without a context. This is a story with drama and excitement that is part of a centuries-old struggle for equal rights in America. It is also part of a more recent struggle whose battles from Montgomery to Selma to Chicago received extensive television and media coverage.

Clearly the lunch counter was well suited to be the centerpiece, or at least an essential artifact, in an extensive exhibition. But even the space seemed to limit what could be accomplished. While there was room for the modest use of large photomurals, there was a concern that despite our best efforts, a hallway could not become an exhibit hall. The exhibit also suffered from the lack of a major visual presence of the people who used the counter. This could be remedied through the use of mannikins, by mounting an array of photomurals, or by peopling the exhibition through video or musical presentations—all quite effective and all possible in another setting.

Yet the exhibition works for several reasons. First, while the NMAH has, in the last fifteen years, strived to reinvent itself as a museum driven by social history, there are still many objects displayed for their iconic or patriotic value. We were struck by how few of these icons were reflective of the diversity of the American populace. We felt that it was important to have a racialized icon that cried, in the words of poet Langston Hughes, "I, too, am America." We hoped that visitors would come to realize that while it is important to revel in museum

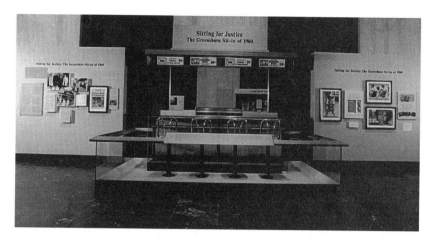

Fig. 7.2. "Sitting for Justice" exhibition, National Museum of American History, Smithsonian Institution. Photo by R. Strauss. Courtesy of the Smithsonian Institution.

icons like the Washington statue, the Ceremonial Court, or Archie and Edith Bunker's chairs, without icons such as the Woolworth lunch counter their visit, like the history they receive, would be incomplete.

The exhibit, though modest, is not without context. Using a marriage of idea, word, image, and object, "Sitting for Justice: The Greensboro Sit-in of 1960" explores the event through the eyes of the participants and examines its impact in 1960. Though centered on the sit-in, the exhibit places the moment within the context of the Civil Rights movement. In an exhibition of this size, we did not try to place the Civil Rights movement in the larger context of racial struggle throughout the late nineteenth and early twentieth centuries. In essence, it tells a limited but complete story. The exhibit was never meant to be a permanent fixture within the shadow of the Star-Spangled Banner. Eventually the lunch counter will become part of a major interpretive exhibition that chronicles aspects of twentieth-century history. Until it is removed, however, it will continue to remind visitors of the recent nature of the struggle for racial equality and the importance of individual participation in the political process. More important, the exhibit is a reminder that the Civil Rights movement is not just a part of African American history but a story that should have meaning for all Americans.

Acquiring and exhibiting the Woolworth lunch counter provided an opportunity to explore and grapple with many of the issues that make interpreting contemporary history in museums so problematic, so challenging and so rewarding. Even though we have already raised many of these concerns in the body of this essay, we want now to call attention to four areas that require careful consideration, thoughtful analysis, and a modicum of flexibility.

THE PRIMACY OF MEMORY

In light of the critical outcry that has been occasioned by many of the museum profession's attempts to explore contemporary history, including the Smithsonian Institution's "*Enola Gay*" and "Science in American Life" exhibitions, it is not surprising that many institutions and their research staff are wary of the recent past. After all, presenting the history of the living means treading on dreams and wrestling with recollections both cherished and painful. It is the primacy of memory, the idea that since one can remember an event, he or she has ownership of that history, that is one contributor to the contested nature of recent public historical interpretation. This sense of ownership means that visitors for whom the episode has direct meaning may be less likely to defer to curatorial prerogative. Usually that means several visitors will complain that "they were there, and they don't remember it that way." But in the case of a value-laden and politicized subject like the dropping of the atomic bomb, this sense of ownership creates a wave of criticism that museums are often unable to handle.

Acquiring and exhibiting the Greensboro lunch counter forced us to face the different and conflicting memories about this event. To some, especially members of the African American community, this episode should be celebrated as the triumph of good over the forces of racism. To others, it was an important but unfortunate occurrence that should not bring dishonor on the city of Greensboro. Many who worked in the corporate headquarters of Woolworth wanted to make sure that the company was not tarred by this event. Others believed that the sit-in changed little. We attempted whenever possible to recognize the legitimacy of these conflicting viewpoints. But we also made sure that their proponents understood that as historians we held the ultimate responsibility for the way the sit-in would be interpreted. We were successful because we listened with respect but made clear, in an unwavering manner, our curatorial role and responsibility.

MEANING AND REPRESENTATION

As curators, what we collect, whose stories we preserve, what interpretations we present, and our mandate to convey those decisions to millions gives us power.

The power to determine who and what has value. The power to save or to forget a people's culture. The power to shape memory. And the power to help determine what is historically meaningful and culturally significant. In essence, curators have the power of choice and the power to convey meaning—powers that should be used judiciously and openly.

It is increasingly difficult, especially in the arena of contemporary history, for curators to wield that power. As audiences have more connection with a historical moment, they are more likely to contest the curators' choices. For example, all artifacts can evoke emotion and memories, but those emotions and memories differ depending on a variety of factors, including age, race, gender, class, place of birth, and an individual's personal history. Part of a curator's task is to choose what artifacts and what interpretations he or she thinks are important for the visitor to experience. As recent history demonstrates, those choices are undergoing greater scrutiny than ever before. Yet that scrutiny must not deter curators and institutions from exploring issues that have multiple or contested meaning.

The lunch counter is an object burdened with many layers of meaning. During the process of collecting that artifact, we often remarked how much of the history of the South one could tell simply by using the Woolworth store. Additional interpretations of the lunch counter include seeing it as a prism to explore how southerners use food, as Roland Barthes has written, "as a system of communication . . . a protocol of usages, situations and behaviors"; the consequences of consumerism on southern culture; the economic impact of luncheonettes; and the rise of southern urbanism. Whenever we were asked how would the museum interpret the lunch counter, the subtext was often, "Who gave you that right?" Rather than fear that query, curators must accept the legitimacy of public questioning and seize the opportunity to communicate to visitors our roles as interpreters of the past and keepers of a public trust. We found that by deconstructing the historical and curatorial processes, explaining how we arrive at decisions about collecting, exhibiting, and interpreting, we could address many of the questioners' concerns. It is essential that we help the public—visitors, politicians, and funders—to better understand that what curators do is based less on whim and personal ideology than on scholarship, research, and considered reflection.

THE PAST IS POLITICAL

Thomas Schlereth has written that "objects have politics." Curators have politics too. And what we learned from the "*Enola Gay*" affair was that politics can be brought to bear to shape historical interpretation. Clearly, exploring contemporary history is a reminder to us all that the past is political. As curators begin to delve into contemporary issues that are unresolved or still painful to the American psyche, they are made more aware of the limits of their institutions, their collections, and their abilities to educate in a museum setting. Visitors to museums often come seeking reaffirmation or answers. Exploring such difficult issues of contemporary history as the dropping of the atomic bomb or the Vietnam War requires great skill—not because museums do not have the collections or the expertise to grapple with these questions but because of the inability of cultural institutions to resolve conflicts that have existed for generations. Curators must continue to contextualize the past in order to give visitors the tools to use to manipulate history so that they might deal better with the present. Our task is not to retreat from this opportunity but to continue to craft exhibitions that give meaning, hope, and understanding, rather than to produce presentations that attempt conflict resolution.

RACE

Until recently, race was one of the last "unmentionables" in the museum profession. Rarely were people of color seen as central to a museum's interpretive, collecting, or educational mission, except for racially specific museums. Within the last decade, much has changed. Museums large and small, from the National Museum of American History to the Geneva (New York) Historical Society, now find ways to include programs, exhibitions, and publications that embrace cultural diversity. While much has improved, many of these efforts falter because of the paucity of racially specific objects in their collections. Exploring race effectively means that museums must dedicate the resources to review and reinterpret their holdings and develop creative collecting initiatives that tap nontraditional sources. Even when questions of race are investigated, the exhibits tend to view groups like African Americans or Asian Americans as outsiders, whose stories, while important and dramatic, are not central to the telling of American history. Or the interpretations tend toward less-critical depictions of "positive images" and "famous firsts."

Exhibiting the lunch counter enabled the NMAH to address many of these considerations. Only through the collaborative efforts of many staff members and the contribution of needed resources by the museum administration was the counter obtained. To remedy the paucity of objects that speak of race, museums must make commitments, and possibly sacrifices, to exert the extra efforts needed to collect successfully in this area. Additionally, by focusing on the story of the sit-in, the museum was able to transcend a romanticized version of American race relations by exploring conflict, struggles, and dreams deferred. The exhibit, both through its location in the building and by its interpretive posture, allowed the museum to place this racially specific episode squarely within the mainstream of American history.

It serves the museum profession well to remember that what it does is public history—a history that is shaped by scholarship and research, by the need to make that information accessible, and by an obligation to be of service to the public. We fulfill that responsibility best in our role as an educational institution. By ensuring that our audiences have the opportunity to explore and to enlarge their understanding of the recent past and its lessons for today, museums can provide a service that makes them vital to our visitors.

Clearly, exploring contemporary history is a dark and bloody ground that is not for the faint of heart. But, oh, the ground is so fertile. Curators must emulate the bravery of the participants in the Greensboro sit-in and summon up the courage and the creativity to face the challenges of collecting and interpreting the recent past.

8

The Unstifled Muse
The "All in the Family" Exhibit and Popular Culture at the National Museum of American History

ELLEN RONEY HUGHES

As a character who maintained that all change was for the worse, Archie Bunker was an unlikely focal point for transformations in twentieth-century American culture.[1] The TV series in which Archie starred reflected and promoted change in network television programming; the exhibition of the show's memorabilia by a Smithsonian museum signaled and accelerated change in history museums as well. More than simply lowbrow joins highbrow, popular entertainment artifact exhibits at the American History Museum[2] denoted an unprecedented endorsement of popular culture as an appropriate subject for a national cultural institution. Not everyone applauded.

Within the American History Museum, the inclusion of national popular culture was part of the shift away from military and technological history and toward social and cultural history. Propelled by critical events in the country in the 1960s and 1970s, from the civil rights movement to the Vietnam War, museum exhibition themes came closer to reflecting the life experiences of their varied audiences. These trends were exemplified in the 1976 exhibition "A Nation of Nations," portraying America's immigrant heritage. The 1980 name change to National Museum of American History from Museum of History and Technology underscored this refocus and suggested that although innovations emanated from the curatorial staff, they were also endorsed by administrators.

New directions were not unanimously embraced, however. Many remained unconvinced that popular culture was either historic or substantive enough to support a compelling interpretation of the American past. And the museum's annual audience, averaging five million visits,[3] did not remain unmoved by the changes but responded in the time-honored ways: writing in praise or protest, staying away or bringing friends, or, in a few cases, threatening to resign their membership in Smithsonian Associates.

The single-case display of props from the popular, iconoclastic television series All in the Family (1971–79) gained significance out of proportion to its tiny size. The exhibition, which opened in 1978, and the resultant publicity added a surprising dimension to the identity of the Smithsonian Institution's American History Museum. Even though more-traditional exhibit themes dominated the halls, over time the museum became famous for popular entertainment, especially after several subsequent, well-publicized exhibitions on similar subjects: "The Ruby Slippers and The Wizard of Oz" (1979 and 1991); "Black Baseball: Life in the Negro Leagues" (1981); "M★A★S★H: Binding Up the Wounds" (1983); "Hollywood: Legend and Reality" (1986); "Sesame Street: The First Twenty Years" (1989).

For years after the donation of the Bunker chairs, Tourmobile operators briefed their tourist passengers on the museum's highlights as follows: "the Star-Spangled Banner, George Washington's sword, the First Ladies' gowns, the ruby slippers, Archie and Edith Bunker's chairs," prompting questions about why those chairs were in the litany of notable artifacts. As political icons, the flag and the sword are expected patriotic attractions; the display of the gowns is among the few historical exhibitions to throw light on women's experiences in the past; and the red shoes have a cultlike following of film buffs; but why, so long after the All in the Family series ended, do these television show props still draw a crowd? " 'All In The Family' is an offensive, degenerative show," wrote one of several irate correspondents in 1979, soon after the museum announced it would accept and display the chairs. "Imagine future generations viewing those chairs as a symbol of American TV comedy?" To her probable amazement, and sometimes to the museum's, a generation later the Bunkers' chairs have become even more eminent—American cultural icons. How this popular culture exhibit came about in a national cultural arena and why it still resonates with meaning for museum visitors are worth exploring.

A museum is read through its exhibitions. They are the posters of a museum's identity, which signify to the public more clearly than publications, mission statements, or even collections what the institution is about—whether it teaches with art, nature, or history, whether it embraces the traditional or promotes the revolutionary. Every museum exhibition articulates a message, usually in line with its audience's expectations, or, less often, it challenges them to think anew.

Museum exhibitions, like the one containing the All in the Family chairs, have three main components: the artifacts, ideas in a text, and the audience's reception. Each component represents a context. First is the context of the makers and users of the exhibited objects. The artifacts may have been used by many and may have served a variety of purposes over the years since they were created. Many men and women may have participated in the design and production, as well as the selling and distribution of the displayed objects. To tell the intentions of these humans and their worldview or to examine changing meanings of the objects is often the point of a museum exhibition.

The second context is the message of the exhibitors, the reasons the museum staff selected particular objects and graphics for display either alone or juxtaposed with others. This message is embodied in the choice of objects and explained in the thematic text label.

The third context is in the mind of the viewer, who brings her own cultural assumptions and often previous knowledge of the objects.[4] Presumptions about objects and about the museum that contains them help shape the audience's interpretation, making possible many different reactions to a single display. Often viewers' reactions reflect cultural conflicts within American society, especially when the message of the exhibition differs from mainstream beliefs or from the audience's assumptions about the identity of the museum.

To understand how and why the Bunkers' chairs became part of the American History Museum, the three contexts—the artifacts, the museum and its interpretation, and the audience's perceptions—all contain compelling testimony. The artifacts—two chairs, one table, a doily, an ashtray, and two mock beer cans—came into the museum as a physical representation of the series and its leading characters. On their own merits, the chairs—lacking in provenance, beauty, or distinction—would never have been accepted by the Domestic Life Division, the area of the museum that curated Anglo-American furniture. The Community Life Division acquired them because they were central props in a television show that was significant on a number of levels: as a leading example of situation comedy, a dominant type of American television show; as a pivotal show that caused change in the genre; as revealing of common beliefs, values, and behaviors in American life during the 1970s; and as a widely shared American cultural experience with passionate fans and detractors.[5]

The All in the Family television series was created by Norman Lear, a veteran writer and producer of variety shows, who founded Tandem Productions with film producer Bud Yorkin. Their industry specialty was comedy with social commentary. Lear purchased the American rights to an edgy BBC sitcom, Till Death Do Us Part, which featured a Cockney father and his son-in-law who fought bitterly over social politics. For his American version, Lear created Archie Bunker, modeled on the original Cockney character—with a dose of his own father thrown in—as a blue-collar worker and bigoted social conservative played by actor Carroll O'Connor. Jean Stapleton acted the part of wife Edith Bunker, Sally Struthers played the daughter, Gloria, who was married to Mike "Meathead" Stivic, Archie's lazy, liberal nemesis, performed by Rob Reiner. At first Lear titled the show Those Were the Days.[6]

From the beginning, the visual centerpiece of the series was a tableau of two old chairs of unequal size flanking a small table purchased from a California used-furniture store. Although nothing is known about their previous life, their common, battered, and homey 1940s look captured the tone of the set. Archie's chair dominated. "Its symbolism cuts across all generations, cultures, races, times," Lear later said. "Everybody's father had a chair, or something akin to it—some place that was sacrosanct to him and him alone. In my father's case, for example, it was a red leather chair. We'd never think of sitting in it—it was *his* place."[7] From his chair Archie spouted his characteristic malapropisms, clichés, and bigoted commentary; it was also where he usually received his comeuppance, often delivered innocently and honestly by Edith, the occupant of the smaller chair (Figure 8.1).

In the late 1960s television executives perceived the shifting social ground in the real world of their audiences and set out to encapsulate the new social realities in innovative shows. CBS president Bob Wood selected Norman Lear's pilot (that ABC had rejected twice) to test his belief that the network needed to appear young, urban, and more realistic yet should retain some of the successful comedy and family formulas. In cleaning the CBS house, Wood jettisoned most of its older comics and rural series: Jackie Gleason, Red Skelton, Ed Sullivan, Jim Nabors, Petticoat Junction, Hee Haw, Gunsmoke, and The Beverly Hillbillies. Although some "relevant" new shows bombed, such as Storefront Lawyers, Lear's gutsy new show, renamed All in the Family, tested very well; it was an instant hit when it premiered in January 1971. A popular and critical success, the series defined quality television—in the sitcom tradition—for the next decade.[8] With the 1969 debut of the Public Broadcasting Corporation, which re-aired many British imports (often called the least worst television in the world), and with 1970's The Mary Tyler Moore Show, the first sitcom to feature an independent woman as its main character, there was a virtual renaissance of comedy on American television.[9]

Norman Lear's All in the Family and many of his later series, such as Maude

Fig. 8.1. Edith and Archie Bunker (Jean Stapleton and Carroll O'Connor) sitting in their chairs on the All in the Family set. Photo by Michael Feder; © 1978 Tandem Productions, Inc.

and The Jeffersons, expanded the idea of domestic comedy by translating the problems encountered by the family in the direction of the social and political. Lear introduced overtly political agenda into the sitcom genre.[10] Archie's attitudes presented a challenge to the broadening of society, as well as to social history. Although intended as social satire, the show opened a dialogue among viewers and provided a common ground for the exchange of different ideas. Not surprisingly, this sitcom revealed that the so-called melting pot had not produced a digestible brew.

Despite the success of All in the Family, the socially conscious series was controversial. Debate centered on bigot Archie's references to minorities as "micks," "spades," or "hebes" and on his long-running arguments with the tolerant housewife Edith and liberals Mike and Gloria. Analysts and critics could not agree, however, on whether the show satirized prejudice or reinforced it.[11] The mainstream press, particularly at the end of the series, generally favored the sitcom. *Washington Post* critic Tom Shales wrote, "Eventually it became the target of repeated and prolonged controversy, but beyond the social significance of the program lies another fact that makes it a landmark in television. Never before has the best comedy show on TV also been the best dramatic show on TV, and that's why none of the weeping and wailing on Friday night [the final show] seemed inappropriate."[12] As representative of domestic life and social change, All in the Family artifacts were ideal to bring into the American History Museum at that time to evoke popular intellectual exploration of the subject.

American History Museum curator Carl H. Scheele attended the All in the Family final episode taping in March 1978 at the suggestion of Rep. John Brademas (D-Ind.), who was serving on the House committee that watched over the Smithsonian. The congressman had contacted Norman Lear, asking whether symbols of the series "could be preserved here as part of the cultural legacy of our country."[13] Lear enthusiastically offered Archie's chair first, then the entire set or any parts thereof. Scheele, with the approval of museum director Brooke Hindle and the museum's acquisitions committee, selected the two chairs and a small table that had been used through all 186 episodes. Scheele and Lear signed a Deed of Gift on the spot, a moment captured in a *Time* magazine photo.[14] After eight years as theatrical props, the chairs began a new life as museum artifacts.[15]

When the Bunkers' chairs arrived at the museum in 1978, they were the only major television series artifacts in the collections, yet the decision to take them was in line with changes in the museum and consistent with the broadening scope of the history profession. New social history, emanating out of American universities at that time, became the model for scholarly inclusiveness. Subjects like popular culture, folklore, women's studies, and labor history began to effect a reorganization of museum collections.[16]

The innovative approach to history within the museum was dramatized and advanced in the exhibition "A Nation of Nations" (1976–91). Beginning with the earliest migrations in 22,000 B.C., the exhibit moved through the Colonial periods and the Revolution on to the mass immigration of the nineteenth and twentieth centuries. It examined the persistence of foreign traditions in America as well as the homogenizing forces that aspired to smooth away or Americanize those traditions. In addition, it searched out America's place among other nations through mass production and mass communications. A wide range of subjects was explored frankly; neither the dark nor the light aspects of the American past were ignored. Above all, it concentrated on the objects and experiences of the common person, paying particular attention to issues of race and class.[17]

The remarkable "A Nation of Nations" exhibition had a direct bearing on the Bunker chairs exhibition in several distinct but related ways. First, the expansive thinking and collecting efforts in creating that exhibition led to the realization that the intellectual organization of the American History Museum was too narrow to accommodate collections reflecting aspects of American life and recent trends in history scholarship, including entertainment history. Second, in highlighting the history of work, sports, and entertainment in that show, Carl Scheele and I began acquiring the collections that formed the new curatorial division, in which the Bunker chairs eventually would reside. The overwhelming favorable response by the museum visitors, particularly to the sections on popular culture, reinforced our ambition to incorporate those subjects into the museum. Finally, "A Nation of Nations" provided the physical and intellectual context for exhibiting All in the Family artifacts. As a location, it was singularly appropriate because many of the same forces that shaped the content of the exhibition brought All in the Family to American television audiences. Both the exhibition and the television series dealt with a distinctly "American" group of experiences, especially aspects of ethnicity and pluralism, and neither was reluctant to examine cracks in the culture where pluralism was resisted.

The Division of Community Life that Carl Scheele and I founded in 1977 was an essential new curatorial unit. Although the collections might have been incorporated into existing divisions, some curators resisted expansion of their subject areas, voicing the concern that museum storage and exhibit space could not expand to accommodate new collections. Further, few were interested in the acquisition of common, twentieth-century artifacts. Therefore, we invented this curatorial entity specifically to study the history of entertainment, leisure, and sports, as well as to pull together objects relating to education, labor, urban life, and other previously marginalized subjects.[18] Convinced that achievements in the performing arts have always been among the more important and lasting cultural contributions of a nation, we launched a study collection of artifacts associated with amateur and commercial aspects of popular culture, including recorded music, theater, radio, television, and motion pictures. An intellectual asylum having been established within the museum, acquiring the sitcom artifacts was a logical step.

In addition to the chairs, table, and doily, Tandem Productions donated an ashtray, two fake beer cans, and six set-design drawings. All the artifacts were shipped to the museum, where the staff fumigated, numbered, cataloged, and photographed them and executed the paperwork necessary to render them government property and accessioned museum artifacts. Although we had anticipated some objections from the museum community, none was voiced. Even Otto Mayr, acting director and traditional historian of technology, penned a warm letter of thanks to Norman Lear, citing the show as "a landmark in the history of entertainment."[19]

The determination to place All in the Family props on exhibition as quickly as possible was driven by the publicity surrounding their donation. Immediately, visitors and press asked to see the chairs. Within the "A Nation of Nations" exhibition an ideal site was identified, adjacent to the American entertainment section on one side and the twentieth-century American home period rooms on the other. After deciding to suggest, rather than re-create the set, we hunted up an old patterned rug at a flea market (on the original set a carpet was painted directly on the floor so the camera crew could move around unimpeded) and found an appropriately patterned wallpaper at a local decorator store. Exhibit designer Richard Virgo planned a sturdy Plexiglas case on a short platform to accommodate the chairs in their familiar position. Because of a not-unusual measurement discrepancy, the chairs and table just barely fit. Scheele supplied a cigar for the ashtray. Set drawings, two photographs, and the text labels completed the exhibit.

To explain the significance of the objects as well as their relevance to the museum was the challenge of writing the exhibit text. The message needed to be brief, specific, and not overponderous, yet it also needed to contain our point of view. Although exhibits are often created by groups and reviewed by committees, labels are ultimately crafted by one or two individuals expressing their interpretation of the objects within a historical context.

The Bunkers' chairs presented the paramount problem of the study of popular culture: how to show the significance of what many consider trivial without overstating the cultural value of the genre.

The label read:

> The "All in the Family" TV series, which began in January 1971, has consistently presented issues foremost in American consciousness. Intolerance in its many forms—frequently ethnic prejudice—was one of the basic themes. Archie Bunker (that arch-bigot) became identified with all that flawed the relationships of our multi-ethnic citizens. The interplay between Archie's bigotry, Mike Stivic's Polish-American liberalism, and Edith's and Gloria's search for tolerance and acceptance reflected that nation's social struggles, holding a dramatic mirror to America's conscience.
>
> Shown here are Archie and Edith Bunker's chairs and end table from "All in the Family." Gift of creator Norman Lear; Tandem Productions, Inc.

Two photographs were captioned—one showing Archie and Edith posed in their chairs and a cast portrait that stated: "Over the years, the cast, production staff, and the show itself have won more than ten Emmy awards." The text was rounded out by a quote from newspaper columnist Abigail Van Buren: " 'All in the Family' has accomplished more about understanding America and what it's all about than any other show that's ever been done on television. *Los Angeles Times,* March 6, 1978."

The text addressed not only fans of the show but also the casual visitor who happened on the sitcom props in the center of a show on American ethnicity. Although comfortable in our decision to acquire and exhibit the chairs, we felt compelled to quell the concerns of the audience segment who disliked the show as well as popular culture critics both within the Smithsonian and in the larger intellectual community. While it is in the Smithsonian tradition to break new ground, new ventures seem automatically to foster a host of questions. We did not have to wait long for a reaction.

The acquisition and exhibit of the chairs received nearly as much press coverage as did the closing of the series. The Washington Post and the *Los Angeles Times* ran big stories mentioning the museum. Newspapers from Florida to Hawaii gave that story several inches. The taking of the chairs became an event in itself.[20] *People* magazine extrapolated, not quite accurately, "No less an arbiter of the national treasure than the Smithsonian Institution formally requested Archie's and Edith's chairs for its archives. 'All in the Family' was not only TV's most popular entertainment series (with unequaled five straight years as No. 1); it was also the most important."[21]

Dignity, as well as the mantle of high culture, was brought to the exhibition by S. Dillon Ripley, secretary of the Smithsonian, who presided exuberantly at the opening event (Figure 8.2). Surprisingly grand, the event attracted a mix of entertainers and politicians that was more exotic in 1978 than today. Actress Bette Davis broadcast a live television show from the exhibit featuring interviews with celebrities like Ripley, Lear, Stapleton, Penny Marshall, and even Scheele and myself. Everyone was a bit startled by the scale.

We quickly found that a museum such as American History is in itself very popular and that many people pay a great deal of attention to what we collect and exhibit. Unfortunately, the people who object to certain programs are among the few who take time to write. Although terse, the public's responses to our popular entertainment exhibitions reveal the varied meanings that artifacts and exhibitions hold. The letters also demonstrate the passionate feeling and expectations that audiences have for their national museum. A particularly interesting aspect of these letters is that protests rarely came from people who visited the "All in the Family" exhibit in person, only from those responding to media coverage. Generally complainants fell into three categories: those who looked down on television as trivial, considering it inappropriate for inclusion in a national shrine; those who did not like the All in the Family series specifically; and those who were either puzzled or amused.

Fig. 8.2. Drawing by D. Fradon; © 1978 The New Yorker Magazine, Inc.

Addressed to various Smithsonian officials, this pithy assortment was fired off around the time the "All in the Family" exhibit was installed. "This morning I learned via the radio news that Archie Bunker's chair was now ensconced in the Smithsonian Institution, near George Washington's effects. How silly can you get? No wonder you are always having to ask Congress for money . . . if the Smithsonian is going to be cluttered up with junk like this."

Another: "Assuming a board or commission was responsible for this idiotic idea, I would recommend that its members be enshrined in your institution as the nuttiest people of 1978. I am not anti-Bunker."

"With deep regret I am sending back to you this application and my will to drop my membership. The reason for this determination is simple, probably wrong, but sincere. In 1969 when I visited the Smithsonian I was amazed of [*sic*] being in front of those millions of relics for which I called myself that Institute a National Shrine, but, when I learnt ARCHIE BUNKER's chair is going to be there in exhibition I got the impression such a sanctuary will be converted, gradually, to another 'pawn shop' or second hand store."

Fig. 8.3. "The Bunkers' Chairs" exhibit in its second location, the first-floor corridor of the National Museum of American History, 1995. Photo by Eric Long, Smithsonian Institution.

Correspondents who had a negative opinion of the show also weighed in. "We want to protest putting Archie Bunker's chair in the Museum. His show is vulgar, constantly using four letter words. Just things that the American people can be proud of should be put there."

"What kind of American society raises a monument to bigotry, slobbiness, and a sneer at all decent American values? The sad part is you are putting this alongside such memorials as the Spirit of St. Louis and other great achievements and seem to feel that it is in its proper place."

A perplexed writer asked about the chair: "What are the criteria for selection to your museum? (Is it considered a museum?) To get back to Archie's chair—what is so 'Americana' about that chair. I am really serious—by what standard was his chair selected? I always thought the Smithsonian was a place for historical memorabilia of America . . . items to be saved so our history would be preserved. . . . If my interpretation is correct though, then what will Archie Bunker's chair from a TV show indicate to future generations?"[22] Humorously representing other puzzled folks, a *New Yorker* cartoon featured a man-in-the-street gazing quizzically at an Archie Bunker chair reproduction sale (Figure 8.3).[23]

Correspondents singled out only Archie's chair as objectionable, never Edith's. One reason was that as the chief provocateur, Archie stood for the entire show. The lack of complaints about her also reflected the traditional family structure portrayed in All in the Family and, indeed, in most television situation comedies. Edith did not stifle herself, but for the most part, she did remain in her place.

Each letter was answered with both the context of the exhibit and our rationale in mind. We clarified that the chairs were part of a display dealing with the history of entertainment and within a larger exhibition that focused

> on many aspects of interracial relationships and prejudices, social mobility and bigotry, opportunities, contributions, achievements and conflicts commonly experienced by Americans, major themes that have been dealt with in the "All in the Family" series for more than eight years. . . . Moreover, the series as a whole has become an important factor in changing programming and censorship policies through dealing squarely with socially controversial issues in the mass medium of television over a sustained period of time. The fact that "All in the Family" was a "popular" series helped to reinforce television's mission as a vehicle for social comment in the best tradition of the drama.[24]

Of the many thousands who enjoy looking at artifacts like the Bunkers' chairs, only a few wrote to express their enjoyment. In 1980 one said, "Archie's chair deserves an special place so future generations can, with some imagination try and visualize what comedy was like in the 1970's and also get some idea of what America thought its heroes should be like."

As we persisted through the 1980s to add to the collections of popular entertainment, other donations of well-known television artifacts and costumes, such as Fonzie's jacket from Happy Days, generated more news coverage and dispatches. Some continued along familiar lines: "I have gone back to college and for an English class I am writing a research paper. I have chosen as the subject, why those chairs are in the museum and why do they typify Americana. . . . What qualifications are required for something to be classified as Americana?"

"I would never join the Smithsonian as long as you have an exhibit of Archie Bunker as part of American culture. Archie Bunker and Norman Lear are racist saboteurs and you are gullible nincompoops." There were even threats: "Please remove the Archie Bunker family exhibit. Some day someone will."

However, a new thread began, with suggestions and demands for additional artifacts: "I am shocked that your institution obviously holds such persons as

Archie Bunker and Fonzie in higher regard than Elvis Aron Presley. . . . I earnestly request, as a taxpayer, that you take steps to acquire something of Elvis' and that it be placed on display as soon as possible." And "There's another TV star who owns something very special, maybe even more than the great pyramids or the great wall of China. That star would be RADAR of MASH [sic] fame, and I think America would like to see RADAR'S TEDDY BEAR in your exhibit right along side Archie's chair and Fonzie's jacket."

MAD magazine featured a two-page spread titled "Future Smithsonian Exhibits from TV Land." Some twenty selections included "From 'Little House' average size Kleenex used by a family of four while watching a typical tearjerking episode"; "From the 'Incredible Hulk', green body make-up"; "From television in the '50's, first dress ever worn by Dinah Shore, first dress ever worn by Milton Berle."[25] These we did not add to our want list; however, "M★A★S★H" did become the museum's next large popular culture exhibition in 1983.

"M★A★S★H: Binding Up the Wounds," the American History Museum's exhibition on the television comedy series set in a U.S. Army field hospital during the Korean War, featured two sets, equipment, props, costumes, and photographs (everything but Radar's teddy bear, which was reportedly lost). Michael Harris of the Medical Sciences Division acquired the show's authentic 1950s medical equipment, while the Division of Community Life sought theatrical objects, including an alcohol still, a Hawaiian shirt costume, and the "Swamp."[26]

For eleven years, 1972 to 1983, the significant characters of the award-winning series were doctors and nurses who, as healers, were against war, refused to carry guns, treated the enemy and compatriots equally, and made fun of the army. With the army as a foil they never ran out of jokes, and the anti-bureaucracy message was one key to M★A★S★H's continuing success. The Vietnam War was the principal social context, providing a humorous liberal response to an extremely divisive situation in America. The show helped the audience deal with that crisis in ways that no other media provided. After the war ended, the show lost its critical edge and eventually died. It made television history as the first sitcom to have a real conclusion—the Korean War ended and everyone went home.[27] It made museum history as the first—and to date, the only—set from a television production accepted in its entirety by the museum.

The "M★A★S★H" exhibition was also controversial, although for different reasons than the "All in the Family" display. The text contrasted the real and fictional wars in Korea, and the relationship of the television series to the Vietnam War.[28] Visitors usually took sides along the national split of feelings for and against the Vietnam War. Nevertheless, the exhibition proved to be an enormous success with the public and the popular press. As always, that was a mixed blessing. The term trivia crept into the debate over the validity of an important museum's collecting effort in the field of entertainment history.

Writing for the *Chicago Tribune,* a critic penned a superficial piece highlighting recently acquired television artifacts under the headline "Smithsonian Treasures TV Trivia."[29] Though it usually would have been just another piece of newspaper ephemera, this article caught the eye of the incoming new secretary of the Smithsonian Institution and resonated with his unease over popular culture. Soon afterward, in his monthly magazine column Secretary Robert McCormick Adams quoted the *Tribune* article and confessed his trouble in seeing enduring value in the television history collections and the "disproportionate attention given to these items by the media." He concluded, "Most people, I believe, come to the Smithsonian and to the museums as places to view treasured achievements that are tangible as well as enduring. But if the relics of TV are accepted as additions to the permanent collections of museums, with accompanying fanfare, is there not some danger that we will contribute to the ongoing erosion of vital standards of judgment and performance in the society at large?"[30]

Never given the opportunity to discuss either the objects in the collection or their position as neither the most nor the least significant objects in the American History Museum, we were unable to present our rationale to the secretary. By chance, the sole letter to the editor (which we did not write, honestly) challenged his opinion. "Dear Sir: Concerning Secretary Adams' Smithsonian horizons . . . One of the strengths of the Smithsonian is the preservation of the past trivia. A fossil sea urchin, a woodland stone point and a First Lady's dress may have seemed trivial in its own time."[31]

Being accused of contributing to the ongoing erosion of American society may have daunted some, yet we understood that this broadside was an intellectual, articulate, and very public rendition of the familiar popular culture controversy. The central tenet of this argument is not against popular culture per se, but a recognition of the power of popular culture materials in museum exhibitions to communicate ideas directly and powerfully to the public as a possible threat to the established social and political order.[32] In addition, such a critique equates the mission of a history museum with that of an art museum—to define, select, and promote the "best" in a culture. Negative aspects of the argument also stress that (1) television is primarily commercial popular entertainment, its shows so ever-present and simple that they neither warrant nor deserve analysis; (2) bringing them into a museum and treating them in a serious way elevates these shows to the same level as traditional political, social, and art museum fare, thereby legitimating them, exaggerating their importance, and possibly perpetuating them; (3) academic analysis renders comedy boring;

(4) television viewing is a harmful activity that should be discouraged, not encouraged.[33]

A number of scholars argue the positive roles of popular culture. Herbert J. Gans, for instance, devoted a weighty portion of his book to refuting the criticism of popular culture. Although his defense was multifaceted, in debunking the charge that popular culture has a negative impact on society, Gans concluded: "Popular culture has played a useful role in the process of enabling ordinary people to become individuals, develop their identities, and find ways of achieving creativity and self-expression. Popular culture has not caused these changes; it has only helped predisposed people to achieve them by providing examples and suggesting ideas."[34]

Writing sixteen years later, George Lipsitz took an even stronger view of how popular culture works for the audience. His students "identified with television program, film, and popular music in a way that they would not even consider about politics. These texts unleashed the memories and experiences suppressed by the dominant rhetoric of their private and public lives. Here hope was still an issue, and happiness was still possible. . . . Not because these films, songs, and shows reflected our lives directly, but, rather, because they reflected the core contradictions of our everyday lives indirectly enough to make discussion of them possible."[35]

British literary critic Raymond Williams wrote in 1972: "More drama is watched in a week or a weekend, by the majority of viewers, than would have been watched in a year or in some cases a lifetime in any previous historical period." That alone renders television an essential subject of study.

Because history museums have less in common with art museums, which focus on the finest examples of a few object types, and are similar in many ways to natural history museums, the commitment to collect and exhibit inclusively persisted. The American History Museum continued to present popular culture, not only in exhibitions but in performances, film series, lectures, and publications. Many programs were presented in connection with the "A Nation of Nations" exhibition, but time and crowds eventually took their toll on that space. For eleven years the exhibition endured indignities, from the poor maintenance of its once theatrical lighting to the closing of major sections to poorly grafted additions. We reluctantly killed the ailing exhibit in 1991. That decision necessitated the temporary removal of all popular culture artifacts from public view. Because those very artifacts had become identified with the American History Museum—and vice versa—the public vigorously expressed its disappointment when they were no longer available, in a flurry of calls, letters, and visitor comment forms.

This time the public's reaction was more tempestuous, but the reverse of our first experience. "We came 3,000 miles to see Archie Bunker's chair. . . . Please bring those artifacts back. They are favored relics of American Popular Culture. What a shame!!!"

"The main reason we came was to see the entertainment in 'A Nation of Nations' which has been closed. I consider this unprofessional and unfair to the public."

"Please bring back the TV & Movie memorabilia. You've taken away the fun by removing those exhibits."

"The past and politics is wonderful but our culture is one of television and should be included as part of our recent times."

"I am most distressed that the exhibit has been discontinued. So many of us come here to see Dorothy's shoes, Archie's chair, Fonzie's jacket, Mr. Rogers' sweater—America as we know it. I can't fathom what would possess you to discontinue this popular exhibit."

My personal favorite was this very succinct note: "Ridiculous that some dumb bureaucrat would eliminate Entertainment & Sports which are such an important part of American Life."

We "dumb bureaucrats" swiftly reinstalled the popular culture artifacts for public view. Presented on their own in a series of cases on television comedy, the Bunkers' chairs required a different interpretation, although they remained in the same case. The new text, written by Charlie McGovern and me, reads:

> "All in the Family," which ran from 1971 to 1979, was one of television's most popular and influential programs. Creative in many respects, it shattered a long tradition in television of portraying happy families living in a world without social strife. Producer Norman Lear made conflicts and wounds in American Life the targets of the show's biting comedy. Archie Bunker, played by Carroll O'Connor, was the bigoted centerpiece of the program and a living symbol of intolerance and ignorance. Archie fought fiercely with his son-in-law, Mike, portrayed by Rob Reiner, and his daughter, Gloria, played by Sally Struthers. Their battlegrounds were the very issues dividing American Society—ethnic prejudice, women's liberation and racism. The show's humor revealed the limits of Archie's bigotry, as well as the self-righteousness of his children. The antidote to Archie's fears and prejudices was the innocence and generosity of his wife, Edith, portrayed by Jean Stapleton.

Today, fewer people relate to the original television production of All in the Family, although it is rerun sporadically on cable television. As a critic said, "When both the nation and the industry grew more conservative in the mid-

1970s, the grammatical innovations of the Lear programs appeared passe as political relevance faded from the sitcom's repertoire."[36] Yet the show went into syndication for years. In the 1990s, the genre of blue-collar social issue sitcom made a small comeback with Roseanne and The Simpsons. In 1991, All in the Family's twentieth anniversary year, CBS aired episodes in prime time as television classics. The following year, a New York Times book review sidebar quoted a new book analyzing and reinterpreting The Mary Tyler Moore Show and All in the Family: "But both turned their backs on the promises of postwar optimism. Both gave up on the ideal of a mass culture, a fully integrated society. They were the twin small comforts of the American audience in a time of deep anxiety. They were just dark enough, just sad enough, to ring true."[37]

If the series is dimming in people's minds and psyches—a whole generation has been born since the last episode was produced—it is because the issues and concerns of the 1970s are not the problems of the 1990s. The "All in the Family" display remains among the most asked-for objects in the museum, although it may have lost the passionate audience it once commanded.[38] The exhibit of the Bunkers' chairs was best understood, and most enjoyed, in the context of a comprehensive American history exhibition, where its serious relationship to entertainment history and other aspects of American life could be appreciated. Without the context of history, displays of popular culture artifacts risk becoming mere attractions. The larger framework gives artifacts greater meaning and allows more compelling interpretations.

Nevertheless, the artifacts and the series retain their importance to museum historians and audiences. The value of any significant artifact of popular culture is as historical evidence of past states of consciousness and the texturing of social and domestic relationships.[39] For historians of twentieth-century culture, the recovery of events and meaning is less a problem than understanding them is. These objects provide access to that understanding. The forms of American popular culture—movies, television programming, country music, broadway musicals, comedy acts—are products of American creativity with worldwide impact and recognition. While individual examples can be poor or even offensive—no one likes it all—in its totality and diversity, popular culture is highly significant.

Displays of American popular entertainment and sporting experiences, a new direction in exhibitions during the 1970s, altered the identity of the museum, signaling a change in the thinking of the staff and attracting new audiences. Although a necessary and healthy passage in the life of a dynamic institution, change proved difficult for both staff and audience who preferred traditional themes. In expressing their concerns about exhibits and the museum, people ultimately have revealed larger concerns about the nation, with their comments often reflecting contemporary ideological divisions in American society. The Smithsonian Institution is one of the uncommon intersections of intellectuals and the general public. At the American History Museum this presents a singular opportunity to articulate the symbols and meaning of American culture to a broad audience. The museum has made a commitment to inclusiveness, to cover all facets of American history; it is the only museum charged with such a broad mission. Researching, collecting, interpreting, and exhibiting the history of entertainment and sports artifacts contributes to the "increase and diffusion of knowledge" in important, if not traditional, ways.[40] Like America itself, its national museum has become intricately identified with popular culture; indeed, the museum is a branch of popular entertainment itself. With Edith Bunker as an example, we did not stifle the exuberant, eccentric voices of American entertainers, entertainment entrepreneurs, and the entertained, nor our desire to represent them. Aw, geez, Archie.

NOTES

1. This essay is dedicated to Carl H. Scheele (1928–1995), my friend and mentor, whose intelligence, humor, courage, and vision as a curator led so many of us to expand the boundaries of America's museums.

2. For simplicity I use the unofficial name American History Museum throughout. The official name has changed from Museum of History and Technology (authorized by Congress in 1955, opened in 1964), to the National Museum of American History (1980), to which the phrase "Science, Technology, and Culture" was added on letterhead and signs but not officially to the name (c. 1985).

3. Statistics for the Smithsonian Institution are compiled by the Institutional Studies Office. The director, Zahava D. Doering, reports that figures represent a loose count of visits, not visitors, that they are approximate, and could be unreliable for the years before 1976.

4. A clear explanation of this process is given in Michael Baxandall, "Exhibiting Intention: Some Preconditions of the Visual Display of Culturally Purposeful Objects," in *Exhibiting Cultures: The Poetics and Politics of Museum Display*, ed. Ivan Karp and Steven D. Lavine (Washington, D.C.: Smithsonian Institution Press, 1991), pp. 33–41.

5. Several books have been published on the series, including Richard P. Adler, ed., *All in the Family: A Critical Appraisal* (New York: Praeger, 1979); Donna McCrohan, *Archie and Edith, Mike and Gloria: The Tumultuous History of "All in the Family"* (New York: Workman, 1987); Spencer Marsh, *Edith the Good: The Transformation of Edith Bunker from Total Woman to Whole Person* (New York: Harper and Row, 1977); Spencer Marsh, *God, Man, and Archie Bunker* (New York: Harper and Row, 1975).

6. Designs for the 1969 set of Those Were the Days were donated by designer

Henry C. Lickel. Smithsonian Institution, National Museum of American History, Office of the Registrar, file no. 1979.0458.

7. John Weisman, "Enshrined Under Plastic: How Archie's Chair Got to Its Final— and Appropriate—Resting Place," *TV Guide,* February 10, 1979, p. 37.

8. Todd Gitlin, *Inside Prime Time* (New York: Pantheon Books, 1984), pp. 206–11; Gerald Jones, *Honey, I'm Home! Sitcoms: Selling the American Dream* (New York: Grove Press, 1992), pp. 193–213.

9. Richard Maltby, *Passing Parade: A History of Popular Culture in the Twentieth Century* (Oxford: Oxford University Press, 1989), p. 173.

10. Jane Feuer, "Genre Study and Television," in *Channels of Discourse, Revisited: Television and Contemporary Criticism,* ed. Robert C. Allen (Chapel Hill: University of North Carolina Press, 1992), pp. 149–55.

11. Michael R. Real, *Mass-Mediated Culture* (Englewood Cliffs, N.J.: Prentice-Hall, 1977), pp. 33–36.

12. Tom Shales, "Meathead and Gloria Break Up an American Family," *Washington Post,* March 6, 1978, sec. B1, p. 11.

13. Weisman, "Enshrined Under Plastic," p. 37.

14. *Time,* March 20, 1978, p. 66.

15. At the last minute the donation ran into a problem. Although two principal cast members, Struthers and Reiner, had resigned, the show was continued for one more season. The Smithsonian could not lend the chairs for that purpose, so the props that Tandem had acquired for about eight dollars were then replicated at considerable expense for use during the final year.

16. From its beginning, the museum dealt with some subjects related to popular culture, but both its collections and its exhibitions privileged technological developments over content. For example, collections held phonographs, but few recordings; televisions and radios, but no scripts, kinescopes, or tapes of programs; pianos, but no popular sheet music. Although collecting policy eventually changed to include content, popular culture hardware and software remain stored and studied in separate curatorial units. A new twist is that exhibitions on technology now usually include popular culture artifacts.

17. Peter C. Marzio, ed., *A Nation of Nations: The People Who Came to America as Seen through Objects and Documents Exhibited at the Smithsonian Institution* (New York: Harper and Row, 1976).

18. We selected the name Division of Popular Culture. For reasons of their own, however, the museum administration grafted onto the new unit the tiny Division of Ethnic and Western History, headed by Richard E. Ahlborn. The amorphous name Community Life was chosen because it embraced almost every topic possible, creating a verbal umbrella for these dichotomous groups. In 1994, Community Life joined Musical History, previously called Musical Instruments Division, in a large Division of Cultural History. Stay tuned.

19. File no. 1979.2146, Office of the Registrar, National Museum of American History, Smithsonian Institution.

20. *Washington Post,* March 6, 1978; *Los Angeles Times,* March 6, 1978; for example, *Honolulu, Hawaii Advertiser,* March 7, 1978.

21. "Up Front: Meathead and Gloria Depart the Bunker Nest in a Cloudburst of Real Tears," *People,* March 27, 1978, pp. 26–31.

22. Letters are in the Correspondence File, Division of Community Life, National Museum of American History, Smithsonian Institution.

23. Dana Fradon, *The New Yorker,* November 6, 1978, p. 46.

24. Carl Scheele, October 31, 1978, Correspondence File, 1978/9, Division of Community Life, National Museum of American History, Smithsonian Institution.

25. Dennis Snee, with illustration by George Woodbridge, "Future Smithsonian Exhibits from TV Land," *MAD,* September 1983, pp. 24–25.

26. File no. 1983.0095, Office of the Registrar, National Museum of American History, Smithsonian Institution.

27. Sarah Kozloff, "Narrative Theory and Television," in Allen, Channels of Discourse, p. 92.

28. *"M*A*S*H": Binding Up the Wounds* (Washington, D.C.: Smithsonian Institution Press, 1983).

29. Marilynn Preston, "Smithsonian Treasures TV Trivia," *Chicago Tribune,* 1985.

30. Robert McCormick Adams, "Smithsonian Horizons: Our Collections May Include Some Trivia, But the Real Emphasis Is on More Enduring Achievements," *Smithsonian* 16, no. 4 (July 1985): 10.

31. Samuel L. Cook, Col. U.S. Army (Ret.), Letter to the Editor, *Smithsonian* 16, no. 6 (September 1985): 18.

32. Carl H. Scheele, unpublished paper, n.d.

33. Herbert J. Gans, *Popular Culture and High Culture: An Analysis and Evaluation of Taste* (New York: Basic Books, 1974).

34. Ibid., p. 58. Also see Russel Nye, *The Unembarrassed Muse: The Popular Arts in America* (New York: Dial Press, 1970); and John Story, *An Introductory Guide to Cultural Theory and Popular Culture* (Athens: University of Georgia Press, 1993).

35. George Lipsitz, *Time Passages: Collective Memory and American Popular Culture* (Minneapolis: University of Minnesota Press, 1990), p. xiv.

36. Feuer, in Allen, Channels of Discourse, p. 154.

37. *New York Times,* January 26, 1992; Jones, *Honey, I'm Home!* p. 213.

38. In 1994–95, 8% of all visitors came to the museum to see a "cultural icon"; of those, 24% specifically mentioned the Bunkers' chairs, totaling 0.95% of all visitors interviewed. This contrasts with the highest of 12.3% of all visitors who come to see the First Ladies Exhibition and 10% for the Transportation Hall (*1994–95 National Museum of American History Visitor Survey Overview,* October 1994 to May 1995, Institutional Studies Office, Smithsonian Institution.

39. E. P. Thompson, *Making History: Writings of History and Culture* (New York: New Press, 1994), p. 204.

40. Numerous scholarly books explore the history and analyze the meaning of television in America. Among the most useful are those cited above, as well as Horace Newcomb, ed., *Television: The Critical View* (New York: Oxford University Press, 1994); and John Fiske, *Television Culture* (London: Routledge, 1989).

9

Zuni Archangels and Ahayu:da
A Sculpted Chronicle of Power and Identity

WILLIAM L. MERRILL AND RICHARD E. AHLBORN

Throughout its history, the Smithsonian Institution has curated its collections according to well-established, albeit evolving, concepts and practices derived from European and Euro-American ideas about the role that museums should play in society.[1] In keeping with this intellectual tradition, the principal responsibility of museum curators has typically been defined as that of organizing, studying, expanding, and preserving the collections for which they are responsible so that these collections will be available for research and public education long into the future.

During the second half of the twentieth century, this vision of museum curation has been seriously challenged by alternative perspectives grounded in the cultural traditions of many of the non-European societies who are represented in the collections. In the case of the Smithsonian (as well as many other American museums), this challenge has been offered most forcefully by members of contemporary American Indian societies. Indian people who visit museum collections frequently are shocked by the techniques that museums routinely employ to preserve items that are of great religious significance to them—fumigation, for example. They also are dismayed to discover that religious objects often are stored among more mundane materials and that anyone examining the collections has access to such sensitive objects, which in their own societies are available to only one or a few individuals.

Most museums, the Smithsonian among them, have attempted to address the concerns expressed by American Indian people by modifying their standard curatorial procedures, storing the objects in ways more consistent with the Indians' cultural practices or providing the Indians access to special objects for traditional ritual purposes. In some cases, however, Indian religious and political leaders have argued that some objects can never be properly curated in museums and, in fact, should never have been removed from the communities within which they were created. These objects, they maintain, should be returned to those communities. As a consequence, repatriation has been added to the traditional responsibilities of museum curators and in many instances has come to overshadow their efforts to build and preserve the collections for future generations.

Representatives of American Indian societies and museums currently are engaged in extensive discussions of the complex issues surrounding the curation of such sensitive objects. To a considerable extent, these discussions have been motivated by two laws enacted by the United States Congress: the National Museum of the American Indian Act (Public Law 101-185) of 1989 and the Native American Graves Protection and Repatriation Act (Public Law 101-601) of 1990. Among other provisions, these laws establish that American Indian societies have legitimate claims to certain kinds of objects housed in museum collections and define the parameters within which these societies can exercise their claims.

The impact of this federal legislation on anthropological and historical museums is unparalleled in the history of museums in the United States, for it requires these institutions to radically redefine their relationship to their collections and their responsibilities to American Indian people; it may eventually set the stage for transforming their relationships with all the people whose cultures are represented in their collections. Yet, while the significance of this legislation is undeniable, it is important to recognize that some museums and American Indian societies began to address the problems that it was intended to resolve years before it was enacted.

Here we will explore one example of repatriation that developed in the decade prior to the passage of this legislation. In this case, the Zuni Indians of New Mexico and the Smithsonian Institution agreed that four carved wooden images taken from Zuni by Smithsonian anthropologists in the late nineteenth century would be returned to the Zuni people. Two of these images are statues of the archangels Saint Michael and Saint Gabriel, which were removed from the altar screen of the Catholic mission church in the center of the Zuni pueblo. The other two images are Ahayu:da, or war gods, which were taken from shrines outside the pueblo.

We summarize here the history of the removal of these four images from Zuni and their return a century later, but our intent is primarily cultural and interpretive, not chronological. We provide a hagiology of sorts, focusing on the lives of these religious images and the multiplicity of identities that have been ascribed to them within the framework of contrasting Zuni and Euro-American concepts of objects, property, and knowledge. These distinct, culturally grounded concepts provide the basis for understanding how the Smithsonian justified removing and subsequently returning these objects and also how the Zunis developed their successful campaign to regain possession of them. We conclude with some thoughts on the relationship of such highly significant objects to more encompassing processes of power and identity as these processes have developed within and between museums and American Indian communities.

THE IMAGES

The Spanish first established Catholic missions among the Zunis in 1629, but Zuni resistance to the Spanish colonial program precluded a stable missionary presence there until near the end of the seventeenth century. During the first four decades of the eighteenth century, the church at the Zuni village of Halona (present-day Zuni Pueblo), which had been destroyed during the Pueblo Revolt of 1680, was rebuilt. Around 1775 the Franciscan friars Silvestre Vélez de Escalante and José Mariano Rosete y Peralta remodeled and refurbished the church, which was known by then as Our Lady of Guadalupe.[2]

Throughout the Spanish colonial period, Catholic missionary activities were supported through the *situado* system of royal patronage developed for the New World missions in the 1500s. In this system, missionaries received stipends and the necessary supplies to hold services, including basic altar furnishings.[3] For more elaborate furnishings, such as a splendid altar screen and its imagery, additional patronage from local sources typically was required. In 1760, for example, Governor Marín del Valle donated a carved and painted stone altar screen for the military chapel recently constructed on the central plaza of New Mexico's provincial capital, Santa Fe.[4] Such important patrons appear to have been lacking for the Zuni mission and its church. According to Fray Francisco Domínguez, an ecclesiatic visitor to Zuni in 1776, the new altar screen was "paid for by Father Vélez and the Indians of the pueblo."[5]

Fray Domínguez provided a detailed description of this handsome, *estípite*-style altar screen.[6] In keeping with arrangements of subjects on Mexican colonial altar screens, the central element was an imported "large oil painting on canvas . . . of Our Lady of Guadalupe, which the king had given before." At the

Fig. 9.1. Statue of Saint Michael after 1992 Smithsonian conservation (Report 5296, Conservation Analytical Laboratory, Smithsonian Institution).

top of the two-level altar screen appeared "a bust of the Eternal Father in half relief." To either side of the Guadalupe portrait were "painted half life-sized" images of the founders of the Dominican and Franciscan orders, Dominic of Guzman (d. 1221) and Francis of Assisi (d. 1226), and, in "lower niches at the sides . . . St. Michael on the right and St. Gabriel at the left, new middle-sized images in the round."

Fig. 9.2. Statue of Saint
Gabriel, about 1942
(negative number 42-706A,
Smithsonian Institution).

These angelic statues reflect a solid familiarity with Hispanic Mexican proto-
types in terms of the selection and use of materials, their scale, and their late
Baroque, provincial style. Pale, tinted skin tones (*encarnación*), garment ornamentation (*estofado*), stylized Roman military attire, European pigments including lake blue and Prussian blue, metallic gold and silver foils, and the finishes of
the statues are all typical features of Renaissance sculpture in Spain and Spanish
America. Moreover, the bold, if not masterful, carving places the statues well
within the range of late Spanish colonial statuary provided for mission churches
without access to master sculptors (*imagineros*) working in metropolitan centers.[7]

Documents identifying the creator of the Zuni altar screen images are lacking, but in 1974 the noted Hispanic New Mexico arts curator E. Boyd concluded that they likely had been produced by Captain Bernardo Miera y
Pacheco (d. 1785), a Spanish-born mapmaker stationed at Santa Fe since 1754.[8]
As a draftsman and explorer in service to the Crown in New Spain, Miera y
Pacheco was acquainted with Hispanic artistic styles and techniques, including
those required by the Church. Fray Domínguez recorded that the captain had
made a sculpture of Saint Philip the Apostle for San Felipe Pueblo, located be-

tween Albuquerque and Santa Fe; later Miera y Pacheco accompanied Domínguez and Zuni's Fray Vélez de Escalante on an exploratory expedition into Colorado and Utah. Thus, Captain Miera made religious images and was well
known to Fray Vélez de Escalante, who was ministering at Zuni by January
1775.[9] If at that time Vélez de Escalante arranged for the altar screen and its
sculptures to be created, Miera y Pacheco would have had nearly two years to
complete the work before Domínguez's visit.

The Spanish missionaries at Zuni presumably regarded these religious images
as devotional and didactic aids that would inspire and focus the Christian faith
of their Indian converts and beautify the church interior, an architectural mass
that differed significantly from native buildings. These intended functions—as
well as the selection of the images as part of the overall theme of the altar screen
and the materials, techniques, and style used to produce them—fully invested
the archangel statues with a Spanish cultural identity.[10]

Over the course of the following century, these images also acquired a distinctive Zuni cultural identity that was not defined by European artistic and the-
ological precepts. Information on how Zunis might have perceived these statues
was not recorded until the second half of the nineteenth century. By that time,
they apparently considered the images to constitute one component of the
church and its adjacent cemetery, which they viewed as having strong symbolic,
spiritual, and physical associations with their ancestors. Much of Zuni religion
is directed toward convincing their ancestors to intercede on their behalf to
bring rain, so these images may have been linked, albeit indirectly, to this central concern of their native religious life.[11]

Like the archangel statues, the Ahayu:da images are carved out of wood and
painted, but their significance and identity are firmly grounded in traditional
Zuni culture with no apparent influence from Spanish or Anglo-American cultural traditions. The Zunis regard these wooden images as living embodiments
rather than mere physical representations of two spiritual beings who were
brought into existence in the ancient past through the agency of the Sun Father.
The purpose of their creation was to aid the Zunis during their migrations in
search of the Middle Place, which they eventually found at the current location
of the Pueblo of Zuni. These beings, who are twin brothers, were endowed
with vast powers that could be directed toward bringing rain and prosperity or
unleashed to help the Zunis defend themselves against their enemies and overcome other obstacles.[12]

Each year at the winter solstice and also when a new Bow Priest, or War
Chief, is initiated, the leaders of the Zuni Deer Clan create an image of the
Elder Brother Ahayu:da (whose name is Uyeyewi) while the leaders of the Bear

Fig. 9.3. Images of the Elder Brother Ahayu:da removed from their cave shrine on Corn Mountain for photographing. James Stevenson, 1881 (negative number 2335, National Anthropological Archives, Smithsonian Institution).

Clan prepare an image of the Younger Brother Ahayu:da (Ma'a'sewi). After these images are created, they are taken to their shrines by the Bow Priests, who place them next to the Ahayu:da produced in previous years. Through prayers, blessings, and constant instruction, these Bow Priests and clan leaders endeavor to direct the destructive powers of the Ahayu:da toward protecting the Zunis and promoting good in the world.[13]

COLLECTING THE IMAGES

The two archangel statues and the two Ahayu:da images were taken from Zuni between 1879 and 1884 by members of the first scientific expedition sponsored by the Smithsonian Institution's Bureau of Ethnology.[14] The principal objective of the expedition was to document the complex cultures of the Pueblo Indians of the American Southwest before their traditional ways of life were further transformed by interaction with the growing numbers of Anglo-Americans who were entering the region.[15] This information, in turn, would assist in interpreting the numerous Pueblo ruins that dotted the Southwest and would provide insights into the evolution of human societies in America and around the world.

The leader of the expedition and, at thirty-nine, its oldest member was Colonel James Stevenson. Stevenson was appointed to the task by John Wesley Powell, the founder and first director of the Bureau of Ethnology, who during the previous decade had directed the natural history surveys of the American West in which Stevenson had participated. The remaining members of the expedition were the thirty-six-year-old photographer John K. Hillers, another veteran of the western surveys; Stevenson's wife, Matilda Coxe Stevenson, ten years his junior, who would become one of the first female ethnographers in the United States; and Frank Hamilton Cushing, twenty-two, a protégé of Spencer F. Baird, then secretary of the Smithsonian Institution. Baird assigned Cushing to the expedition to conduct intensive research on one Pueblo society, to be selected during the course of the expedition.

On August 5, 1879, the expedition members boarded a train in Washington and a month later arrived at the terminus of the Atchison, Topeka, and Santa Fe Railroad at Las Vegas, New Mexico. From Las Vegas they traveled by mule to the territorial capital at Santa Fe and then on to the U.S. Army outpost at Fort Wingate. Finally, in late September, they arrived at the Pueblo of Zuni in western New Mexico; they set up camp on the outskirts of the pueblo and began establishing contacts in the local community. A month later, Cushing moved from the expedition's quarters into the home of Palowahtiwa, the governor and, as such, the principal civil official of Zuni Pueblo.

For the next five years, Cushing lived almost continuously in the pueblo. During the same period, the Stevensons combined their work at Zuni with visits to other pueblos and ruins in New Mexico and Arizona as well as several return trips to Washington. After James Stevenson's death in 1888, Matilda Stevenson continued to pursue her research and writing on Zuni and other New Mexico pueblos until her own death in 1915.[16]

This research produced an impressive record of Zuni life in the late nineteenth century, documented in photographs, monographs, and a collection of several thousand artifacts, but the work of the expedition was plagued by intense interpersonal conflicts between Cushing and the Stevensons. Cushing shared with some other southwestern ethnographers a dislike for the Stevensons, centered "on their high-handed manner with the Indians, their supposed failure to

Fig. 9.4. Watercolor by Richard H. Kern of proper right side of Zuni church altar screen showing Saint Michael and *estípites,* 1851 (Beinecke Library, Yale University).

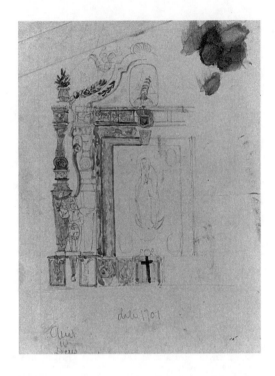

give proper credit to informants, their essential lack of respect for the pueblo peoples, and their political connections."[17] For their part, the Stevensons apparently regarded Cushing as an arrogant self-promoter who was not above distorting and even fabricating data to fit his view of things. After Cushing's death, Matilda Stevenson characterized him as "the biggest fool and charlatan I ever knew."[18]

Their conflicts aside, both Cushing and the Stevensons abused the confidence that the Zunis placed in them by publishing information that the Zunis regarded as secret and by failing to respect Zuni wishes that certain kinds of objects not be removed from their lands. Among these objects were the four carved wooden images that these anthropologists took from Zuni and later deposited in the Smithsonian collections.

In November 1879, only two months after their arrival at Zuni, the Stevensons took the statues of Saint Michael and Saint Gabriel and two other carvings from the altar screen of the mission church and shipped them back to Washington. By that date, the church had been neglected by Catholic authorities for

Fig. 9.5. Stereo view (left side) of Zuni apse and altar screen showing the archangel sculptures in place. Timothy H. O'Sullivan, for the "Expedition of 1873," led by Lieutenant George M. Wheeler (Bancroft Library, University of California at Berkeley).

over half a century. Catholic priests had stopped residing at the Zuni mission after Mexico gained its independence from Spain in 1821, and they visited it only periodically until around 1848, when New Mexico was annexed by the United States.[19] During this period and the following years, the church building deteriorated, but the altar screen and two freestanding statues remained in fair condition, as documented in watercolors produced in 1851 by Richard Kern and photographs taken in the early 1870s by Timothy H. O'Sullivan.[20]

Details of the circumstances surrounding the removal of these images is available primarily because Cushing used them as ammunition in his efforts to discredit the Stevensons.[21] In 1896, he reported:

A party of Americans who accompanied me to Zuñi desecrated the beautiful antique shrine of the church, carrying away "Our Lady of Guadalupe of the Sacred Heart," the guardian angels, and some of the painted bas-reliefs attached to the frame of the altar. When this was discovered by the Indians, consternation seized the whole tribe; council after council was held, at which I was alternately berated (because people who had come there with me had thus "plundered their fathers' house"), and entreated to plead with "Wasintona" to have these "precious saints and sacred masks of their fathers" returned to them.[22]

Cushing published these claims after James Stevenson's death, and there is no evidence that Matilda Stevenson responded to his charges until after Cushing himself had died, and then only indirectly. In a 1904 publication, she wrote:

> Two images of saints and portions of the altar of the old Catholic church were obtained, the enamel finish on the face and limbs of the figures showing much artistic skill. The church objects were in the custody of one Mauritio, and in order to determine whether they might be removed a council of religious and civil officers was held. It was finally decided that it would be well to have these objects go with the other Zuñi material to the "great house" (National Museum) in Washington, where they would be preserved.[23]

While it is impossible to determine whose account is closer to the truth, James Stevenson himself provided strong support for Cushing's accusations. In a letter written on November 21, 1879, Stevenson remarked that the archangel images had been taken from the church "in the dead hour of night."[24]

In light of his own collecting activities, Cushing's righteous indignation at the Stevensons' actions is better regarded as self-righteous hypocrisy. He removed the ancient church records from Zuni and in conjunction with the Stevensons made an extensive collection of Zuni "fetishes" for the Smithsonian, which he described in detail in an 1883 publication.[25] He also collected one Ahayu:da for the Berlin Museum, another that became part of the Smithsonian collections, and carved a third for the British anthropologist E. B. Tylor, apparently in an effort to gain his support in his conflicts with the Stevensons.[26] In a letter to Tylor, Cushing wrote:

> Ere writing I have been waiting several weeks that I might inform you of the completion of the war-god. Now tell me frankly, pray, if you disapprove of what I have been doing. Finding on trial that the half-decayed surface of the idol I gave you would not take paint, I carved a facsimile of it, colored it properly, and then, using as models several articles in a collection I made for the Museum of Berlin, I restored as completely as possible the paraphernalia of the god that his fetish might be presented to you just as it is annually to the populace of Zuñi, by the Priesthood of the Bow. To me this task was easy as each year since my initiation into that order it has been my elected province to make one or another of the self-same things.[27]

Cushing probably took the Ahayu:da that became part of the Smithsonian collections during his residence at the pueblo between 1879 and 1884, although

Fig. 9.6. Shrine of the Younger Brother Ahayu:da, Corn Mountain. Adam Clark Vroman, 1899 (negative number 2330-a-2, National Anthropological Archives, Smithsonian Institution).

it is possible that he removed it during later visits to the pueblo between 1886 and 1889. Matilda Stevenson wrote that her husband acquired an Ahayu:da in 1881 through the Zuni Elder Brother Bow Priest, Nai'uchi, who was a friend and collaborator of the Stevensons. The Smithsonian catalog records indicate that both Ahayu:da were taken from shrines on Corn Mountain, a large mountain that dominates the view from Zuni to the east.[28]

What the Zunis regard as living spiritual beings the Stevensons and Cushing saw as elaborate artifacts of singular importance to Zuni religious life and, as such, of considerable scientific value. At the same time, these anthropologists may also have viewed the Ahayu:da images in a rather different and less professional light. Neither James Stevenson nor Frank Cushing included the Ahayu:da in the extensive collections that they deposited at the Smithsonian, keeping them instead in their private collections, where they remained until after the two men had died.[29] This curious fact suggests that Stevenson and Cushing may have regarded these images as ethnographic trophies or souvenirs that, because of their exotic appearance and esoteric associations, enhanced their own image as explorers with access to the most hidden corners of American Indian culture. In fact, these images appear to have been favored collectors' items for many of the explorers and tourists who passed through Zuni during the late nineteenth and early twentieth centuries, even though they almost certainly realized that the Zunis opposed the removal of the Ahayu:da from their shrines. At least eighty Ahayu:da eventually ended up in museum collections.[30]

Cushing presumably did not condemn the Stevensons for taking the Ahayu:da image because he was also removing Ahayu:da from shrines, but it is possible that both he and the Stevensons regarded the Ahayu:da as less valuable because new Ahayu:da images were created every year, while the archangel statues were unique.[31] Moreover, it appears that the Zuni populace as a whole was not aware that the Ahayu:da had been removed from their shrines. Unlike the reaction in the case of the archangels, there was no public outcry that Cushing could use in his attacks on the Stevensons.

The Stevensons and Cushing apparently felt justified in removing the archangels and Ahayu:da from Zuni because they believed that Zuni traditional culture, like that of the other southwestern pueblos, was doomed to disappear as a result of the influx of Anglo-Americans to the region. For them, the importance of documenting these cultures and creating a scientific record of human cultural diversity outweighed any desire that the Zunis might have had to keep these images for their own use. The three anthropologists also were confronted by the prospect that if they did not take these images themselves, the objects would fall into the hands of tourists and collectors working for other museums, particularly museums in Europe. The archangels were kept in the old mission church that was collapsing around them, and the Ahayu:da reposed in isolated shrines located at some distance from the pueblo. While the anthropologists clearly realized that the images continued to have great significance for the Zunis and had in no sense been abandoned by them, they perhaps felt that in these locations the images were especially vulnerable to other collectors.

The motives of the anthropologists for removing the images from Zuni cannot be justified in terms of modern museum ethics, but they were very much in keeping with accepted collecting practices and the Victorian presumption of cultural authority and superiority of the late nineteenth century. Knowing what their motives were does not, however, reveal how they had the opportunity to collect the images. The existing records are full of gaps and at times contradictory, but a general picture of the circumstances that enabled the objects to be acquired can be reconstructed.

From the point of view of Zuni religious leaders in the late twentieth century, holding a religious office did not confer on Cushing, Nai'uchi, or anyone else the right to remove Ahayu:da from their shrines or to produce Ahayu:da and their associated paraphernalia for museum collections. It is likely that the Zunis of the late nineteenth century shared this perspective, but there is some evidence of ambivalence, or at least a diversity of opinion, on these matters.

Matilda Stevenson reported that, while the majority of people at Zuni adamantly opposed any photographing of their religious ceremonies, "the priests and other high officials favored photographing the ceremonials—in fact, seemed eager to serve the expedition in every way."[32] This attitude of the Zuni leadership may have reflected their concern about the growing presence of Euro-American settlers, traders, soldiers, government officials, and missionaries in the region. Such concern, which perhaps was greater than that of the general Zuni populace, may have caused the leaders to adopt a position of guarded tolerance toward the anthropologists as part of a more general political strategy designed to deal with this potential threat.[33] They apparently hoped that the Stevensons would promote Zuni interests in Washington, and they endeavored to maintain good relations with them. As a result, they may have allowed them access to some areas of their culture while keeping other areas hidden from them, areas that in many cases were restricted even among the Zunis themselves.

Cushing overcame these restrictions somewhat by successfully maneuvering to be initiated in 1881 into the Bow Priesthood, an appointment that he characterized as perhaps "the greatest of all the achievements of my life" because it gave him access to "all the other secret, medicine, or sacred orders of the Tribe."[34] Why the Zunis acquiesced to Cushing's desires is not entirely clear, but their reasons probably were related to the Bow Priests' primary responsibility to protect the pueblo and people of Zuni from outside threats. By allowing Cushing access to esoteric knowledge and practices through the Bow Priesthood, the Zunis gained in return an ally whom they perceived to have important connections in Washington and who would be obliged to assist them in their efforts to defend themselves against local Anglo-American settlers and neighboring Navajos.[35]

If the Zunis did in fact tolerate the collecting activities of these anthropologists for political reasons, their strategy was successful; the Stevensons and Cushing *did* defend and further Zuni interests both locally and in Washington. Yet there were other factors that enabled them and others to take items that most Zunis agreed should not have been removed. For example, it was standard practice for collectors to offer Zuni individuals money and goods in exchange for items that could not be acquired otherwise, thereby exploiting the poverty that the Zuni people were experiencing at the time. Also, they may have pressured the friends they had gained at Zuni to acquire such objects for them as personal favors.[36] It also is possible that the Zunis let them take the objects as a way of

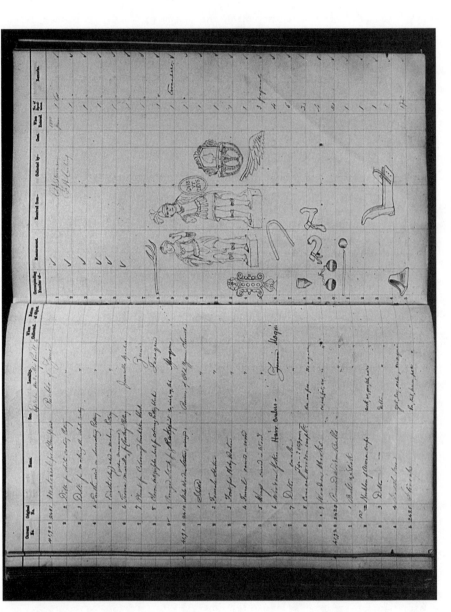

Fig. 9.7. Drawing of the archangel figures, entered into the Smithsonian catalog in 1881 (entries for accession number 9899, catalog numbers 41910 through 41915, catalog ledger books, vol. 9, Department of Anthropology, Smithsonian Institution)

"getting them off their backs," so to speak, using the objects as a buffer to protect more esoteric areas of knowledge and practice from them.

AT THE SMITHSONIAN

The images of Saint Michael and Saint Gabriel arrived in Washington in 1880 and were accessioned into the collections of the Smithsonian's U.S. National Museum in 1881, accompanied by two other objects from the altar screen: a crown-over-heart cartouche and a polychromed carving consisting of feathers, C-shaped scrolls and circular bosses.[37] Matilda Stevenson incorporated the Ahayu:da collected by James Stevenson into a collection of artifacts that she had acquired at Zuni in 1897 and deposited at the Smithsonian the same year. Three years later, shortly after Cushing's death, his widow sold the Ahayu:da that he had taken from Zuni to the Smithsonian, along with other items from his private Indian collection.[38]

In the Smithsonian context, the images acquired a new cultural identity as museum artifacts of anthropological, historical, and artistic significance to be preserved for scholarly study and public education.[39] As such, their associations with Zuni and Spanish cultures became part of the intellectual framework within which they were understood rather than the foundation for their primary identities.

The Ahayu:da sold to the Smithsonian by Cushing's widow remained in storage until it was returned to the Pueblo of Zuni in 1987, but the archangel images and the Ahayu:da acquired by James Stevenson were destined for public exhibition. All three images were first displayed in the original United States National Museum building (now the Smithsonian's Arts and Industries Building) around 1898. While the archangel images were simply placed with other mission artifacts in a elegant display case, Matilda Stevenson used the Ahayu:da acquired by her husband as the centerpiece of an elaborate exhibit that recreated the Ahayu:da altar as it had appeared in the home of the Elder Brother Bow Priest at the winter solstice of 1896. She went to great lengths to ensure that this exhibit was accurate, preparing a sketch of the altar at Zuni and convincing Zuni religious leaders to prepare "models" of all the items associated with the Ahayu:da when they are created and installed in their shrines.[40] Her attention to detail no doubt reflected her desire to present a scientifically accurate exhibit, but it also is likely that she used these objects and her knowledge of their proper arrangement to validate her authority as an ethnographer and to confirm her status in a profession totally dominated at the time by men.

Fig. 9.8. Saint Michael and Saint Gabriel in an exhibit case in the U.S. National Museum, about 1898 (negative number 2526, Smithsonian Institution).

Smithsonian records do not reveal how long this Ahayu:da remained on exhibit at the Smithsonian. It definitely was not incorporated into the American Indian exhibit halls installed during the 1950s in the second U.S. National Museum building (which soon after became the National Museum of Natural History).[41] In contrast, the image of Saint Gabriel (presumably selected over the image of Saint Michael because it was more complete), along with the cartouche taken from the Zuni church, was included in these new exhibits as part of a display case titled "Pueblo Indians Accepted Christianity Without Giving Up Their Traditional Nature Worship." In 1965 this case was consumed by an electrical fire and both objects were completely charred. Later the same year, all the Zuni church artifacts were loaned (and in 1987 officially transferred) by the National Museum of Natural History to the National Museum of American History as outstanding examples of the Spanish-Catholic crafts found in Hispanic New Mexican village churches and fraternal meetinghouses, in Indian mission churches, and increasingly in the homes and folk art shops of "Anglo" (non-Indian, non-Hispanic) romancers of the Southwest.[42]

Fig. 9.9. Matilda Stevenson's re-creation of the Ahayu:da altar, on display at the U.S. National Museum in 1905. De Lancey Gill, 1905 (negative number 2363, National Anthropological Archives, Smithsonian Institution).

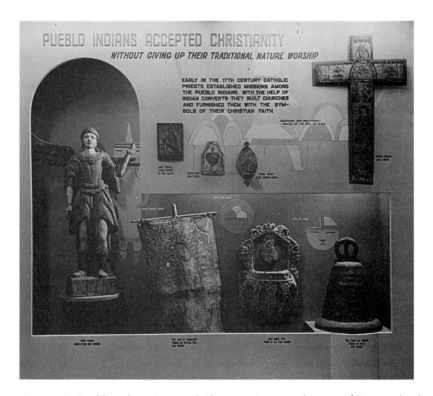

Fig. 9.10. "Pueblo Indians Accepted Christianity" case with statue of Saint Gabriel in the American Indian Halls of the U.S. National Museum, about 1955 (negative number 43373-d, Smithsonian Institution).

RETURNING THE IMAGES

While some Zuni people may have accepted and even contributed to the removal of the archangel and Ahayu:da images in the nineteenth century, the religious and political leadership of the pueblo in the twentieth century insisted that these images should never have been taken from Zuni. In two documents that the religious leaders submitted to the Smithsonian in the 1980s, they explained that the Ahayu:da must be returned to their shrines because only there could their destructive powers be controlled. In fact, some Zuni religious leaders had concluded that the disasters that had plagued the world since the removal of the Ahayu:da from their shrines might have resulted because the proper religious officials had been unable to direct the power of these Ahayu:da to more positive ends for the benefit of all humanity, in keeping with the goals of Zuni religion. In addition, they insisted that by preserving the Ahayu:da, museums and private collectors were upsetting the natural entropic processes of the universe. The appropriate fate of the Ahayu:da images is their gradual disintegration through exposure to the elements in their shrines.[43]

The Zunis may also have maintained a similar perspective with regard to the archangel statues, at least in the nineteenth century. As Cushing noted, they made no effort to protect these images and other altar objects from the elements, and they firmly rejected his entreaties to repair the church, even though it was in danger of collapsing. According to Cushing:

> They said they could not repair the church. It was the house of their fathers and they could no more bring their fathers back to life as bring the church back to its original condition. How, if they took it away, would the fathers know their own? It was well that the wind and rain wore it away, as time wasted away their fathers' bones.[44]

By the second half of the twentieth century, however, this attitude toward the church had changed. In the 1960s, the Pueblo of Zuni joined forces with the Catholic Church and the National Park Service to repair the church building, and in 1970 the Zuni artist Alex Seowtewa began decorating its interior walls with elaborate murals depicting Zuni kachinas at different points throughout the Zuni religious year. As part of this renovation project, the Zunis requested that the archangel statues and other altar objects be returned.[45]

In March of 1987, the Smithsonian returned the two Ahayu:da images to the Zuni after both images had been documented in detail at the Smithsonian with the permission of the Pueblo of Zuni. In a ceremony held on March 14 at the School of American Research in Santa Fe, Robert McC. Adams, secretary of the Smithsonian at the time, transferred the Ahayu:da to the appropriate Zuni religious leaders, who, upon arriving back at Zuni, placed them in a shrine outside the pueblo.[46]

Ten days later, Robert E. Lewis, governor of the Pueblo of Zuni, wrote Secretary Adams, formally requesting that the objects taken by the Stevensons from the church also be returned and that the items damaged by the 1965 fire be restored or reproduced. In 1991, after receiving no reply, Lewis wrote Adams again, repeating the request. Adams responded that the 1987 correspondence from Governor Lewis could not be located but indicated that the Smithsonian acknowledged that the Zunis' claims to these objects were legitimate and would "investigate appropriate methods and costs for making a reproduction" of the damaged archangel image. At the same time, he asked their permission to include the image of Saint Michael in a quincentennial exhibition at the National Museum of American History scheduled to open the following year. The exhibition as a whole explored cultural encounters in New Mexico, and the archangel image was to be incorporated into a unit called "Christianity: Faith and Defiance," which focused on the process of Indian missionization. The Zunis loaned the image to the Smithsonian for this exhibition and allowed scientific material analysis and stabilization of it to be completed.[47] In October 1995, the image was removed from the exhibit, to be returned to Zuni, while efforts were initiated to identify costs and methods to reproduce the damaged image of Saint Gabriel.

The Smithsonian agreed to return the Ahayu:da and archangel images to the Zuni people on the grounds that the institution did not hold good title to them because they were owned communally by the Pueblo of Zuni as a whole and no evidence existed to indicate that the Pueblo had agreed to their removal. However, while acknowledging that this justification was appropriate within the framework of American jurisprudence, the Zunis indicated that it did not correspond to their own thinking, particularly in regard to the Ahayu:da. From their perspective, the Ahayu:da and other Zuni religious objects embody knowledge that belongs to the Zuni people as a whole and is held by specific individuals only in trust. As a result, all objects produced on the basis of this knowledge, even if they are made by non-Zunis outside Zuni lands, derive their existence ultimately from Zuni knowledge and thus belong to the Zuni people.[48]

The Zuni religious leaders developed their perspectives on these objects during a series of lengthy discussions held on the Zuni reservation in the 1970s and 1980s. While continuing to recognize the traditional right of the different Zuni religious societies and priesthoods to formulate their own policies regarding the specific objects for which they are responsible, they also developed a single

Fig. 9.11. "Missionization" case in the "American Encounters" exhibit with statue of Saint Michael, National Museum of American History, 1992 (negative number 92-15472, Smithsonian Institution).

official position on general issues of repatriation that, as a group, they had never explicitly articulated or made available to non-Zunis before. In the process, they supplanted or suppressed any diversity of opinion on these issues that might have existed within the Zuni community at that time or in the past. This position provided the basis for the Zunis' successful campaign to secure the return of Ahayu:da and other objects from a number of museums and private collectors across the country.[49]

CONCLUSIONS

Over the course of their existence, the images of the Zuni Ahayu:da and arch-angels have been endowed with a series of identities, each of which summarizes and expresses complex cultural and social historical traditions. The statues of Saint Michael and Saint Gabriel began as material representations of spiritual beings central to Catholic ideology, as implements in the conversion of the Zu-nis to Christianity, and as aesthetically powerful objects intended to inspire both missionaries and converts alike. As the Zunis accommodated mission Catholi-cism to their indigenous religious and cultural traditions, they apparently recon-textualized the statues within the framework of their ancestor-oriented religious practices. The removal of these statues from the mission church and their incorporation into the Smithsonian's collections transformed them into anthropological and historical artifacts, and also art objects that were used both to document and to educate the public about the interactions between the Zunis and European missionaries and, subsequently, about Hispanic culture in the American Southwest. By the second half of the twentieth century, the statue of Saint Gabriel had been reduced to a charred post, but it (or the memory of it) had become, along with the image of Saint Michael, an object of cultural patrimony for both the Catholic Church and the Pueblo of Zuni, as well as an element in the formulation of a new cooperative relationship between the Pueblo of Zuni and the Smithsonian Institution.

The Ahayu:da have shared with the images of the archangels many of these same identities: physical embodiments of spiritual beings, anthropological artifacts, educational tools, art objects, and, perhaps, ethnographic souvenirs for their collectors. These multiple identities have not replaced one another in succession, but rather each has been added to previous identities as the images have moved through space and time. For the Zunis, the images never lost their original significance, and because Zuni religion has persisted relatively unchanged from the nineteenth century to the present, the conceptual and physical spaces that these images originally filled were preserved for their return.

By the same token, even though the images have been (or, in the case of the archangels, will be) returned to the Pueblo of Zuni, they will continue to have significance for non-Zunis as objects of scientific, historical, and aesthetic value. They persist outside Zuni in written descriptions, photographs, and drawings and as the subject of discussion and reflection in essays like this one. They have achieved an existence that, in a platonic sense, transcends their material substantiation and extends beyond the cultural contexts within which they were originally created.

A constant feature of these objects throughout their history has been their special relationship to power in its multiple expressions. They have been inextricably linked to the spiritual power of the universe as that power is understood by both Zunis and Catholics and also to the power relations of international politics associated with Spanish and American imperialism and Zuni resistance to it. They have served as tokens in the politics of anthropology, both to validate the professional status of the people who removed them from Zuni and to undermine their reputations. They have been the focus of controversy within the Pueblo of Zuni, but they also have served as a rallying point around which the Pueblo and its religious and political leadership have been able to forge a united front with respect to museums and other outsiders. The repatriation of these images also signals the success of the Pueblo of Zuni within the political and legal arena of late-twentieth-century America and constitutes a major step toward their achievement of greater political and cultural sovereignty.

The history of these images is emblematic of the evolving relationships between anthropologists and American Indians over the past century. The Stevensons and Cushing were both advocates for and victims of an approach to anthropological research that subordinated the wishes of the people they studied to the goals of documenting human diversity and furthering an understanding of humanity. While these are commendable goals, the arrogance of anthropology and its practitioners in the formative years of the discipline—an arrogance characteristic of science in general in the nineteenth and early twentieth centuries—poisoned the relationship between American Indian people and anthropologists for many generations thereafter. Perhaps if Zuni traditional culture had disappeared, as these anthropologists assumed it would, criticism of their collecting activities would have been muted and their efforts to preserve a record of Zuni culture would have been lauded by Zunis and non-Zunis alike. But the Zuni people and their culture do survive and thrive today to challenge not just the propriety of the methods of these and other scholars but also the accuracy of their reports.

Indians, anthropologists, and historians are all part of enormously complex social, political, and economic processes that are constantly undergoing transformation. As these processes unfold, the prospects for future interaction among non-Indian scholars and American Indians become increasingly brighter. The National Museum of the American Indian Act of 1989 and the Native American Graves Protection and Repatriation Act of 1990 gave strong support to American Indian societies in their efforts to secure from museums objects of great cultural and religious significance to them that had been acquired improperly.[50] In the early stages of the formulation of this legislation, its drafters viewed the relationship between Indian communities, on the one hand, and museums and anthropologists, on the other, as necessarily adversarial. Yet for decades many Indian communities and museum scholars have recognized that they share a number of interests and goals, particularly in the area of cultural preservation. Many Indian tribes that formerly refused to allow researchers into their communities are now hiring non-Indian scholars to pursue research programs that the tribes themselves have decided are important and that employ methodologies that they have determined to be appropriate. At the same time, many anthropologists and historians have become stronger advocates for Indian rights, firmly committed to respecting Indian perspectives and wishes. These changes in attitudes and approaches provide the framework within which the curation of American Indian collections and cooperation between Indians and non-Indian scholars will be defined in the future.

NOTES

1. The authors would like to express their gratitude to Roger Anyon, T. J. Ferguson, H. Richard Hart, Edmund J. Ladd, and William C. Sturtevant for their assistance in the preparation of this essay.

2. Frank H. Cushing, *Outlines of Zuñi Creation Myths*, in *Thirteenth Annual Report of the Bureau of Ethnology to the Secretary of the Smithsonian Institution, 1891–1892* (Washington: Government Printing Office, 1896), pp. 327–40; Louis R. Caywood, *The Restored Mission of Nuestra Señora de Guadalupe de Zuni, Zuni, New Mexico* (St. Michael's, Ariz.: St. Michael's Press, 1972); John L. Kessell, *The Missions of New Mexico since 1776* (Albuquerque: University of New Mexico Press, 1980), pp. 206–14; David L. Weber, *Richard H. Kern: Expeditionary Artist in the Far Southwest, 1848–1853* (Albuquerque: University of New Mexico Press, 1985); E. Richard Hart, "Alex Seowtewa's Murals in the Old Zuni Mission," *Zuni History, Victories in the 1990s,* sec. 2 (1991): 28; T. J. Ferguson to William L. Merrill, personal communication, December 4, 1995.

3. Amy Turner Bushnell, *Situado and Sabana: Spain's Support System for the Presidio and Mission Provinces of Florida,* Anthropological Papers no. 74 (New York: American Museum of Natural History, 1994).

4. E. Boyd, *Popular Arts of Spanish New Mexico* (Santa Fe: Museum of New Mexico, 1974), pp. 58–60, 109, 162.

5. Eleanor B. Adams and Fray Angélico Chávez, trans. and eds., *The Missions of New Mexico, 1776: Description by Fray Francisco Atanasio Domínguez* (Albuquerque: University of New Mexico Press, 1956), p. 198.

6. Ibid., pp. 195–201. For illustrations and a history of the two archangel figures, see Boyd, *Popular Arts,* pp. 100–102. An *estípite* is a column, often attached to the altar screen, in the form of an ornamented, inverted pyramid; see Victor Manuel Villegas, *El Gran Signo Formal del Barroco: Ensayo Histórico del Apoyo Estípite* (Mexico City: Universitaria, 1956), and Gonzalo Obregón, "Barroco Estípite," *Artes de México* 106 (1968): 40–57. The Sevillan architect Jerónimo de Balbás introduced the *estípite* to America about 1718 in Mexico City's cathedral. Accenting both altar screens (*retablos*) and facades, it was especially popular in northern New Spain. By 1780, neoclassical columns were replacing this late Baroque element in central Mexico, but the *estípite* lingered on in provincial and folk forms in New Mexico. The Zuni *estípite* altar screen was described by Domínguez in 1776, but its *estípite* style was not illustrated until 1851, in watercolors by Richard Kern; see Weber, *Richard H. Kern,* pp. 64, 156.

7. See H. W. M. Hodges, John S. Mills, and Perry Smith, eds., *Conservation of the Iberian and Latin American Cultural Heritage: Preprints of the Contributions to the Madrid (IIC) Congress, 9–12 September 1992* (London: International Institute of Historical and Artistic Works, 1992), especially the chapters on Spanish American sculpture. Practices established by 1700 for selecting and grouping subjects for Mexican church altar screens were extended to frontier missions in what is now the United States. See

Richard E. Ahlborn, *The Sculpted Saints of a Borderland Mission: Los Bultos de San Xavier del Bac* (Tucson: Southwestern Mission Research Center, 1974), and Barbara Anderson, "Figural Arrangements of Eighteenth-Century Churches in Mexico" (Ph.D. diss., Yale University, 1979).

8. Boyd, *Popular Arts*, pp. 100–102. Based on Domínguez's 1776 report, Boyd noted a second local image maker, Fray Andrés García, who visited Zuni in 1773 (Adams and Chávez, *Missions of New Mexico*, p. 333), but his known carvings do not reflect the skills needed to create the Zuni archangels. At Taos, Domínguez criticized Fray Andrés's images: "It is a pity that he should have used his labor for anything so ugly . . . as bad as the ones at [Santa Cruz de] La Cañada]" (ibid., p. 104). The skill of Miera y Pacheco is being reconfirmed by art historian Donna Pierce in her study of the *estípite*-style stone altar screen created for Santa Fe's military chapel in 1760; see Carmella Padilla, "Hot on the Trail of an Art History Mystery," *Santa Fe Reporter*, July 26, 1995, pp. 13–19; and Boyd, *Popular Arts*, p. 55.

9. Adams and Chávez, *Missions of New Mexico*, pp. xv–xvi. Assigned through the Franciscan college in Durango, both Vélez de Escalante and Rosete y Peralta were present at Zuni during Domínguez's visit on December 9, 1776.

10. David Freedberg, *The Power of Images* (Chicago: University of Chicago Press, 1989); and Ramón A. Gutiérrez, *When Jesus Came, the Corn Mothers Went Away: Marriage, Sexuality, and Power in New Mexico, 1500–1846* (Stanford: Stanford University Press, 1991).

11. In folk Catholicism, religious statuary often has important intercessory functions, but there is no evidence that the Zunis used the archangel statues for such purposes. Before the eighteenth century, they likely regarded any Catholic religious images housed in the churches as symbols of Spanish religious and political oppression. In 1632 and 1680, for example, they destroyed the mission churches and their furnishings, also killing the missionaries stationed there (Cushing, *Outlines of Zuñi Creation Myths*, pp. 326–32). Cushing provides an overview of Zuni ideas about the mission church and its altar in the late nineteenth century, including their association of the church with their ancestors (ibid., pp. 335–39; cf. C. Gregory Crampton, *The Zunis of Cibola* [Salt Lake City: University of Utah Press, 1977], p. 57n). For information on the possible associations between the church, ancestors, and rain, see E. Richard Hart, "A Brief History of Religious Objects from the Old Zuni Mission," unpublished report in Merrill's possession, pp. 19–20, 33.

12. For information on Zuni ideas about the Ahayu:da, see Cushing, *Outlines of Zuñi Creation Myths*, pp. 417–24; Matilda Coxe Stevenson, *The Zuñi Indians: Their Mythology, Esoteric Fraternities, and Ceremonies*, in *Twenty-third Annual Report of the Bureau of American Ethnology to the Secretary of the Smithsonian Institution, 1901–1902* (Washington: Government Printing Office, 1904), pp. 34–49; Elsie C. Parsons, "War God Shrines of Laguna and Zuñi," *American Anthropologist* 20 (1918): 381–405; Wilfred Eriacho and T. J. Ferguson, "The Zuni War Gods: Art, Artifact, or Religious Beings: A Conflict in Values, Beliefs, and Use" (paper presented at the symposium "New Directions in American Indian Art History," University of New Mexico, Albuquerque, October 26, 1979); and William L. Merrill, Edmund J. Ladd, and T. J. Ferguson, "The Return of the Ahayu:da: Lessons for Repatriation from Zuni Pueblo and the Smithsonian Institution," *Current Anthropology* 34 (1993): 523–67.

13. Eriacho and Ferguson, "Zuni War Gods"; Matilda Coxe Stevenson, "Zuñi Games," *American Anthropologist* 5 (1903): 468–97; M. Stevenson, *The Zuñi Indians*, pp. 44–51, 576–607; and Parsons, "War God Shrines."

14. For information on this expedition and its members, see James Stevenson, *Illustrated Catalogue of the Collections Obtained from the Indians of New Mexico and Arizona in 1879*, in *Second Annual Report of the Bureau of Ethnology to the Secretary of the Smithsonian Institution, 1880–1881* (Washington: Government Printing Office, 1883), pp. 307–465; James Stevenson, *Illustrated Catalogue of the Collections Obtained from the Pueblos of Zuñi, New Mexico, and Wolpi, Arizona, in 1881*, in *Third Annual Report of the Bureau of Ethnology to the Secretary of the Smithsonian Institution, 1881–1882* (Washington: Government Printing Office, 1884), pp. 511–94; M. Stevenson, *The Zuñi Indians*, pp. 15–18; Frank H. Cushing, *My Adventures in Zuñi* (Santa Fe: Peripatetic Press, 1941); Nancy O. Lurie, "Women in Early American Anthropology," in *Pioneers of American Anthropology*, American Ethnological Society Monograph 43, ed. June Helm (1966): 29–81; Curtis M. Hinsley, *Savages and Scientists: The Smithsonian Institution and the Development of American Anthropology, 1846–1910* (Washington: Smithsonian Institution Press, 1981); Don D. Fowler, *The Western Photographs of John K. Hillers* (Washington: Smithsonian Institution Press, 1989); Jesse Green, ed., *Zuñi: Selected Writings of Frank Hamilton Cushing* (Lincoln: University of Nebraska Press, 1979); Jesse Green, ed., *Cushing at Zuni: The Correspondence and Journals of Frank Hamilton Cushing, 1879–1884* (Albuquerque: University of New Mexico Press, 1990); and Phil Hughte, *A Zuni Artist Looks at Frank Hamilton Cushing* (Zuni, N.M.: Pueblo of Zuni Arts and Crafts and A:shiwi A:wan Museum and Heritage Center, 1994). According to Green (*Cushing at Zuni*, p. 32), Hillers joined the expedition in St. Louis.

15. Although Spanish explorers reached the Zuni area by 1540, the lack of mineral wealth delayed Hispanic evangelization and settlement until the end of the century. During the first colonial era in New Mexico (1598–1680), Hispanic trade was dominated by the needs and authority of the Franciscan mission. With the return of Hispanic settlers and government following the Pueblo Revolt (1680–92), officials and merchants reestablished trade, including contraband. With Mexican political independence in 1821, Anglo-American traders opened a trail from the United States to Santa Fe that linked up with the colonial *camino real* south to Chihuahua and beyond. The United States annexed New Mexico through the Treaty of Guadalupe Hidalgo in 1848 in order to advance nationalistic military, legal, and commercial interests. The railroad reached Albuquerque in 1879, providing increased access for traders, Protestant evangelists, health seekers, tourists, writers, artists, and scholars. Many of these newcomers shared Victorian American notions of their cultural superiority and the myth of the vanishing Indian.

16. Lurie, "Women in Early American Anthropology"; Hinsley, *Savages and Scientists.* Hillers continued photographing the people and landscapes of New Mexico and Arizona until 1883, working primarily with James Stevenson. In 1885, he joined John Wesley Powell for one last trip to the American Southwest and then spent most of the remaining years of his life in Washington as a photographer at the Smithsonian Institution. He died on November 14, 1925. For details of Hillers's life and work, see Fowler, *Western Photographs.*

17. Hinsley, *Savages and Scientists,* p. 197.

18. Stevenson's description of Cushing is preserved on the back of a photograph of Cushing attired in his version of traditional Zuni clothing. The photograph is housed in the Hodge-Cushing Collection of the Southwest Museum in Pasadena, California. The complete comment is as follows: "Frank Hamilton Cushing in his fantastic dress worn while among the Zuni Indians. This man was the biggest fool and charlatan I ever knew. He even put his hair up in curl papers every night. How could a man walk weighted down with so much toggery?" (Green, *Cushing at Zuni*, p. 351, n. 31).

19. The Catholic mission with a priest in residence was reestablished in 1921 (Hart, "A Brief History," pp. 17–19). John L. Kessell (*Kiva, Cross, and Crown: The Pecos Indians and New Mexico, 1540–1840* [Albuquerque: University of New Mexico Press, 1987]) provides an engaging history of the Catholic missions in New Mexico.

20. Timothy H. O'Sullivan, *Wheeler's Photographic Survey of the American West, 1871–73* (New York: Dover Publications, 1983); Weber, *Kern*, pp. 64, 156–57. O'Sullivan was a member of the George M. Wheeler Expedition, which explored the American Southwest in the 1870s.

21. The Zunis surely were aware of the conflicts between Cushing and the Stevensons, but while some Zuni individuals had closer ties with either the Stevensons or Cushing, as a group they appear never to have taken sides.

22. Cushing, *Outlines of Zuñi Creation Myths*, p. 337. The party of Americans to which Cushing refers obviously were the Stevensons and Hillers. His characterization that they had accompanied him to Zuni rather than the reverse reveals the attitude that so infuriated the Stevensons. We are unable to confirm Cushing's claim that the Stevensons removed the large central painting of Our Lady of Guadalupe. The Stevensons do not mention the painting in their writings, and there is no record that it ever reached the Smithsonian.

23. M. Stevenson, *The Zuñi Indians*, pp. 16–17; cf. Matilda Coxe Stevenson, *Zuñi and the Zuñians* (Washington: n.p., 1881), pp. 9–11.

24. James Stevenson to James C. Pilling, Fort Wingate, November 21, 1879, BAE Correspondence, Incoming, 1879–1888, National Anthropological Archives, Smithsonian Institution; published in Green, *Cushing at Zuni*, p. 64. Reports from other sources regarding whether the Stevensons received permission from Zuni officials to remove the archangel statues also are contradictory. In 1883, Adolph Bandelier claims that the church had been "plundered by the Washington party in the most shameless manner, and falling to ruin in consequence," but it is likely that he acquired his information and perspective directly from Cushing, who through Bandelier was making a collection for the Berlin Museum (quote from Charles H. Lange and Carroll L. Riley, eds., *The Southwestern Journals of Adolph F. Bandelier, 1883–1884* [Albuquerque: University of New Mexico Press, 1970], pp. 40, 371–72, n. 109). See also Green, *Cushing at Zuni*, p. 15; and Frank H. Cushing, "Katalog einer Sammlung von Idolen, Fetischen und priesterlichen Ausrüstungsgegenständen der Zuñi- oder Ashiwi-Indianer von Neu-Mexiko (U.S. Am.)," *Königliches Museum für Völkerkunde, Veröffentlichungen* 4 (1895): 1–12. Taylor F. Ealy, the Presbyterian missionary at Zuni during the 1879 expedition, confirms Matilda Stevenson's claim that they received permission to remove the images, but Ealy may have welcomed the elimination of these vestiges of Catholicism from the pueblo. See Norman J. Bender, ed., *Missionaries, Outlaws, and Indians: Taylor F. Ealy at Lincoln and Zuni, 1879–1881* (Albuquerque: University of New Mexico Press, 1984), p. 127.

25. Robert W. Delaney and Myra E. Jenkins, *Guide to the "Lost" Records of the Mission of Nuestra Señora de Guadalupe de Zuni, 1775–1858* (Santa Fe: New Mexico State Records Center and Archives, 1988); and Frank H. Cushing, *Zuñi Fetishes,* in *Second Annual Report of the Bureau of Ethnology to the Secretary of the Smithsonian Institution, 1880–1881* (Washington: Government Printing Office, 1883), pp. 3–45. The Zuni mission records taken by Cushing are now housed in the Manuscript Division of the Library of Congress, under the classification "Zuni Indian Mission Records." The Library of Congress purchased the records in 1903 from Frederick W. Hodge, who acquired them the previous year from Cushing's widow. See Henry P. Beers, *Spanish and Mexican Records of the American Southwest: A Bibliographical Guide to Archive and Manuscript Sources* (Tucson: University of Arizona Press in collaboration with the Tucson Corral of the Westerners, 1979), pp. 82–83.

26. Cushing, "Katalog."

27. Frank H. Cushing to E. B. Tylor, copy of undated letter, envelope 80, Hodge-Cushing Collection, Southwest Museum. Tylor donated this Ahayu:da to the Pitt Rivers Museum at Oxford University in 1911 (Linda Cheetham to William L. Merrill, personal communication, July 17, 1987). The Ahayu:da taken by Cushing from Zuni, which his wife later sold to the Smithsonian, is notably weathered. Perhaps it is the one that he originally intended to give to Tylor.

28. Catalog cards 176544 and 206426, Department of Anthropology, National Museum of Natural History, Smithsonian Institution. See also M. Stevenson, *The Zuñi Indians,* p. 116, n. b; Green, *Zuñi;* and Green, *Cushing at Zuni.*

29. The Ahayu:da taken by James Stevenson was accessioned into the collections of the U.S. National Museum in 1897 as part of a collection of Zuni artifacts made in the same year by Matilda Stevenson (accession number 31983; catalog number 176544). The Ahayu:da removed by Cushing was sold to the U.S. National Museum by his widow, Emily Magill Cushing, shortly after his death in 1900 (accession number 36918; catalog number 206426).

30. While there is no doubt that the Stevensons kept the Ahayu:da image in their private collection between 1881 and 1887, it does not appear in a series of undated photographs taken of the interior of their home, which they adorned with numerous Indian objects (negative numbers 4910-a–4910-g, National Anthropological Archives, Smithsonian Institution; negative number 4910-g is published in Hinsley, *Savages and Scientists,* p. 198). For a lurid account of the theft of an Ahayu:da image from its shrine by a private collector, see G. Wharton James, "With the Zunis in New Mexico. II. The Religious and Ceremonial Life of the Zunis," *The Theosophical Path* 4 (1913): 25–41. A list of the Ahayu:da recovered by the Pueblo of Zuni by 1992 appears in Merrill et al., "Return," p. 527, table 1. Since 1992, the Pueblo of Zuni has recovered four additional Ahayu:da from museums in the United States. Seven other Ahayu:da images have been located in museums in Canada and Europe (Roger Anyon to William L. Merrill, personal communication, November 28, 1995)

31. The statues of the archangels also may have been older than the Ahayu:da, having been created about a hundred years before the Stevensons removed them from the church. If the Ahayu:da collected by Stevenson and Cushing were taken from open shrines, it is possible that they were no more than about fifty years old, the approximate amount of time that wooden articles exposed to the elements endure in the Zuni area

(Roger Anyon to William L. Merrill, personal communication, February 1995). It might be suggested that the Stevensons and Cushing valued the archangel statues more than the Ahayu:da because the former were expressions of a European cultural and religious tradition. It appears, however, that they regarded both sets of images as primarily Indian in cultural context if not origin and of value for their ethnographic rather than their religious significance.

32. M. Stevenson, *The Zuñi Indians*, p. 17.

33. Given this apparent discrepancy between the leadership and the populace of Zuni, it is possible that the Pueblo leaders gave the Stevensons permission to remove the archangel statues but later reversed their decision if, as Cushing reports, the Pueblo as a whole expressed dismay at what had taken place.

34. Cushing to Spencer F. Baird, Zuni, December 4, 1881 (Green, *Cushing at Zuni*, pp. 196–201).

35. Triloki N. Pandey, "Anthropologists at Zuni," *Proceedings of the American Philosophical Society* 116, no. 4 (1972): 323–26. In the 1960s, a Zuni woman told Pandey (ibid., pp. 323–24) that three Zuni religious leaders were killed because they had been responsible for Cushing's appointment as a Bow Priest, an event that Pandey dates as having taken place in May 1889. He also notes that a decade before Cushing's appointment, the Zunis had asked Albert Franklin Banta, an American pioneer in the area, to become a Bow Priest, an invitation that he declined. Fred Eggan ("Foreword," in Green, *Zuñi*, xi–xiv) and Green (*Zuñi and Cushing at Zuni*) suggest that the Zunis saw Cushing as a useful mediator with the new external forces that were impinging on them.

36. Among the most prominent of the Stevensons' Zuni friends were Nai'uchi, a Bow Priest and Rain Priest who provided them extensive access to religious objects and knowledge, and the transvestite We'wha, who defended Matilda Stevenson while she was in the pueblo and visited the Stevensons in Washington in 1886; see Pandey, "Anthropologists at Zuni," pp. 326–29, and Will Roscoe, *The Zuni Man-Woman* (Albuquerque: University of New Mexico Press, 1991).

Pandey, "Anthropologists at Zuni," pp. 326–28, concludes that Matilda Stevenson was generally disliked by the Zunis because she was demanding and disrespectful and that when her few friends and supporters died, the other Zunis opposed her. Cushing's relations with the Zunis appear to have been more congenial, although they clearly had ambivalent feelings about him. To acquire Zuni objects, he seems to have relied less on personal friendships than on the access he had achieved to Zuni life. His collecting activities, in any case, were minimal when compared to those of the Stevensons. See Pandey, "Anthropologists at Zuni," pp. 322–26, and Green, *Cushing at Zuni*.

37. The church objects taken from Zuni by the Stevensons were accessioned into the Smithsonian collections in 1881 as accession number 9899, and sketches of them were included in the museum's catalog ledger book. The figure of Saint Michael and his shield were cataloged as numbers 41910 and 41911; Saint Gabriel and his wings as 41912 and 41915; the crown-over-heart cartouche as 41913; and the scroll carving as 41914. Although visible, neither the cartouche nor the decorative carving is clearly shown in Kern's 1851 watercolors or O'Sullivan's 1873 photographs of the altar; see Weber, *Kern,* and O'Sullivan, *Wheeler's Photographic Survey.*

38. Records for accessions 31983 and 36918, Department of Anthropology, National Museum of Natural History, Smithsonian Institution.

39. Caywood, *Restored Mission;* and Hart, "A Brief History."

40. M. Stevenson, *The Zuñi Indians,* p. 116, n. b.

41. John C. Ewers, "New Ethnological Exhibits, United States National Museum, Washington, D.C.," *Museum* 9 (1956): 28–36; and John C. Ewers, "A Century of American Indian Exhibits in the Smithsonian Institution," in *Annual Report of the Smithsonian Institution for 1958* (Washington: Smithsonian Institution, 1959), pp. 513–25.

42. In the 1955 exhibit, the cartouche was wrongly mounted as a font. The charred remains of the Saint Gabriel statue and the cartouche were stabilized by the Conservation Laboratory of the National Museum of History and Technology (now the National Museum of American History) under the direction of Robert Organ. Illustrations of exhibits containing the archangels and an early engraving of Saint Gabriel were published in Richard E. Ahlborn and Harry R. Rubenstein, "Smithsonian Santos: Collecting and the Collection," in *Hispanic Arts and Ethnohistory in the Southwest: New Papers Inspired by the Work of E. Boyd,* ed. Martha Weigle with Claudia Larcombe and Samuel Larcombe (Santa Fe: Ancient City Press, 1983), pp. 241–79.

43. Merrill et al., "Return," pp. 546–47.

44. Cushing, *Outlines of Zuñi Creation Myths,* pp. 337–38.

45. Hart, "Alex Seowtewa." See n. 46 for a list of the correspondence related to the Zunis' request for the return of the church objects.

46. Merrill et al., "Return."

47. The letters from Robert E. Lewis to Robert McCormick Adams are dated March 24, 1987, July 5, 1987, January 10, 1991, and May 28, 1991. Adams's responses to Lewis are dated March 21, 1991, and July 5, 1991. The material analysis of the Saint Michael image added substantial evidence for a Spanish origin of the artistic traditions and practices embodied in it. The results of this analysis are available at the Smithsonian's Conservation and Analytical Laboratory (Report 5296).

48. Merrill et al., "Return," pp. 542–43.

49. Ibid.

50. A possible unintended consequence of these acts is the repatriation of objects regarded today as inappropriate for museum collections that were, nonetheless, acquired properly according to both Indian and non-Indian standards at the time of collection.

10

Ambassadors in Sealskins
Exhibiting Eskimos at the Smithsonian

WILLIAM W. FITZHUGH

"The Polar Eskimo: The Northernmost People in the World"

Standing near the elephant in the Rotunda of the National Museum of Natural History one catches a glimpse of a tall Eskimo figure with his walrus harpoon thrust into the snow. Beside him, his wife and children are poised as though frozen in time. A sled stands ready, and its dogs fix their gaze on a small seal lying on the ice in front of a young hunter. The boy has called for help to bring his game home, and his family rushed to greet him at the seal hole. But after seeing the small size of the seal, the father cries out, "Call that a seal???" Attention is riveted on the moment of interaction as the family laughs while the proud young man, chagrined, learns a lesson the Eskimo way.

"Hey, lookit the Eskimo Indians!" a child yells out to his classmates as he turns a corner in the Hall of American Indian Peoples and encounters the Polar Eskimo diorama.
  "This is how they hunt from the sea," says a teacher. "Then they freeze their meat!"
  "Who would want to live way up in the Arctic?" says a student.
  "Are those wolves in there?" says another, seeing the sled dogs.
  "Do they live in igloos today?" says a third.

POLAR ESKIMO
THE NORTHERNMOST PEOPLE OF THE WORLD

Fig. 10.1. One of the Smithsonian's most popular exhibits, the Smith Sound Eskimo life-group was created by William Henry Holmes for the U.S. Government display at the Buffalo Exposition of 1901. It created a sensation there and was later moved to Washington, where it has been seen at the Smithsonian's National Museum for nearly one hundred years. This rendition dates from 1957 to present. (NMH-035)

This essay illustrates the dilemmas faced in exhibiting northern cultures at the Smithsonian's National Museum of Natural History from its earliest days to the present.[1] It illustrates problems in conveying past and present views of culture and cultural history, demonstrates how collections have influenced research and exhibition strategies, explores problems in the use of authoritative rather than reflexive voices, and discusses stereotypes that have been created and reinforced by the Smithsonian's arctic exhibits. It also presents a curator's personal dilemma in balancing conflicting professional, curatorial, public, and Native interests in a large natural history museum with ancient traditions and bureaucratic structures.

The subject matter is the Smithsonian's Eskimo[2] exhibits, which for more than 150 years have helped to educate the public while at the same time instilling a stereotyped Eskimo persona. How and by what means have Eskimo cultures been represented to the public? How and for what reasons have these representations changed through time? And what have been the responses and outcomes of this educational program? In this exploration of the larger subject of Eskimo culture in the media,[3] this essay documents the history of Eskimo representations at the Smithsonian. The scene is the National Museum of Natural History (formerly the United States National Museum), the Smithsonian entity that has been primarily responsible for presenting America's Native cultures to the public in Washington. While the focus here is on arctic peoples, their history at the Smithsonian is similar to that of Smithsonian representations of other Native cultures on exhibit.

ESKIMOS AND THE PUBLIC

Public fascination with arctic peoples, animals, and environments has a long history in Western culture. England's first encounter with Inuit in 1576 and 1577, when Martin Frobisher returned with first one and then three Inuit from his historic voyages to Baffin Island in search of the Northwest Passage, were widely publicized.[4] While the Baffin Inuit whom he captured and displayed in London in 1576 were the first known to have been brought to England[5] and the first to be publicly exhibited, information about arctic peoples had existed in Western and Northern Europe at least since Viking times. As early as the ninth century Harald Fair-Hair had recorded stories of arctic peoples of northern Scandinavia who hunted great tusked beasts and white bears in the waters of northern Norway and the White Sea.[6]

Knowledge of northern regions remained relatively limited and esoteric, however, until British and American explorers began intensive geographic surveys of central arctic regions in the mid-nineteenth century. Starting in the 1820s and continuing until the culmination of Vilhjalmur Stefansson's explorations a hundred years later, the European and North American public was fed a constant diet of personal drama and scientific discoveries as explorers investigated the most minute crannies of unmapped arctic lands and seas.[7] Spurred by nationalism and vamped by a voracious hero-building media, the era of arctic exploration pitted European technology and personal hubris against the unbridled arctic wilderness. The successes and failures of these enterprises became sensations that made expedition journals and narratives hot sales tickets and brought the Arctic and its hardy, quaint residents into the public spotlight. In time, what had begun as fascination with a harsh, alien land that tested the wills of staunch explorers evolved into a broad curiosity about Eskimo culture. How could these "uncivilized" peoples thrive under conditions that mocked the notion of European superiority and technological mastery?

By the time museum collecting began in the 1860s, with the Smithsonian in the vanguard, the public was thirsting for information about Eskimo culture and flocked to experience it firsthand at expositions and museums. Through this process the public came to equate "Arctic" with the Eastern Canadian Arctic, and its resident Inuit became the stereotype for arctic peoples in general. Even the opening of the Western Arctic to Russia between 1741 and 1850 and to Euro-American society after 1850 did little to change the firmly rooted perception of a homogeneous "Eskimo" ethnicity, and the western groups, even the culturally and linguistically distinct Bering Sea Yupiks, Aleuts, and Alutiiqs of the Pacific coast became "Eskimo" also.

Perhaps there is something deeper here as well, something psychological that taps into our evolutionary history as hunters and pioneers. Whether we are Europeans who abandoned this way of life ten thousand years ago or Native Americans whose ancestors migrated from Asia through Alaska, many of us were once ice age "arctic" hunters. Whoever we are, we find ourselves at one time or another confronted with the reality of a stark existence—of being alone in a frigid darkness with a family of loved ones and facing the shriek of a polar gale, the threat of starvation, the crack of a thin ice sheet, or the stealthy approach of a predator.

For whatever reasons, Eskimo life has become a standard element in elementary school curricula that teach children lessons about cultural diversity. At the same time the simplistic way in which these materials are often presented has created a characterization of a happy, carefree, resourceful, technologically adept, and stoic people. Ethnographic exhibits, as well as movies, Mark Twain stories, and gold rush tales, have played an important role in forming such views, often in concert with school programs. These attitudes are not limited to Western culture. Eskimos are possessed in some part by hundreds of millions of admirers who have learned something significant from their example and about their environment. They remain the quintessential arctic people whose image as ambassadors in sealskins has been created largely through museum representation.

THE BUFFALO EXPOSITION

William Henry Holmes, head curator of the Department of Anthropology of the United States National Museum, created the Polar Eskimo life-group of a Smith Sound Inuit family in 1901 and titled it "The Happy Eskimos." The scene was one of twelve groups he developed to illustrate the Native peoples of the Americas for the government display at the Pan-American Exposition in

Buffalo, New York.[8] In an interview after the show was installed later at the National Museum, Holmes commented: "By some means the false notion has gained ground that the Eskimos are a morose, gloomy, and dismal people as a result of the rigors of their inhospitable climate and surroundings. This is a great mistake, for, on the contrary, they are the most cheerful and mirth-loving people you ever saw. In this group I have endeavored to give a truthful representation of the Eskimo as he is."[8]

One of the surprising features of this display is the mystery surrounding the origin of the ethnographic materials. Although the objects are clearly from the Smith Sound area, Department of Anthropology records contain no accession data on them. Nor are there any cataloged collections from this region of Greenland. It is therefore assumed, because the date of the exhibition's fabrication coincides with that of Robert E. Peary's explorations here, that the collections originated from Peary or from Henry G. Bryant's United States Peary Relief Expedition of 1897. In the absense of catalog data in our files, we assume that clothing, sled, dog whip, and weapons were collected from the Smith Sound Eskimos living near Thule, Greenland, and were transferred to Holmes directly without going through the cataloging process.[10]

At eighty degrees north latitude, the Polar Eskimos were the northernmost indigenous people in the world. Holmes prepared the rendition and supervised the sculpting of the mannikins using field notes; he also probably had available photographs and descriptions made by the collector. Holmes's artistic guidance even extended to the poses of the dogs, which also had been collected and which were rendered in natural, lifelike attitudes—one asleep, another with his nose to the ground as though scenting something, while the others, ears erect, intently watched the landing of a seal. "So lifelike are these groups," one reporter commented, "that children visiting the museum with their parents invariably steer clear of the case . . . thinking the wolfish-looking dogs are alive."[11] They appear so to many young museum visitors today, as we discovered in our monitoring program.

The Smith Sound group was the keystone of the Buffalo exhibit series that represented race, costume, and handicrafts of Native peoples in their natural settings throughout the Americas. The groups ranged from the Eskimo of North Greenland to "the wild tribes" of Tierra del Fuego. "With such a set of groups geographically arranged upon the exhibition space it was conceived that the student, and even the ordinary visitor, might, by passing from north to south or from south to north through the series, form a vivid and definite notion of the appearance, condition, and cultures of the race or peoples called American Indians, the race so rudely and completely supplanted by the nations of the Old World."[12]

Holmes began to develop ethnographic life-groups as a major focus of the ethnology displays at the National Museum after he returned from five years' employment at the Field Columbian Museum in Chicago, taking charge of the Department of Anthropology in 1897. His approach was later described by Walter Hough, who succeeded Holmes as head curator and credited him with being the genius behind this work:

> In designing a lay-figure group[13] the necessary studies of the peoples to be represented are made. Individuals are selected to illustrate the salient features of the people, their arts and industries, their costumes, and their physical characteristics; and such features of their environment as can be utilized within the available space are added. The end sought is to assemble the figures as in a picture, which will tell the story forcibly and at once.[14]

In addition to being an excellent scientist, Holmes was a consummate artist whose works ranged from detailed geological drawings of the Grand Canyon to scientific illustration of artifacts. His sense of drama and skill in theatrical design gave him unique qualifications for revolutionizing the dreary and confusing ethnology exhibit program at the National Museum. What was needed, he realized, was emotional appeal that would excite the viewer's interest and kindle a desire to learn. Holmes found the process challenging: "Satisfactory costumes were not always available, and collections illustrating arts and industries were found to be deficient . . . the exhibit is not yet complete . . . many changes will be necessary to bring it up to a satisfactory standard." Having moved beyond earlier (and unsatisfactory) experiments involving wax figures, glass eyes, and papier-mâché models, Holmes had settled on plaster sculptures as the best vehicle to represent "more-perfect" racial types[15] than the life casts previously used for exhibit figures, as long as they were modeled scientifically, under curatorial direction, using drawings and field photographs:

> Life masks, as ordinarily taken, convey no clear notion of the people. The faces are distorted and expressionless, the eyes are closed and the lips compressed. Like the ordinary studio photograph of primitive sitters, the mask serves chiefly to misrepresent the native countenance and disposition; besides, the individual face is not necessarily a good type of a group. Good types may, however, be worked out by the skillful artist and sculptor, who alone can adequately present these little-understood people as they really are and with reasonable unity in pose and expression.[16]

As to costs, Holmes's goal of placing before the public a new, dramatic, and permanent type of museum display paid off in spades. He had experimented with preparing papier-mâché figures modeled after the exquisite mannikins donated to the United States by Japan in the Matthew Perry Collection, but the results were so poor that this effort was abandoned.[17] Earlier attempts to refine the presentation of ethnic peoples employed sculptural techniques and plaster of Paris. A French sculptor named Achille Colin, who had been living in Washington since 1881, had produced a new style of figure for the museum "in accordance with the rules of sculpture," using plaster for the hair and body, and the sculptor's eye instead of the staring glass eye. The figures were then painted by a portrait painter who had spent his life portraying Indians.[18] Later, this model was advanced by Holmes, using another Washington sculptor, U. S. J. Dunbar, who modeled the figures, cast them in plaster, and added wigs. A large number of groupings in this new style was created for the 1893 exhibition, including Zuni, Navajo, Kiowa, Sioux, Hupa, and Kutchin.[19] In a later report Walter Hough estimated the cost of creating a standard twelve-by-eight-by-nine-foot case with mannikins in 1920 dollars to be $2,500, exclusive of collecting and specimen purchase. Although expensive, some of these groups, like the Polar Eskimo, are still in use today.[20] Holmes also had other hints for would-be preparators: "If the figures are to be clothed, the work is expedited and made cheaper by employing [a] framework of wood, which is filled out with tow, burlap, etc., and the exposed parts, as the head, hands, and feet, [are] modelled, painted, and added to the figure. In some instances the hands are cast from the living model."[21]

For American museology, the 1893 breakthrough at the Chicago World Columbian Exposition was startling:

A new feature of the greatest interest was, however, introduced among the figures prepared for this occasion, and a set of groups, unique and full of interest, was the result. These[,] shown in the cases surrounded by proper environmental accessories and engaged in the occupations peculiar to the tribes which they represented, were no longer pieces of sculpture but pictures from life. The success of these groups is due to the supervision exercised by Prof. W. H. Holmes, artist as well as ethnologist, who gave life and pictorial expression to the figures already accurately modelled and costumed by Museum preparators.[22]

The report cautioned museum men not "to make such groups except under the eye of an ethnologist who has been among the people to be represented." Brand-new, the method had never before been used for exhibiting the American Indian and permitted "a more sure means of preserving certain of the most precious memorials of the primitive races of mankind."[23]

The Chicago fair also represented the epitome of an earlier exposition presentation style that can be traced back to the days of Martin Frobisher's exhibitions of Baffin Inuit for Queen Elizabeth's royal court.[24] In terms of public interest, the displays of live exhibits of Native peoples were among the most exciting exhibitions to be offered at American World's Fairs since 1876, but they came with a high price, both to the Native peoples involved and to the organizers who responsibly (or irresponsibly) looked after them. The fate of many of these visiting groups was disastrous. Twelve families, including fifty-seven men, women, and children, were brought from Hamilton Inlet and other northern Labrador villages to the Chicago Exposition. A village and a trading post were set up, and Inuit dressed in sealskin clothing (despite the sweltering Chicago summer) threw harpoons, shot arrows, and pulled tourists by dogsled. Following the exposition, the Inuit were returned destitute and diseased by schooner to Newfoundland, from which they had to make their way home, still 800 miles distant. Many either never completed the journey or subsequently died of typhoid. The experience was summed up by one Inuk as follows: "We are glad to be at liberty once more, and not to be continually looked at as if we were animals. We shall never go again."[25] Later, however, the same man responsible for bringing the Labrador Inuit to Chicago convinced another group of thirty-three to tour to Europe, Algeria, and America between 1889 and 1903. Only six Inuit returned from this harrowing experience.[26]

This trend of exhibiting live Native groups in ethnographically reconstructed settings, begun in Europe in the 1880s, reached its zenith in America in Chicago. But by the time of the Buffalo Exposition of 1901, the complications and huge costs in the care and feeding of live exhibits had convinced Holmes and Smithsonian officials to continue their previous trend toward exhibits that were more adaptable and longer-lasting. Holmes, as a government servant, wanted an inexpensive and permanent solution that could become the core of a dramatic new exhibition at the Smithsonian's permanent exhibits once the show was over.

> It is well understood that for exposition purposes the assemblage of family groups—or larger units—of the living peoples would be far superior to lay-figure groups. The real family, clothed in its own costumes, engaged in its own occupations, and surrounded by its actual belongings, would form the best possible illustration of a people; but such an exhibit, covering the whole American field, would require much time for its preparation as well as the expenditure of large sums of money. Furthermore, from the museum point of view, the creation of a set of adequate and artistic lay-figure groups forms a permanent exhibit which, set up in the museum, continues to please and instruct for generations; whereas the real people, howsoever well assembled, must scatter at the close of

the exposition, and nothing is left for future museum display. Such assemblages of our native peoples as those of the World's Columbian Exposition, the Trans-Mississippi, and the Pan-American expositions are highly instructive, but their influence is soon lost, since they reach only the audience of the season.[27]

Here was a new credo for a burgeoning Smithsonian Institution that was soon to move from its cramped centennial building into a lavish new edifice, the monumental National Museum.[28] In the process Holmes's innovations in the crafting of dramatic life-groups set a standard that has been the centerpiece of anthropological exhibition at this museum ever since.

Confirmation of the results was not confined to the pages of the *Annual Report*. The popular press lit on the creations as masterpieces of popular education:

Near the middle of the main Government building . . . there stand some figures that no visitor is able to pass without looking at. They are the figures of Indians grouped in big glass cases. They are of life size, and each group gives the impression of an Indian family suddenly stiffened and made immobile in the midst of its work and play, with all the implements of its daily occupations scattered about. It is like the palace of the Sleeping Beauty; life is there without movement. Around the cases, all day long, eddies a curious throng. The blanketed redskin from the Indian village, and the spectacled man from Boston, the woman in the shirt waist and the trim soldier, elbow each other and look into the cases. All alike understand the spectacle and enjoy it; it is science made easy.[29]

From another source comes a more museological note, with a hint of things to come:

The curators of the museum believe that these groups convey an understanding of the nature of given peoples to the beholders more quickly than any other form of teaching ever devised. They have made these groups in such a way that they should last for centuries before falling into decay and can be copied when that time comes. So will these lifelike reproductions of the peoples of today and yesterday be handed down to the end of time to those that worry long after we, and the tribes modelled, have gone on the happy hunting ground.[30]

The idea that the exhibits should be as faithful as possible to traditional Native American culture was firmly rooted in the Smithsonian's perception of its mission of recording and displaying for posterity the dying cultures of Native Americans. Writing of the proposed Smithsonian contribution to the Philadelphia Centennial Exposition, Assistant Secretary Spencer F. Baird said:

So far as the ethnological display is concerned it is quite reasonable to infer that by the expiration of a second hundred year period of the life of the American

republic, the Indians will have entirely ceased to present any distinctive characters, and will be merged in the general population. It is more than probable that
the ethnological collection now being made by the Government will be the
only exposition of the past; and with each succeeding year these specimens will
become more valuable and more highly appreciated.[31]

Now past the fateful second centennial, these predictions all have come true:
Native American cultures have lost many original distinctive features, especially
technology and economy; the museum collections have been greatly appreciated; and several of Holmes's life-groups are still standing. On the other hand,
Native American cultures are by no means dead; although transformed, they retain much distinctiveness. Baird did not anticipate this outcome.

INSTALLATION IN THE NATURAL HISTORY MUSEUM

After the close of the Buffalo Exposition, the life-groups were returned to
Washington, where they were installed in the old Arts and Industries (Centennial 1876) Building. From there they moved to the new National Museum
across the Mall after that building opened in 1910.[32] By this time the gaps in the
Buffalo series had been filled with a number of new arctic offerings, including
a new family group of Western Eskimo and two arctic "dwelling groups."
Among the latter was a model (Figure 10.2) of a central Eskimo winter village
on the sea ice, showing kayaks perched on their storage racks, a dogsled being
prepared for a trip, and Inuit constructing snowhouses. A second dwelling
group (Figure 10.3) illustrated a pair of domed semisubterranean log and sod
houses of the western Alaskan Eskimos, with fish-drying racks and an elevated
storehouse. This scene was elaborated into a full life-group featuring a family of
seven Western Eskimo from the Yukon-Kuskokwim region engaged in a variety of tasks (Figure 10.4). Their caribou fur, duckskin, and gutskin parkas are
styles from Norton Sound and Nunivak Island. A young hunter holding a bolas
talks with an older hunter stringing a sinew-backed bow; a woman approaches
the storehouse with a grass basket of fish; two young girls converse while playing with toys; a man carves a wood bowl with a crooked knife; and a woman
cooks a meal in a pottery vessel over an oil lamp. Accessories, including hunting gear and sealskin storage bags are displayed. The lively domestic scene illustrates a moment in the life of an Alaskan Eskimo family and teaches the visitor
much about their cultures, crafts, and technology. The exhibit draws heavily on
the artifacts, documentation, photographs, and publications of Edward W.
Nelson from his work for the Smithsonian here during 1877–81.[33] The perfect

Fig. 10.2. This "Central Eskimo" dwelling group (ca. 1901), probably developed with information from Franz Boas's research (1888), depicts a Canadian Inuit winter village on the sea ice. Such reconstructions supplemented artifact displays but were later eclipsed by full-scale life-group reconstructions. This group depicts kayaks on storage racks, a dogsled being prepared for a trip, and Inuit constructing snowhouses. (SI 22773)

rendition suggests that Nelson, an ornithology associate of the Smithsonian, and W. H. Dall, honorary curator of mollusks in the museum and the person who initiated Smithsonian ethnological collecting in western Alaska, consulted extensively on the production.

Following its installation in the new National Museum building, the Smith Sound Eskimo and other life-groups, dwelling groups, and individual lay-figures remained untouched for many years. Although some renovations may have been made, it was not until the late 1940s and 1950s that the Eskimo displays came under major refurbishment under the direction of John C. Ewers, with assistance from Henry B. Collins, previously curator of arctic archeology at the museum but by this time a member of the Bureau of American Ethnology. Ewers's

Fig. 10.3. This dwelling group illustrating domed log and sod houses of the western Alaskan Eskimos was created about 1901 with information from E. W. Nelson's and Lucien Turner's ethnography. The houses, elevated log storehouse, and fish drying on racks carried the dominant message, with artifacts and human figures taking a secondary role. (SI 30233)

Fig. 10.4. This western Alaskan Eskimo scene was created by Holmes about 1910 for installation in the new National Museum building, now the National Museum of Natural History. Holmes's genius for transporting the viewer into a "moment frozen in time" is evident in this busy family scene showing social interaction and utilizing the museum's rich collection of Alaskan Eskimo artifacts, naturalistic human figures, and architectural surroundings. (SI 28133)

installation reused many of the individual Eskimo lay-figures from the Holmes hall; others were retired or refitted with new heads to use in other Indian exhibits. At this time the Western Eskimo life-group was retired, probably because space permitted only one Eskimo life-group, and the dramatic Polar Eskimo assumed center stage. This group was installed more or less exactly as Holmes had prepared it, but with a different label. "The Happy Eskimo" of 1901 had become the "northernmost *known* Eskimos" when erected in 1902.[34] It was now retitled in a more definitive way: "The Polar Eskimo: The Northernmost People in the World." The original situation label, "Call *That* a Seal???" remained in place. Despite attempts to portray the diversified nature of North American Eskimo groups by exhibiting clothing and technology from each region, the lack of clear geographic distinctions and the centrality of the Smith Sound diorama gave the visitor the impression of a single unified northern Eskimo culture, epitomized by the Polar Eskimo.

After the "new" exhibit was installed, it remained in place until the present. Starting about 1980, however, I began to receive letters or messages from visitors who complained about terminology. By 1970, Canadian "Eskimo" groups wanted to be known by their own self-designation, Inuit. Greenland Eskimos, who call themselves *Kalaadlit,* are accustomed to the Danish- and English-language term *Greenlander* or *Eskimo.* In Alaska the term *Eskimo* remains in use in educational literature because the only other term, *Native Alaskan,* does not distinguish them from Athapascans or Aleuts. However, when designating specific groups, Alaskan peoples use the self-designations *Inupiak* (northwest Alaska), *Yupik* (southwest Alaska), *Siberian Yupik* (St. Lawrence Island), *Unangan* (Aleut), *Alutiiq* (Kodiak), and *Chugachmuit* or *Sugpiak* (Prince William Sound). *Eskimo* still remains the only term other than *Arctic Peoples* to designate all indigenous arctic dwellers. Since the National Museum of Natural History's Indian halls were scheduled for renovation "in the near future," and because only a portion of the displays represented Canadian Inuit, a decision was made to delay corrections until that fairy-tale time arrived.

Today, Holmes's Smith Sound Eskimos live on, transported at least partly into immortality by ninety-five years of observation by Americans of all stripes and colors and by foreign visitors of every nationality and ethnicity. All who pass before these sculpted Inuit eyes find themselves conducted into an arctic Native past of unknown age, but they leave perplexed as to whether these timeless people still exist. They wonder what has happened to Eskimos since these early days, whether they still wear fur clothes, live in igloos, hunt seals. Last year the NMHH Inughuit, as Polar Eskimo peoples prefer to call themselves today, were visited by a large part of the three million who enter our doors annually expecting to learn what is "natural" in America: its rocks, animals, insects, and dinosaurs. Major attractions have always been the Hope Diamond and, until removed from display recently, the mummies, including the "soap" man, and the man with the thirty-seven-foot beard, which he "grew" into a bag for safekeeping. Along with these wonders were displayed the Native Americans.

ORIGINS OF MUSEUM ANTHROPOLOGY: 1870–1893

The exhibition development unveiled in Buffalo and in the new USNM building had not been created overnight by Holmes and his team of curators, taxidermists, and sculptors. Rather it represented a long process of experiment and change that had been under way for almost two decades. The first experiments with setting figures into an appropriate environment had been tried at the Louisville (1884) and New Orleans (1885) World's Fairs.[35] Nor did the presentation of life-groups supplant other types of displays that were the legacy of earlier struggles to discover the hidden meaning that curators Otis Mason, Holmes, Rau, and others at the museum believed lurked below the surface in their huge collection of objects. Mason, in particular, had been searching ever since he came to the museum for principles that could unite disparate cultures into a single theoretical framework. Having large collections at his disposal, among which the Eskimo holdings were among the largest and the best documented, with wide geographical dispersion, Mason searched for principles in the ordering, across space, of "types" (adapted from biological classification) and functionally equivalent forms of material culture. His method, like that of the biological curators at the USNM, was to impose order through systematics and taxonomy. Once order was imposed by the physical arrangement of types in space, patterns would emerge and theory would become explicit. Breaks in type distributions were critical points of interest in this procedure.

The Eskimo collections were the ideal body of material to use for this study. As a result of Spencer F. Baird's efforts, beginning in 1858, the Smithsonian had assembled Eskimo collections from almost every region of the North American Arctic: William J. Fisher in Kodiak (1879–85); Lucien Turner in the Aleutians (c. 1880) and Ungava (1882–84); William Healy Dall in Nunivak (1874); Edward W. Nelson from the Kuskokwim to Kotzebue (1877–81); John Murdoch in Barrow (1881–83); Robert Kennicott, Roderick MacFarlane, and Bernard Ross in the Yukon Territories and Mackenzie (1858–67); and Charles F. Hall from East Baffin (1860–62). Other collections had been acquired by exchange and donation from Labrador and Greenland. Spanning more than 5,000 miles and encompassing numerous geographical and ecological subdivisions, these collections provided Mason with an exceptional database from a relatively unified and isolated group of cultures under relatively similar environmental conditions of geography, climate, and animal life. Prospects for ethnographic synthesis were therefore ideal.

For Mason, the exhibit floor of the Arts and Industries Building was a kind of exhibition "laboratory" to explore the meaning of similarity and variation. Arranging the Eskimo specimens in gridlike patterns, row upon row, he laid out his synoptic series displaying fifteen regional ethnic groups along one axis and types or "inventions" along the other, and by this means he compared and contrasted implement forms by culture and region throughout the Arctic.[36] The resulting displays, so ordered, type by type, culture by culture, and region by region, had the potential for creating order out of the National Museum's diverse and growing collections of ethnographic specimens.

As it happened, however, the grand theory of material culture order that Mason hoped to identify failed to emerge. His work demonstrated the basic unity of the Eskimo culture area, with variation ascribed to adaptation to regional environmental variation, contact with adjacent groups (especially Northwest Coast), and unique inventive responses. But it did not answer the question of *cause*. For that, anthropology would have to wait several more decades. Eventually, however, Mason's work led him to formulate the "culture area" concept, which he eventually came to see as largely unified by a combination of environment and, following the publication of J. W. Powell's linguistic map of North America, language. But Mason, like Holmes, Hough, and their assistants, was not a theoretician. His work remained largely at the descriptive level, and his exhibits failed to inspire new generalizations. He longed for comparable order and evolutionary themes such as he had seen on a trip to England in 1889 at the Pitt Rivers Museum, with its developmental "Three Age System" approach to human history.[37] In American ethnology, no such system could be identified. Mason's exhibits of thousands of specimens created a taxonomic dictionary of material culture, but beyond exhibiting principles of invention, diffusion, and homology as ordered by the ethnic principle of culture area, they offered no further instruction. This was certainly the case for the public, for whom the exhibits remained curious, inscrutable, overwhelming, but somewhat pedantic. The problem was acute, since it was in these days that the Smithsonian was recognizing a serious need for education to justify its programs to Congress and the public for the first time.

The Smithsonian was changing. By the late 1800s the grand era of world's fairs and expositions had arrived. The new facilities of the Arts and Industries

(Centennial) Building provided a permanent showcase for public exhibition, anointing manifest destiny and public appetite for knowledge of the new frontiers of an expanding nation. Curators were becoming acutely aware of the need to find new roles for museum specimens. With many collections described and classified,[38] it fell to the staff to find other educational and scientific uses for them. Exchange programs provided one answer, distributing "excess" collections to other U.S. and foreign institutions and receiving, in return, collections from regions not represented in Smithsonian collections.[39] Mason and Holmes were also beginning to feel heat directed at them by a very knowledgeable—and outspoken—arctic scholar, Franz Boas, who had been employed by the American Museum of Natural History. Boas knew the Smithsonian Eskimo collections and had different views about how to present ethnology to the public. In particular, he took issue with the principles of environmentalism, cultural continuity, and human unity that underlaid the USNM exhibit program.[40]

PUBLIC EDUCATION: 1893–1910

Although Holmes and Mason did not abandon their environmental views, a practical solution to the public's confusion over Mason's exhibits gradually emerged from the increasing use of lay-figure displays. Lay-figures had been introduced into the displays in the early 1870s as a method to represent peoples and cultures in ways that showed physical type and costume, adornments and handicrafts. Originally made of wax, lay-figures provided a diversion from the orderly but intellectually sterile ranks of cherrywood cases crammed with artifacts and busts of morbid life casts. One of the earliest figures was of the famous arctic explorer Elisha Kent Kane, which was displayed as early as 1870.[41] Kane had returned from being frozen in the ice pack for two years (1853–55) with his vessel in Smith Sound, Northwestern Greenland. The tale of his exploits, including a miraculous escape and triumphant return south created a sensation in the United States.[42] Probably for this reason, a national frenzy was at work promoting arctic exploration, and the figure of Kane was enthroned, flanked by two famous Inuit, "Joe" and his wife, "Hannah" (Figure 10.5). Joe's Inuktitut name was Ebierbing, and Hannah's was Tookoolito. Both were famous for sustaining the lives of a portion of C. F. Hall's crew on the North Polar Expedition in 1873 when their ship, *Polaris,* was crushed and sank. With Ebierbing's and Hannah's assistance they survived for six months, during which their melting ice floe drifted from Smith Sound to southern Labrador.[43] In a photograph from this era taken in the Castle, we see a full-bearded Kane in his European-style

Fig. 10.5. "Dr. Kane and the Esquimaux." One frame of a stereoptic pair bears the inscription: "Entered according to act of Congress, A.D. 1873, by Chas. Pollock in the office of the Librarian of Congress at Washington, C. Seaver, Jr. Photog." One of the Smithsonian's earliest "lay-figure" displays, it depicts the famous arctic explorer Elisha Kent Kane and his two Inuit companions, "Joe" and "Hanna." (copy neg. SI 82-11680)

Inuit-made exploration clothing, with Joe and Hannah on either side. They are clothed in Eskimo garments, but not, as one might imagine, in Polar Eskimo clothing. Rather they appear to be wearing Alaskan garments from Norton Sound. Since the museum had not yet acquired any Greenland collections, it seems that Dall's Alaskan collections must have been used instead.[44]

In hindsight, this early Smithsonian attempt to venerate national heroes, promote arctic exploration, and present ethnic views was seen as a trial run that was to be quickly forgotten. A gruesome "post-op" view on the Kane exhibit appeared in the *Annual Report* following the Chicago success: "It is scarcely worthwhile to mention the ghastly wax figures of Kane, the explorer, and his companions, in costumes of fur. . . . These, and the equally crude mannikins of Eskimo Joe and his wife Hanna, made in 1873,[45] have long since been discarded and have no place in the history of recent efforts."[46]

A photograph from about 1874 (Figure 10.6) shows a group of lay-figures titled "Western Eskimo" that must have been created about this time, or slightly later. This image, which has no documentation, shows three figures, a man and woman in Norton Sound dress and an Anderson River Inuit woman with a standing child.[47] The figures appear to have been brought together for a photo record shot before installation. The Norton Sound man is wearing West Greenland boots. A different Western Eskimo group illustrated in the *Annual Report* for 1903 describing the Buffalo Exposition display shows another group of "Western Eskimo" figures:

> The third case contains three lay figures of the Western Eskimo, who inhabit the shores of the northwestern seas from the mouth of the Mackenzie River around Alaska to Mount St. Elias. Their mode of dress and living varies according to the animals on which they depend and the contact they have had with other races. This illustration shows an Anderson River Inuvialuit woman dressed in caribou fur with a child on her shoulders (B. R. Ross collections, 1858–62); a man, probably dressed in a Barrow garment (Murdoch's Barrow collection, 1881–83); and a Bristol Bay or Kodiak woman in marmot furs (McKay, 1881–1883; or Fisher, 1879–94). The Mackenzie and Bristol Bay people are out of touch with the great fleet of whalers, and their arts are not greatly modified, but the Norton Sound Eskimo have been under instruction of Russians and Americans for more than a hundred years.[48]

Somewhat contradictory information is contained in a 1922 publication of the same plate,[49] with text that describes five Western Eskimo figures: "a woman from Anderson River region, Canada, with her child standing in front [the child is actually shown on her shoulders]; a man and a woman from Point Barrow, also dressed in deerskin [i.e., caribou]; a man from St. Michaels, Alaska; and a woman from Kadiak Island wearing a costume made of spermophile skin and ornamented with marmot and beaver's fur." The discrepancy may result from Hough's describing a new installation of the original 1893 group of three plus a Barrow woman dressed in a Murdoch garment (1881–83) and the

Fig. 10.6. This group from about 1874 is the first presentation of lay-figures of the Western Eskimo. Probably clothed in Kennicott's and Dall's collections, they represent a woman and man of Norton Sound (left center) and a woman and child of the Mackenzie River Inuvialuit (right). Expressionless but less stiff than the Kane group, they model racial features and clothes but show little humanity and could not engage public visitors. (SI 8360)

Norton Sound man from the 1873 group in the new National Museum building, for which he had no new photograph.

A second group of three standing lay-figures representing Inuit of the Eastern Arctic ("Eastern Eskimo") may also have been prepared in the mid-1880s. Both Western and Eastern Eskimo lay-figure groups were used as surrogates for life-groups that Holmes did not have time to complete for the Buffalo Exposition in 1901. The *Annual Report* on the Buffalo group describes two early lay-figure groups.[50] The "Eastern Eskimo" group (Figure 10.7)

> represents the Eskimo who inhabit Greenland, the shores of northern Labrador, and Hudson Bay adjoining. The figure at the right is that of a young woman of southwestern Greenland, her dress resembling that of a Lapp. Her people have been under instruction of Moravian missionaries for generations. The middle figure represents the native right-hand man of the intrepid whalers, who before the discovery of coal oil ransacked Hudson Bay for oil and baleen. The woman at the left is from Ungava Bay and is dressed in aboriginal costume of reindeer fur, little modified by outside influences. Her loose, roomy garments correspond with those figures by the early voyagers. In her left hand she carries a large wooden plate, while the right is lifted to ease the headband which passes around the forehead, sustaining the babe held in the hood behind. The eastern Eskimo are especially interesting on account of their association with the exploring ex-

Fig. 10.7. This lay-figure group of "Eastern Eskimo" was probably created in the 1880s and was used in the 1901 Buffalo Exposition (this photograph). It shows an Ungava Inuit woman, a Baffin Inuit whaler whose dress shows his contact with whalers, and a Greenlandic woman seen admiring herself—and her Danish-influenced clothing—in a mirror. Later twentieth-century exhibits almost universally "naturalized" Inuit people by showing them without European influence. (SI 13882)

peditions sent out in the last century to search for the northwest passage and the North Pole.

These documents reveal much about the attitudes of Smithsonian curators at this early point in the Institution's history. In relation to nationalistic notions about "intrepid whalers who ransacked Hudson Bay for oil and baleen," we can wonder if the museum staff considered the impacts of whale predation on the Native Inuit. In this very year, 1903, the Sadlermiut of northern Hudson Bay died out from diseases introduced by the whalers. But we also find the museum considering the effects of several decades of whaler contact on Baffin Inuit clothing styles; of Moravian "instruction" and influence on "generations" of Greenland Inuit culture, especially on its highly decorated female clothing styles; and of similar variable patterns of contact among the western Alaskan Eskimos owing to the isolation of some groups from Russian traders and settlers and American whalers. These comments suggest receptiveness in considering culture change and European-Native contact as interesting scientific questions. But this interest appears to have been short-lived and is not raised in the post-

Columbian exhibition programs as the Bureau of American Ethnology program in salvage ethnology and romanticization of the aboriginal past took root in the heart of most Smithsonian Indian programs.

Goode's report for 1893 also provides perspectives on the progress noted since the 1876 exposition program. In the interim between Philadelphia and Chicago, Smithsonian staff had prepared materials for exhibition at fairs in Berlin, London, New Orleans, Cincinnati, Louisville, and Madrid. Mason's trip to Europe to view the Paris exposition in 1889, in particular, was a revelation. In addition to visiting the Pitt Rivers Museum, the most advanced exhibition and research center of its day, he found that the live Parisian exhibits of Polynesian and African peoples and villages had a huge impact on his views. Mason returned home more convinced than ever of the need to advance science through taxonomic classification while at the same time portraying cultures through life-group environmental dioramas.

Mason's plan for the National Museum's contribution to the program of the Columbian exhibition in Chicago was a major step forward from his earlier didactic displays of cultures, comparative technology, and inventions. Stimulated by Powell's progress in the mapping of Native language groups of the Americas, Mason tried to conceive of the diversity of ethnographic cultures as a function of linguistic affinity. As he began to apply Powell's classification to material culture, he noted broad similarities in material culture within linguistic groups and found frequent breaks in these distributions that corresponded with linguistic units. He experimented with this technique in organizing the Chicago displays, displaying ethnographic materials arranged by tribe and language with Powell's map hanging from the ceiling above as an organizing principle for the entire presentation. But, as Ewers notes:

> For several months Mason [had] struggled with the difficulties presented by this challenge. Some of the linguistic stocks of North America could not be interpreted through objects because there were no artifacts made by the speakers of those languages in the Museum's collections. Either the tribes had become nearly extinct or their ways of life had become so modified through white contact that it would be impossible to obtain a group of objects that would portray their traditional customs. Some of the most prominent linguistic stocks were represented by tribes spread out over vast areas in quite different geographical environments so that the contrasts in material traits among tribes of the same language stock were greater than those between neighboring tribes speaking quite different languages.
>
> Mason compared the distribution of traits of Indian material culture with Dr. C. Hart Merriam's biogeographic map of North America published by the

Department of Agriculture and found that the distribution of artifacts corresponded much more closely with it than with Powell's linguistic map. He concluded that "the materialistic activities were controlled by the environment."[51]

Mason's culture area concept had begun to take shape. This was to be his most lasting contribution to anthropological theory. His ideas emerged directly from a need to discover a higher meaning and pattern in the museum's huge collections of ethnographic material and to communicate this knowledge through public exhibition.

The Chicago exhibition was a major turning point for Smithsonian anthropology in two important ways. The emergence of the culture area concept with its environmental and linguistic correlates provided both contrasting and correlative paradigms suitable for researching and exhibiting cultural similarity and diversity in the museum's extensive archaeological and ethnographic collections. It was used by Ewers to organize the new NMNH ethnology halls in the 1950s and will certainly be featured in future renovations. Equally important, Holmes's life-groups ensured that the museum could present the results of its research and collecting programs in an orderly but dramatic new way that would attract the public and provide a context for learning and education. Together with the return of many exhibits to Washington, especially those donated by foreign nations, the Smithsonian was launched forcefully into the organization of its collections for public instruction.

"THE IGLOO ESKIMOS": A NATIVE VIEW

In gathering data for this essay I asked Sven Haakanson, a Native of Kodiak Island who has been working with me at the Arctic Studies Center, to spend some time in the exhibit hall to gather visitor comments and reactions. His report in this section, in his words, provides a reality check on public response to our Eskimo exhibit today:

Sven Haakanson (SH): "Hey! Look at the Eskimos!" a child cries out as a group enters the exhibit area. Several adults comment about how the "Eskimo" lived, never thinking about how they might live today or who they really are. These ideas and understandings are from the last two centuries of images that have been written about, filmed, photographed, and studied—all perpetuating the image of "Nanook of the North."

I shook my head, wondering how much longer such exhibits would continue to misinform the museum's visitors about arctic peoples.

GROUP 1: A group of tourists encounter the Smith Sound Eskimo exhibit.
"Wow! Eskimo Indians! Look!"
"Oh, my gosh! There's wolves over there!"

GROUP 2: A woman is reading the text "Call *That* a Seal???" next to the Smith Sound Eskimo diorama.
"Who would want to live way up in the Arctic like the Eskimos?"
"Look at the arrows, Mommy. They use two at a time!"
"Wow!" another boy says to his mother, encountering the bow and arrows.

SH: They're taking a lot of misconceptions home about these people. They accept what they read in the text as being true and take this home.

I ask groups of tourists—Korean, Swedish, Japanese, Danish, and Spanish—what they think of the display.

GROUP 3: An older woman who had just spent two hours in the museum comments: "I like it. I'm impressed that they know how to survive. The gutskin rain coat surprised me."
"It's neat!
"All ages come to this exhibit; some stop, some continue walking."
"Eskimos! Eskimos! There's a boat here!"
"Oh! Look at the igloo!"
"The northernmost people!"

SH: The exhibit doesn't say that these people are still around and that they have adapted to the new or modern world while maintaining their traditions.

GROUP 4: A group of teachers walks through the exhibit with numerous young children.
"Eskimos from Alaska!"
"This is how they hunt seals" (referring to the kayak display).
"I could not understand how they live in ice houses. Ain't it cold? But then I realized it became warm."

GROUP 5: I interview students from George Mason University who have been sent to look at the Indian exhibits as part of their anthropology course and ask them why they have come to see these exhibits.
"It's an interesting culture."
"Alaskan Eskimo art."
"Too much information."

"Stereotype."

"It's misrepresentation."

"How old is it? They're shown living in the past."

"Why don't they use the term *Inuit*? Using *Eskimo* is an insult, isn't it? Why don't they change the name of the exhibit?"

"Why are these people exhibited in the Natural History Museum?"

SH: The main problem with this exhibit is that it perpetuates the image of the "igloo" Eskimo. The ethnographic material does a wonderful job of demonstrating the types of tools, clothing, and ritual materials. What the displays and text don't do is teach about who the "Eskimo" peoples really are. The visitors are taking the wrong information home, and this continues the misunderstanding of who the northern peoples are, from the Canadian Inuit to the Alaskan Yupiks. There is no text that explains why northern peoples do not like the term *Eskimo* and prefer *Inuit* or local linguistic terms today instead.

GROUP 6: I am sitting very still on the floor in front of the display cases, and a woman and her son look at me in surprise when I look up. As they pass, the boy says, "I thought he was part of the exhibit."

"I did too," says the mother.

Sven's general comment:

Sitting in the arctic exhibit area, I overheard several comments, from children and adults, about how the "Eskimo" people live—hunting cute seals, eating raw meat, living in igloos. Yes, this was true, and in some areas, still is; but most arctic people have changed with the influx of Western ideas and modern technology. We don't live in the past today, as this exhibit leads people to believe. Most "Eskimos" have never seen or built an igloo. However, as the museum's visitors walk past this 1957 "Eskimo" exhibit they take home this old stereotyped image of Nanook and the blubber-eating igloo dwellers that is now fifty years out of date. Why hasn't the museum changed this exhibit to teach people who these northern people really are today? There's no shortage of information or materials to show. What's missing is context for these old materials and something that tells about arctic people's lives today.

Here I am, an "Eskimo" too, but from thousands of miles west of these Greenland Inuit. Our people in Kodiak Island, Alaska, call ourselves *Sugpiaq*. I am wondering if I should tell these kids, tourists, and students that this *Eskimo* term is wrong. It doesn't say who we are anymore. We're not a single unified culture. We don't even speak the same language as the Polar and Canadian Inuit.

I've never seen a polar bear or an igloo; our sea doesn't freeze in winter, and it hardly ever snows.

What can be done about this exhibit? At least we need to change the labels and use the names these northern peoples call themselves today. But these exhibits are so old and stereotyped that label changes won't solve the basic problem of getting people to understand the diversity of our people and lands. We need to change people's attitudes about who "Eskimos" are—more diverse, with different traditions and languages and beliefs—without losing the idea that we are still, in one sense, a closely related culture and people.

In the past four years my studies have taken me to museums across North America, from the Peabody Museum in Cambridge to the Field Museum in Chicago, to the National Museum of *Natural* History at the Smithsonian. In each place I took time to visit the exhibits on "Eskimo Peoples," and every time I left disappointed because they have not changed the name "Eskimo" or the idea of that all northern peoples are not represented by a "Nanook-like" culture. I've italicized *natural* because even the name of our National Museum creates a mind-set of arctic Native peoples being of the "natural" and "historical." In my view both are wrong.

NATIVE AMERICANS AND NATURAL HISTORY

From our perspective in the late twentieth century it is difficult to understand why anthropology and the study of Native and non-Western cultures, and those alone, are part of a museum whose other academic departments include entomology, botany, mineralogy, paleobiology, and zoology. While the Department of Anthropology maintains a high level of scholarship and is recognized as one of the leading institutions conducting anthropological research, our public face to millions of visitors every year projects an antiquated facade that fails to represent arctic peoples, or other peoples of the Americas, in respectful, modern terms. The voice of the display is that of the omniscient curatorial "expert" of the early to mid-1900s. The displays do not embody Native voices, and Native people had no role in interpreting or participating in the decisions about what collections are shown and what messages are delivered. While the exhibits display a variety of cultures, the diversity of arctic peoples is not presented. Rather, emphasis is on technology and environmental adaptation across the entire North American Arctic, and little attention is given to religious views and the rich spiritual life that is one of the most remarkable features of the cultures of northern peoples. As Haakanson points out, the exhibit projects a view of a stereotyped high arctic "Eskimo" culture rather than emphasizing the diversity within this remarkably widespread group of peoples.

The cause of these problems is rooted in the institutional history and structure at the NMNH and the larger Smithsonian, but is not limited to our institution. Anthropological departments were originally founded in most large natural history museums of Europe and North America, and these institutions continue to conduct research and present displays of indigenous cultures from their collections today. The fact that a similar organization survives in our large natural history museums in the United States is rooted in the history of anthropology, which began as a museum discipline devoted to the preservation and recovery of Native American (and other) cultures and languages before they vanished from the face of the earth. Only after its establishment in acquisition-minded museums did anthropology develop a second life in universities.

As Curtis M. Hinsley Jr. has shown in *Savages and Scientists,* anthropology has been an important feature of Smithsonian science since the Institution's founding in 1846. Although not organized as a cohesive field at that time, archeology, ethnology, somatology, mythology, and philology all enjoyed support from Joseph Henry, Spencer Baird, and other early administrators who viewed the origins and history of the Indians as important fields of science. The appearance of *Ancient Earthworks of the Mississippi Valley,* by Ephraim Squier and Edwin Davis, as volume 1 of the Smithsonian Contributions to Knowledge series in 1848 affirmed this, and was followed by Samuel Haven's review of American archeology in 1856. Soon after, ethnology, somatology, and philology studies were organized, but staffed only as unpaid positions.

The roots of ethnological collecting actually preceded the founding of the Institution. The Commodore Matthew Perry Collection[52] from the Japan Expedition (1853–54) was the first ethnology accession of the Smithsonian, but it had been preceded by the Wilkes Collection from the U.S. Exploring Expedition of 1838–42.[53] Thereafter, ethnology developed following two courses: as a field collection program carried out by naturalists and biologists under the direct supervision of Spencer Baird, assistant secretary of the Smithsonian, and as a curatorial and publication program carried on in the museum. Although none of Baird's naturalists had anthropological training, all collected ethnological material. The first of these comprehensive collecting programs was initiated when Baird sent Robert Kennicott north to British North America in 1858 to collect natural history and ethnological specimens from this unknown frontier.[54] Working with local Hudson Bay traders and Native Inuit and Dene, Kennicott and his collaborators, principally B. R. Ross and R. MacFarlane, secured more than 10,000 specimens, including 600 ethnological pieces with detailed documentation. Among these were many MacFarlane specimens from the Anderson River Eskimos living in the lowlands east of the Mackenzie Delta. These were among the first arctic ethnographic collections accessioned by the Smithsonian. They were joined about the same time by a small ethnological collection submitted by Charles Francis Hall from southeast Baffin Inuit, but with less documentation. Following Kennicott's work in the Mackenzie region, he led the Smithsonian's Western Union Telegraph Expedition in Alaska. During this project, in 1865–66, he and his team, which included William H. Dall, collected materials from the Yukon River Ingaliks, Yupik, and Inupiat Eskimos.[55] After the Alaska purchase, these tentative collecting programs expanded rapidly and brought large numbers of ethnographic specimens into the museum from the 1870s through the 1890s.

Unfortunately, few of Baird's naturalists published their ethnology collections. As a result of his efforts, however, these collections gradually filled with unpublished materials from all over the Arctic. Even with the expansion in the curatorial ranks after 1870, Otis Mason and his assistants did not have the expertise to prepare detailed publications on each collection. Rather they analyzed portions of them, type by type, from Alaska to Greenland, in cross-cultural perspective: oil lamps, tobacco and smoking implements, masks, etc. Such work supported exhibit goals but produced few important scholarly results.[56]

A major development occurred when the Bureau of American Ethnology (BAE) was established in 1879 as an affiliate of the Smithsonian. Its founder, Major J. W. Powell, instituted a vigorous program of field studies in Native American linguistics and ethnology. Initially established to record and publish data on vanishing Native American cultures, BAE staff also made collections that, after publication, were transferred to the USNM for curation and exhibition. This structure guaranteed rivalry between the BAE and USNM staffs, with the BAE holding a position of perceived superiority because of its freedom to pursue field studies and publication without the frustrations of curation and museum work. This dual structure in Smithsonian anthropology persisted until 1964, when S. Dillon Ripley abolished the BAE and folded its remaining staff into the museum's Department of Anthropology. In order to preserve some aspects of the BAE's social anthropological program a Center for the Study of Man was created within the museum, and this unit administered the *Handbook of North American Indians* until the center was disbanded and its remaining staff became part of the Department of Anthropology. Another milestone in the history of the museum was the transferral of its European-derived historical and technological collections to the newly created National Museum of History and Technology, later to be renamed the National Museum of American History.

While providing focus for American history, the partition created new dilemmas as Lapp (Saame) ethnography became "European" rather than indigenous (i.e., "natural history"), and Zuni Christian art was transferred from anthropology to become part of Spanish history in the American Southwest.

Throughout this century the staff of the museum gradually grew and diversified. While Americanist studies remained dominant, Oceanian, Asian, European, and African ethnographic collections grew, often in response to the need to present museum displays of other non-Western cultures. Like Holmes, curators began to see the exhibits as "timeless," and they (curators and exhibits) quickly became rooted in the architecture of the National Museum. The three-to-five-year planning process that accompanied the production of each hall, the high cost involved, and the long term that passed as the exhibit program moved through the anthropology, biology, paleo, and mineral sciences renovation cycle meant that halls remained in place for forty or fifty years at a time. As "a certain sense of stability" settled over the anthropology displays, curators came increasingly to describe them as the "permanent" halls, and so they have become. Isolated from the halls and freed from the vexations that exhibits work entails, in which months—even years—of effort can be (and have been) blown away by administrative fiat, anthropologists at the museum turned increasingly toward the more productive work of creating knowledge. In one sense, Holmes's system had worked too well. It created an exhibit program that documented traditional native cultures as static entities, frozen in time in the early contact era. Cultural uniqueness, not processes of change, was emphasized. The NMNH's ethnological exhibits had become a visual dictionary of cultures, presented in idealized fashion. The real guts of real native history as now recognized through knowledge of cultural, biological, and environmental interactions were completely absent. Even less was spoken of Native relations with Europeans, Asians, Blacks, and other agents of change. No one imagined that these cultures would survive and change and that one day the contact-era "freeze-frame" representations would themselves become "archeological." Nor did museum curators of that time foresee that Native peoples would become interested in how their cultures were represented in Washington.

INUA AND CROSSROADS: A REPRIEVE

In the 1980s, a long-range exhibit plan was developed that gave priority to renovating a series of paleo halls that were badly out-of-date. The anthropology halls were to follow thereafter. Simultaneously, smaller temporary shows were discouraged as being too expensive to produce and of little lasting value. But at the same time, a new temporary exhibit hall, the Evans Gallery, was established on the ground floor to accommodate traveling shows. Here, finally, was a solution to a serious problem that NMNH had faced for many years. Since the "permanent halls" were indeed quite permanent, there were few opportunities to change them or to exhibit collections or topics that fell outside the scheme of synoptic geographic cultural overviews. Nor could we host traveling shows produced outside the museum.

In the wake of the successful traveling exhibit "The Far North," produced by the National Gallery of Art ahd the Amon Carter Museum,[57] the establishment of the Evans Gallery provided an opportunity for developing and exhibiting a "homegrown" Smithsonian arctic show. With the encouragement of NMNH director Richard Fiske, I decided to prepare a special exhibit featuring the remarkable but little-known ethnographic collections made by E. W. Nelson in western Alaska in 1877–81, before the region came under strong influence from missionaries, the gold rush, and other developments. With no hope of changing the permanent halls for many years, Susan Kaplan and I put a selection of Nelson's 10,000 ethnographic specimens on special exhibit at NMNH in 1982.[58] "Inua: Spirit World of the Bering Sea Eskimo" later toured to nine cities: Washington, Juneau, Anchorage, Ottawa, Chicago, Seattle, Winnipeg, Detroit, and Boston in 1982–84. A smaller version, "mini-Inua," was prepared for tour to twenty local villages and culture centers in Alaska in 1984–85 with the assistance of the Alaska State Museum. After this tour the show traveled to locations in northern Canada and Greenland. In 1987–88 a second and more elaborate "mini" Inua show was prepared by Susan Rowley with the USIA's Arts America Program and toured eight cities in Eastern and Northern Europe.

While the Inua exhibition programs were under way we began planning a second, more elaborate, exhibition project that would present a broader panorama of cultures around the North Pacific rim. "Crossroads of Continents: Cultures of Siberia and Alaska"[59] required an elaborate study and inventory program involving collections from American, Canadian, and Soviet museums. Archaeological, ethnographic, historical, and art materials from eight traditional cultures on both sides of the Bering Strait were assembled, illustrating the history and relationships of these cultures. The project took nearly ten years to plan and carry out, but it was a major success and toured widely in North America, including Alaska. As in the case of "Inua," "Crossroads" was followed by a smaller local exhibit, "Crossroads Alaska," that toured for two years in Alaska and is now scheduled for Russia in 1996–97.

In 1988 our efforts led to the establishment of the Arctic Studies Center as a permanent feature of the NMNH program. The ASC conducts research in anthropology, biology, and other northern natural sciences; engages in publication, training, and educational programs aimed at increasing access to NMNH collections and archival data to northern populations and Native groups; prepares exhibits; and conducts outreach programs. A central tenet of the ASC program is to conduct these activities in collaboration with northern groups and institutions. To facilitate these goals, the ASC established a regional office at the Anchorage Museum of History and Art in 1993. Current plans call for developing a series of exhibit projects with Alaska Native groups based on NMNH collections and to use these programs as vehicles for scholarship, instruction, and public education. The first of these projects, "Looking Both Ways: The Rebirth of Alutiiq Identity," exhibits the William J. Fisher Collection of Kodiak Island. A second (as yet untitled) presents Inupiat views on traditional whaling in northwest Alaska. A third, "Science North: Collectors, Traders, Natives, the Origins of Museum Anthropology," is being developed with Canadian Dene and Inuvialuit featuring the collections of Robert Kennicott and Hudson Bay Company traders of 1858–67. Other projects will be planned with Tlingit, Athapascan, and Aleut groups. We hope that each of these projects will be exhibited at NMNH after completing local tours in Alaska and Canada. All will be multimedia projects and will have exhibit, catalog, education, and curriculum material, video, CD-ROM, and internet components.

The traveling exhibits "Inua" and "Crossroads" brought NMNH and other collections to a wide audience in North America and gave special access in Alaska to these materials. The outcome of this program has benefited all parties. It has provided curators with ways to share the museum's rich collections with Native peoples whose ancestors produced these materials in the first place, and it helped educate a broad audience about the diversity of arctic peoples, especially the Eskimo cultures of Alaska who have not been featured prominently in our permanent hall. The special exhibits gave us a chance to do things that could never have been accomplished in the museum's permanent exhibits during the period when it was impossible to upgrade the Native cultures hall and its northern displays. By this route we arrive at the present and a new "crossroads" in our arctic exhibition program—the reinstallation of the Eskimo exhibitions as part of the new hall of North American cultures.

PROSPECT FOR CHANGE

Five years ago, increased funding for Native American programs resulting from passage of the National Museum of American Indian and Repatriation Act stimulated a plan to reinstall the North American ethnology exhibit. Complete reconceptualization would be required. Planning was carried out by a core team of curators coordinated by Berkeley-trained anthropologist Jo-Allyn Archambault, a Lakota Sioux who had joined the Anthropology Department in the mid-1980s. Special funds were allocated to the NMNH Exhibits Program for this purpose. Following a series of background research and preliminary design studies, plans for consolidating both halls into the single large axial hall, Hall 10, were developed by museum staff in collaboration with representatives of the seven Native groups that were to be featured in the new hall, with the design services of Applebaum Associates. "Changing Cultures in a Changing World" would emphasize themes of tradition, dynamism, and change that characterize North American Indian and Inuit societies today. History, archeology, environment, and other themes would be incorporated.

The new plan called for a bold departure from the previous tradition of ethnographic exhibiting at the Smithsonian, in which native peoples were displayed as frozen in the ethnographic present of the late nineteenth century. Like the Smith South Eskimos, the viewer was transported back to an era, seemingly before white contact, when Native life existed in a kind of timeless suspension of reality. Today's visitors are still being transported back into that dimension. They appreciate the variety and complexity of Native American culture, of its rich artistic tradition and its myriad technologies, and they sense the importance of environment as a molder of cultural tradition. What they do not sense is the dimension of time, the impact of European contacts, of local intercultural contacts, or of the role Native groups played in altering their environment and surroundings. The devastation brought down upon Indian peoples by the advancing wave of European peoples and cultures by disease, military defeat, loss of land, confinement, and impoverishment is not treated, nor are the impacts of later African and Asian immigrants presented in even a passing manner. Native American cultures, as portrayed in our ethnographic displays, still carry the message and values of a national policy of manifest destiny of the nineteenth century.

The fact that the NMNH persists in projecting this view of its native peoples and native history as we near the turning point of a new millennium, and the 150th anniversary of the Institution, is deplorable. We have reached a state in which our exhibits have lagged so far behind social reality and educational need that their only legitimate purpose can be for instruction in Native arts of a bygone era. Worse still, by continuing to display Native American cultures in a natural history context of a former national agenda, and under a discredited social evolutionary paradigm, we do great injustice to Native peoples. What discipline can survive such "dinosaurs" in its public relations facade? What about the future? What do Native American history and current circumstance tell of things to come?

Eskimo groups were to be featured as one of the seven North American groups in the new hall. The plan called for using the museum's rich collections of Western Eskimo Inupiat, Yupik, and Alitiiq as the core of an exhibit that would emphasize Alaskan peoples in contrast to the 1957 display that gave prominence to Canadian and Greenlandic arctic peoples. An additional focus would balance concepts of environmental and technological adaptation with spiritual and religious ideas that are so well embodied in Alaskan Eskimo art, dance, and ceremonial life. For instance, an annual ceremony in a Yupik *qasgiq*, or dance house, could feature a diorama displaying Yupik culture at the time of E. W. Nelson's visit, with the "man who collects good-for-nothing things" (Nelson's Yupik name), who might be portrayed trading for artifacts while the ceremony takes place around him. Such an exhibit would provide a specific date and circumstance documented from Nelson's field notes and would illustrate both traditional life and the Native-European interaction that was beginning to transform Native life from its pre-Western to its post-contact existence. This is only one of several options that might be considered in consultation with Alaskan Yupik groups. Other displays would feature aspects of culture important to other Alaskan groups and would illustrate the wider diversity of Eskimo cultures in other areas of the North American Arctic.

Provisional plans for Hall 10 do not utilize Holmes's Polar Eskimo life-group because the current design provides room for only one Eskimo diorama. Given our national constituency and the dominance of Alaska in our collections, an Alaskan focus seems necessary. Nevertheless, the Polar Eskimo display is now, itself, a national treasure that has been seen by hundreds of millions of visitors since its creation for the Buffalo Exposition in 1901. Is this birthright not a legitimate basis for its continued existence? Can we retire such a prominent historical feature of our national cultural landscape—one that still continues to inspire and that is a testimonial to one of the most brilliant achievements of Native peoples in the New World, a people's existence as the hemisphere's most northern permanent residents?

These issues have to be carefully considered as we enter the next phase of our planning. It is only one aspect of the tragedy facing the Native American Halls at NMNH in the near future as we confront the dogma of modern museum administration that "less is more," reducing display real estate to a fraction of what was formerly on display, far less than is needed for a reasonable exhibition on Native American and world cultures. At issue is the reduction of forty-two distinct culture exhibits in more than seventy-five cases into a new space of only half that size displaying only seven of the New World's Native cultures. The percentage of objects on exhibit is even more shocking: less than one percent of about 300,000 cataloged ethnological specimens and a much smaller percentage of the archaeological collections. This stark elimination of the capacity of the museum to present the unique cultures of the Americas, using the great collections at our disposal, is a grievous loss not only to our visitors, both national and foreign, but to the Native peoples whose ancestral cultures can be displayed only at the few institutions having resources such as ours. As the museum grows more complex and requires more integration of environment and modern components in displays of traditional culture, it seems inevitable that hard choices have to be made. But the losers, those native peoples whose cultures cannot be presented for their own edification and for the benefit of Americans and foreigners who come to Washington to see the Smithsonian's legendary exhibits, are increasing in number as our capability to present the nation's finest ethnological collections declines.

One hopes there will be another solution. If our wonderful collections cannot be displayed, if we are forced to destroy the Polar Eskimo display, if we cannot find adequate ways to preserve, protect, and exhibit these treasures for the benefit of scholars, Native peoples, and the public—can we justify keeping them in storage, where they are accessible only to scholars and a small number of Native visitors? Should we return these objects, now national treasures belonging in part to every American and citizen of the world, to Native groups, where they will be greatly treasured also but seen by few? The dilemma is unresolved. The NMNH Eskimo collections are among the earliest, largest, and best documented of any institution in the world. They are also one of the largest, earliest, and most comprehensive ethnographic collections in the museum. They have been gathered by field-workers with painstaking care and dedication since the "biblical" times of Smithsonian history. They should not be allowed to languish, unseen and without purpose, in our storerooms. Rather, they should be made to "sing," as our former leader, Secretary S. Dillon Ripley once said of the Institution's collections of musical instruments. This responsibility exists not only with respect to our arctic collections but also to our other wonderful collections of Native American materials. Today many of these collections have been "orphaned" by the process of history, losing not only their original makers and owners but also, increasingly, their curators and their public, as funding cuts reduce curatorial staffs and exhibit space.

It is time to reverse this trend. Recent efforts to re-store the anthropological collections have given them a new lease on life. They are now readily accessible for study and use. The Arctic Studies Center has shown that reconnecting these treasures with Native constituents can give new life and meaning to collections that have lain dormant for a hundred years and that can have huge impacts through cultural legacy programs conducted in collaboration with Native peoples. The fulfillment of an educational plan of exhibition that does justice to these collections should be the goal of our next generation of administrators and curators, many of whom we hope will be of Native ancestry. This cannot happen by fine-tuning an already disastrously compressed exhibition plan. It must come from bold new moves that will provide opportunity for expansion and for inclusion of the many features of Native American life that should find integration with the traditional materials filling the shelves and cabinets of the museum. We do not have the luxury to create institutions that subdivide and fragment the Native American experience in American history. We should work to build a new concept in which our Native cultures can be seen in their fullest form, where archaeological and traditional ethnographic displays need not be isolated from each other or from presentations of language, mythology, spiritual life, art, oral history, and modern social and political life; where these cultures can also be seen in relation to the larger American experience, historical, modern, and future. This is not too much to dream for and to plan for in a day when ethnicity and cultural identity have surfaced as prime movers of world history. And it need not, should not, be limited to the cultures of the Americas, for the Smithsonian has global resources to bring broader formulations to reality. Among these are a new vision of America as a multicultural society.

"CHANGING CULTURES": CONFLICTED PLANS

In 1993 a "Bubble" plan and a model of the proposed hall, with two of seven cultural units developed in some detail, was presented to NMNH director Frank Talbot and Smithsonian administrators, including Secretary Robert Adams and Under Secretary Constance Newman. Presentations were also made to Richard West, director of the Museum of the American Indian and to its board. All agreed that the Archambault plan was an excellent, innovative, and forward-looking concept and initial design based on curatorial and Native collaboration.

During the next year object selection and scripting for the Tlingit and Plains Indian sections of the plan were developed by Archambault and Rosita Worl, a Tlingit who is also on the national board of NMAI. Despite much progress, in spring 1994 further planning was terminated because of the need to concentrate on renovating the much-criticized African Cultures Hall and because the NMAI and Castle believed that fund-raising activities for the new hall would compete with higher priorities for the drive to fund construction of the NMAI and its collection facility. As a result, plans for the American Indian Hall have been postponed indefinitely. Since it now appears that the funding drive for the NMAI will extend beyond its initial term into the post-2000 era, prospects for renovating the Indian halls in the near future remain, at best, unclear. In addition to funding problems, issues of repatriation and ambiguities concerning the Department of Anthropology's relationship to the NMAI and other cultural units within the Smithsonian family have not been resolved.

In the meantime, the installation of a new IMAX theater in the West Court of the NMNH has presented a new and unexpected crisis. The entry for this new complex will pass through the Eskimo displays. Unless alternative spaces can be found, Holmes's "Happy Eskimos" and the accompanying Eskimo exhibit cases will be replaced by temporary displays that will be inadequate to represent the diversity of Eskimo cultures in North America.

Today the anthropological exhibits at the National Museum of Natural History face an uncertain future. Pressures to consolidate and reduce the numbers of cultures represented, to incorporate archaeological materials, to illustrate environments and modern social and cultural adaptations all create challenges that cannot be resolved under current conditions of space, funds, and organization. Funding difficulties and a long rotational cycle needed to change permanent exhibits (generally forty to fifty years) pose significant hurdles in today's rapidly shifting world of cultural representation. Many believe that these problems are irreconcilable without new structure and new facilities, that the National Museum of Natural History is too large to function effectively as a single unit; that its dominant biological focus cannot accommodate the growth, complexity, and public interest in museum anthropology; that—simply put—after 130 years, new organization and new space are needed.

Fundamentally, the intellectual context for anthropology today is not environmental. As Boas understood a century ago, cultures are inherently social and historical constructs that are influenced, however strongly, by biology and environment. But more important, the native cultures that are presented in the NMNH are alive and well and are experiencing a rebirth of interest in all aspects of culture, past and present. They do not see their cultures as appendages of natural history any more than American immigrants from Europe, Africa, or Asia see theirs in this context. Many nations have recognized the need to present history, culture, and art in appropriate settings. As we approach a new millennium and a 150th birthday, the Smithsonian should look again at the oft-revisited subject of a Museum of Culture. The resources for such a museum are scattered about the Institution in nooks and crannies where they are not able to do justice either to their specialties or to serve a greater purpose of cross-cultural understanding of human societies in their richness and complexity.

History and circumstance have taken us a long way from the Smith Sound Eskimos. Nevertheless, they are symbolic of the larger picture, of the need to integrate past and present and to share Smithsonian resources with the broadest possible audience. Our past is before us. Together with the modern representatives of these cultures, we must find ways to keep the history, interrelationships, and diversity of cultural traditions alive and prominently exhibited to the nation and to the world. Cultures are not dying; they are changing. Anthropology is not dead; rather, its collections and resources are in greater demand than ever before as Native students become anthropologists themselves to better tap the roots of their history and tradition. We should ensure that our ambassadors in sealskins and their modern descendants remain with us and before the public into the distant future. No less should be said of the many other cultures of the Americas and the rest of the world.

NOTES

1. I would like to thank Jo-Allyn Archambault, John C. Ewers, Adrienne Kaeppler, Stephen Loring, William Merrill, and William C. Sturtevant for comments on an early draft of this paper; Amy Henderson and Adrienne Kaeppler for persistent and successful editorial prodding; and Paula Fleming and Jane Walsh for assistance in locating photographic materials and archival sources. I especially thank Sven Haakanson for his "fieldwork" in the NMNH exhibits and resulting texts.

2. There is no universally accepted term to designate all the peoples of the North American Arctic. In this essay the term *Eskimo* is used as a general label for the group of cultures more properly identified today as Alutiiq, Yupik, Inupiat in Alaska, Inuit in Canada, and Inuit, Kalaadlit, or Greenlander in Greenland. Although *Eskimo* is no longer used to describe individual arctic cultures, it continues to be used as a collective term, especially in historical contexts. See Ives Goddard, "Synonymy," in *Handbook of American Indians,* Arctic volume (Washington, D.C.: Smithsonian Institution, 1984), pp. 5–7.

3. Ann Fienup-Riordan, *Freeze Frame: Alaska Eskimos in the Movies* (Seattle: University of Washington Press, 1995).

4. William C. Sturtevant and David Quinn, "This New Prey: Eskimos in Europe in 1567, 1576, and 1577," in *Indians and Europe: an Interdisciplinary Collection of Essays,* ed. Christian Feest (Aachen: Rader Verlag), pp. 61–140; Neil Cheshire, Tony Waldron, Alison Quinn, and David Quinn, "Frobisher's Eskimos in England," *Archivaria* 10 (1980): 23–50.

5. A (probable) Labrador Inuit woman and child, kidnapped by French sailors, were brought to France in 1566, but little knowledge of them remains other than sketchy

details and an illustration from a handbill publication. See William C. Sturtevant, "The First Inuit Depiction by Europeans," *Etudes/Inuit/Studies* 4, nos. 1–2 (1980): 47–49.

6. Tette Hofstra and Kees Samplonius, "Viking Expansion Northwards: Mediaeval Sources," *Arctic* 48, no. 3 (1995): 235–47.

7. Prime figures in this drama of nineteenth- and early-twentieth-century Eastern Arctic exploration include Ross, Parry, Lyon, Franklin, Hall, Kane, Peary, Cook, and Stefansson. Arctic exploration was not exclusively an English and American concern; other European powers, even the Spanish and the Italians, caught "arctic fever." See L. H. Neatby, "Exploration and History of the Canadian Arctic," *Handbook of North American Indians,* Arctic volume (Washington, D.C.: Smithsonian Institution, 1985), pp. 377–90; Beau Riffenburgh, *The Myth of the Explorer* (Oxford and New York: Oxford University Press, 1994).

8. The groups presented included: North Greenland (Cape York/Smith Sound) Eskimos; Eastern Eskimos; Alaskan Eskimos; Chilkat Indians, Alaska; Hupa Indians, California; Sioux Indians, the Great Plains; Navajo Indians, the Southwest; Cocopa Indians, Sonora, Mexico; Maya-Quiche Indians, Guatemala; Zapotec Indian woman, Oaxaca, Mexico; Jivaro Indian man, Brazil; Piro Indian man, Brazil; Tehuelche Indians, Patagonia. Of these, the Eastern and Alaskan Eskimos, and the Zapotec, Kivaro, and Piro Indians were not completed as family groups in time for the Buffalo Exposition and were displayed as groups of individual lay-figures.

9. *Washington Post,* March 2, 1902.

10. Renovation and reinstallation of this exhibit, which is scheduled to take place in 1996 or 1997, will give us our first chance to inspect these materials directly since the early 1950s; we hope then to find clues to their origin.

11. *Washington Post,* March 2, 1902.

12. William Henry Holmes, in True, Holmes, and Merrill, *Annual Report of the United States National Museum* (1903), p. 200. Hereafter cited as *AR-USNM.*

13. The term *lay-figure* came to be used in reference to "stand-in" figures for the live displays that had been featured in many early expositions.

14. *AR-USNM* 1920, p. 613.

15. Anthropologists at the USNM were influenced by their biological colleagues in the natural sciences to "define" races by typified physical features. For museum biologists, identification of a single individual whose features best represented "the type specimen" was a standard practice in classification method of the day. "Types" were the standard unit of description and comparison and were applied to humans, artifacts, and cultures in the museum much as they were applied to species, landforms, and minerals. "Types" were visually identified in the ethnology collections with small green tags. The concept seems ludicrous today, but it represented early attempts to apply "scientific" methods to anthropological materials.

16. *AR-USNM* 1901, p. 201.

17. The *Annual Report* for 1895 reports: "These [four Japanese mannikins given to the Smithsonian in 1875] were exceedingly spirited and effective, and when examined in detail showed such conscientious workmanship and such thorough fidelity to nature that they have served as an inspiration and a model for our workmen up to this day. Two of these figures, representing an actor and an actress in the costume of Japanese nobility, were carved in wood, and seem to show the extreme limits of this material in

the construction of the human model. The other two, a laborer and his wife (pl. 42), are in papier-maché and are satisfactory in the highest degree. The material is brought to an extreme of hardness, strength, and delicacy of line which no American workman has been able to rival" (p. 53). The two actor figures are still on exhibit in the NMNH Asian Ethnology Hall.

18. *AR-USNM* 1895, p. 53.

19. John C. Ewers, "A Century of American Indian Exhibits in the Smithsonian Institution," *AR* 1958 (Washington, D.C: Smithsonian Institution, 1959), p. 519.

20. *AR-USNM* 1920, p. 613.

21. Ibid.

22. *AR-USNM* 1895, p. 54.

23. *AR-USNM* 1893, p. 55–56.

24. Sturtevant and Quinn, "This New Prey"; Cheshire et al., "Frobisher's Eskimos in England."

25. W. G. Gosling, *Labrador: Its Discovery, Exploration, and Development* (New York: John Lane Company, 1910), p. 312.

26. The personal tale of a young Inuk's survival of the Chicago ordeal and later death is told in *Pomiuk: A Waif of Labrador* (1903).

27. W. H. Holmes, in *AR-USNM* 1903, p. 201.

28. Ellis L. Yochelson, *The National Museum of Natural History: 75 Years in the Natural History Building* (Washington: Smithsonian Institution Press, 1985).

29. *Buffalo Express,* August 1901.

30. Du Puy, 1913.

31. *AR-USNM* 1875, p. 70.

32. For a history of the "New" Natural History Museum (National Museum of Natural History), see Yochelson, *The National Museum of Natural History.*

33. Edward W. Nelson, *Eskimos about Bering Strait,* Bureau of American Ethnology, Annual Report 18 (Washington: Smithsonian Institution, 1899); William W. Fitzhugh and Susan A. Kaplan, eds., *Inua: Spirit World of the Bering Sea Eskimo* (Washington: Smithsonian Institution Press, 1982).

34. Selection of the words *northernmost known* may have been in reference to Peary's continued explorations of northernmost Greenland and Ellesmere, which might, until 1909, have found Inuit living even farther north.

35. Curtis M. Hinsley Jr., *Savages and Scientists: The Smithsonian Institution and the Development of American Anthropology, 1846–1910* (Washington: Smithsonian Institution Press, 1985), p. 108.

36. Ibid., p. 97.

37. The Pitt Rivers Museum displays were based on the archaeological "Three Age System" originally formulated by the Dane Thom. Thompson but substantially expanded in scope to include prehistoric, historic, and ethnological dimensions.

38. This was a condition more of the biological side of the museum than in anthropology, where types seemed to have infinite variation, and classification was unwieldy and unproductive. In addition, many of the Smithsonian's arctic collections remained undescribed because they had been collected by naturalists and biologists who had little, if any, anthropological training and who rarely prepared reports on them. As a result, the work of publication fell frequently to museum curators who were ignorant

of the crucial field data and tended to produce material culture treatises of limited theoretical value. These works did, however, perform an important service in gathering and publishing collection and specimen documentation that otherwise was not available.

39. In one of many such transactions, southwestern archaeological materials and Alaskan Eskimo materials collected by Nelson, Murdoch, Dall, and others were exchanged with the Danish National Museum for archaeological collections from West Greenland and a portion of the Gustav Holm Collection from the Angmassalik Eskimo of East Greenland.

40. Hinsley, *Savages and Scientists*, p. 98.

41. Thomas Kavanagh (ca. 1990) assembled a photographic inventory of Native American lay-figures and life-groups in Smithsonian exhibitions ("Brief History of the Manikins, Statues, Day-Figures, and Life-Groups Illustrating American Ethnology in the National Museum of Natural History"). While not researched or documented in detail, his report, held in the National Anthropological Archives, provides valuable information on this history. Susan Rowley also prepared an inventory of current the North American ethnology halls.

42. Beau Riffenburgh, *The Myth of the Explorer: The Press, Sensationalism, and Geographic Discovery* (London and New York: St. Martins Press, 1993).

43. United States North Polar Expedition, under command of Charles Francis Hall of the *Polaris*. See Chauncey Loomis's profile "Ebierbing," *Arctic* 39, no. 2 (1989): 186–87.

44. Identification of subjects and specimens on exhibit or seen in photographs of early figures and life-groups is difficult because catalog numbers were not recorded. In fact, the earliest mannikins show little concern with accurate cultural or racial representation. Lacking life casts, curators treated mannikins as mounts for garments rather than as depictions of real people. Garments were frequently shifted from one mannikin to another, and absence of full costumes in the collections necessitated piecing costumes together from various collections and locations, often with bizarre results, e.g., Norton Sound Eskimos wearing Greenlandic boots (Figure 10.4).

Kennicott's collections include Dene and Inuvialuit materials from British North America and the Yukon Territory collected in 1858–67 in one of the first systematic ethnology and biological collecting ventures in the Americas. Stimulated by Kennicott and Baird, several Hudson's Bay Company factors, including Bernard Ross, Roderick MacFarlane, and others, also collected for the USNM during this period. See Henry B. Collins, "Wilderness Exploration and Alaska's Purchase," *The Living Wilderness*, December 1946; Debra Lindsay, *Science in the Subarctic: Trappers, Traders, and the Smithsonian Institution* (Washington: Smithsonian Institution Press, 1993).

45. The discrepancy of dates for Joe and Hannah needs researching. It seems to result from replacement of the early wax figures by new figures in 1873. The Joe and Hannah figures seen with Kane in Figure 10.5 (copy neg. 51-82-11680) appear to be the same as those in the early Western Arctic lay-figure group (neg. 8360; Figure 10.6). Researching this history is confounded by lack of records, questionable and unsigned attributions on archival photographs, mannikin swapping, and errors in published *AR-USNM* descriptions.

46. *AR-USNM*, p. 52.

47. The Anderson River figures wear garments from the Smithsonian's Kennicott-

Baird project that produced its first arctic accessions, collected by R. MacFarlane in 1861–67. The bedraggled fur suggests that the garments had come recently from storage without conservation.

48. Photo source: True, Holmes, and Merrill, *AR-USNM* 1922, plate 25.

49. *AR-USNM* 1920, plate 6, p. 616.

50. True, Holmes, and Merrill, *AR-USNM* 1903, p. 203.

51. Ewers, "A Century of American Indian Exhibits," *AR-USNM* 1958 (Washington: Smithsonian Institution), pp. 520–21. See also William H. Holmes, "The World's Fair Congress of Anthropology," *American Anthropologist* 6 (October 1893): 423–34 (reprint; Washington: Judd and Detweiler, 1893).

52. Chang-su Houchins, "Artifacts of Diplomacy: Smithsonian Collections from Commodore Matthew Perry's Japan Expedition (1853–54)," Contributions to Anthropology (Washington: Smithsonian Institution, 1995), p. 37.

53. Horatio Hale, *United States Exploring Expedition, during the Years 1838–1842. Ethnography and Philology* (Philadelphia: S. Sherman, 1846); Herman J. Viola and Carolyn Margolis, eds., *Magnificent Voyagers: The U.S. Exploring Expedition, 1838–1842* (Washington: Smithsonian Institution Press, 1985).

54. Debra Lindsay, *Science in the Subarctic: Trappers, Traders, and the Smithsonian Institution* (Washington: Smithsonian Institution Press. 1993).

55. William W. Fitzhugh and Ruth O. Selig, "The Smithsonian's Alaska Connection," in *Alaska Journal: A 1981 Centennial Collection*, ed. Virginia McKinley (Juneau: Alaska Northwest Publishing Company, 1981), pp. 193–208.

56. See n. 37 above.

57. See Henry B. Collins et al., *The Far North: 2000 Years of American Eskimo and Indian Art.* "The Far North" was organized by the Amon Carter Museum and was assembled and curated by C. Douglas Lewis of the National Gallery. I had opportunity to experience the preparation of this exhibit by association with this project as a "lender" to the show and as an associate of Lewis.

58. Fitzhugh and Kaplan, *Inua.*

59. William W. Fitzhugh and Aron Crowell, *Crossroads of Continents: Cultures of Siberia and Alaska* (Washington: Smithsonian Institution Press, 1988); William W. Fitzhugh and Valerie Chaussonnet, eds., *Anthropology of the North Pacific Rim* (Washington: Smithsonian Institution Press, 1994).

11

Curators as Agents of Change
An Insect Zoo for the Nineties

SALLY LOVE

Biodiversity conservation is the premier environmental issue of our time
because it is so massive in scope, accelerating, potentially damaging,
and irreversible.

—E. O. Wilson

Do natural science museum exhibits reflect people's changing attitudes toward
nature? Can they influence them? They may have in the late nineteenth century,
when the massive growth of cities and towns increasingly swallowed open land
and wildlife. Museums had collected and preserved biota and made nature available to town populations by developing exhibition techniques that kept people
in touch with the world that lay outside the city limits. These museums presented a "fragmented and exotic natural world, stuffed and mounted to show
nature's curiosities and people's domination over them."[1] Today, as we learn
more about biodiversity and global health, we face a new set of challenges, one
that calls for a change in the way we exhibit the natural world. These developments are reflected in the evolution of the Insect Zoo, where there has been a
decided shift away from the depiction of insects and their relatives as curiosities
of nature to their use as tools to teach the interconnectedness of organisms and
the natural world.

The museum's exhibits are direct by-products of its research, and the focus of that research has changed in the last hundred years. The critical research mission of the National Museum of Natural History—to discover, name, and classify the biological, geological, and human world—is being increasingly augmented by explorations into the evolutionary processes and patterns responsible for the diversity of life. NMNH's researchers will always be concerned with surveying biodiversity, but the way that information is used becomes crucial as we learn how species extinctions dismantle ecosystems. The study of biodiversity, unlike the rest of science, has a time limit, particularly when one considers that 99 percent of all the species that ever lived are now extinct.[2] Our exhibits should reflect this. Public education is vital to conservation—the better biodiversity and its processes are known, the less likely that it will be destroyed.[3]

THE PAST EDUCATIONAL ROLE OF TAXIDERMY IN NATURAL HISTORY MUSEUMS

The increasing quality of exhibit interpretation parallels the development of new taxidermy techniques in the late nineteenth century. Earlier in that century, government-sponsored museums such as the British Museum of Natural History and NMNH (then known as the National Museum), which were primarily interested in the collection of scientific data, maintained what they saw as purely scholarly exhibits with animals statically arranged in rows according to their classification. Curators preferred bird skins and wired skeletons to animal groups and cared little for exhibits that would appeal to the public.[4] "Spread-eagle styles of mounting, artificial rocks and flowers, etc, are entirely out of place in a collection of any scientific pretensions. Birds look best, on the whole, in uniform rows, assorted according to size, as far as classification allows."[5] A few nineteenth-century natural history museums, however, used taxidermy to animate a frozen natural moment, creating dramatic animal displays to entertain the general public. Many times, these displays had more in common with theater than with reality.

In the mid-nineteenth century, as more natural history museums began to experiment with theatrical taxidermy, museum attendance rose. Visitors were enticed by the opportunity to view exotic animals in dramatic settings. The emphasis on theatrics began to change in 1869 when the American Museum of Natural History, wanting to develop exhibits that explained nature more effectively, purchased a reality-based taxonomic group. The National Museum wasn't far behind, with the purchase in 1883 of William T. Hornaday's "Battle in the

Fig. 11.1. An early National Museum exhibit, ca. 1880s.

Treetops," depicting two male orangutans in territorial conflict and produced by Hornaday for Ward's taxidermy establishment. Ward's was training its preparators in the importance of "fidelity to nature" as opposed to theatricality.[6]

Increasing environmental awareness among scientists soon called for updating the taxonomic group method to expand its educational function. Habitat groups resulted, within which were the plants and animals that belonged together, as well as painted backgrounds to depict the interaction between wildlife and habitat. The synthesis of art and science in these habitat groups helped to illustrate basic ecological principles.[7]

The concept of using habitat groups to give people something comparable to an outdoor experience was espoused by Harvard zoologist and naturalist Louis Agassiz, who wanted to popularize the study of nature. George Brown Goode, Agassiz's former student and director of the National Museum (1878–96), saw several different functions for a natural history museum: to record, to research, and to educate. He created two sets of collections—one for research and the other for public education and exhibition.[8] Goode had come to the Smithsonian in 1873 as an ichthyologist and became the protégé of then Assistant Secretary

Fig. 11.2. The Insects Exhibit, ca. 1880s.

Fig. 11.3. W. T. Hornaday's taxidermy lab, 1880s.

Fig. 11.4. Hornaday's American Buffalo group, completed in 1888, was the second habitat group to be produced in the United States. Hornaday's emphasis was not so much on conveying scientific information as on evoking an emotional response in the viewer to recognize the need for wildlife protection.

Spencer F. Baird, himself a strong natural history advocate and prodigious collector. When Baird became secretary in 1878, he appointed Goode as assistant secretary, in charge of the National Museum. Goode quickly became a "museum man" and was soon widely regarded as a leading specialist in museum administration and in exhibit preparation, which he developed as a field unto itself.[9]

Realizing the educational value of exhibit taxidermy, Goode created the position of chief of exhibits, the first official recognition of exhibition design within the museum.[10] Museum taxidermist Hornaday was one of the finest in his field and can be credited with helping to establish the National Zoo and with being the among the first in the United States to develop the concept of placing specimens in their natural settings. A turning point for exhibits at the museum was Hornaday's "American Bison Group" exhibit, created after he returned from a collecting trip to Montana with enough material to fashion a realistic environment: "The group, with all its accessories, had been prepared so as to tell . . . the general visitor . . . the story of the buffalo, but care has been taken to secure an accuracy of detail that will satisfy the critical scrutiny of the most technical naturalist."[11]

Fig. 11.5. Habitat group exhibit of mountain sheep.

By the turn of the century, the natural world was declining rapidly. Attempting to raise public awareness by demonstrating what was at stake, the museum created pristine habitats in its exhibit halls. The impact of those exhibits on the public's attitudes cannot be accurately measured, but they "reflected the desire of the layman and scientist alike to accept nature whole. . . . Conservation was taking the place of use [of the environment] as the ultimate motive."[12] Habitat group exhibits and the sentiments they represented did have a measurable effect on Congress, however, by successfully contributing to legislative reform for wildlife protection. When the Migratory Bird Treaty Act (1918) was being considered, Hornaday sent each member of Congress a copy of his book *Our Vanishing Wildlife,* which, along with a strong anti–sport hunting appeal, contained evocative images of his habitat groups.[13]

In the 1920s, Rochester Museum director Arthur Parker was part of a museum movement to view exhibits as ideas illustrated by dioramas, models, lifegroups, or an orderly, systematic arrangement of objects. This was a step toward using exhibition techniques to teach scientific concepts, but education was still "viewed as a passive endeavor: the visitor was expected to have an educational experience merely by standing in front of an object and absorbing its meaning through some magical process of osmosis."[14] There was room for improvement.

BEYOND HABITAT GROUPS: BIOLOGICAL DIVERSITY EXHIBITS

The exhibits at NMNH in the 1990s are on the brink of a philosophical shift as scientific and ecological illiteracy has reached dangerous levels. Natural history museums have the scholarly resources, and as they have grown and matured, so has their role as institutions of public learning. The public has come to expect museums not only to preserve and display objects but also to provide their context in the natural world. Exhibits that once illustrated taxonomic relationships and the components of habitats are giving way to ones that explain the history and diversity of life. Among the central concepts of new exhibits will be the evolutionary patterns and processes that have created past and present biodiversity, what we understand about evolutionary relationships, how we know about the natural world, and the environmental context—the complex interconnections and interdependencies that characterize ecosystems.

But how does one effectively exhibit complex concepts? Many times, curators select objects and write the text explaining their importance to our understanding of the general phenomenon in question. They are developing the concept, while the visitor is allowed to absorb only the end product of the curator's learning. Some curators complain of visitors' ignorance, but one reason may be that they are excluded from the learning process.[15]

Museum educators now view visitor experience, rather than instruction, as fundamental to the type of informal learning that lends itself to museums. This new paradigm shifts the focus of the educational message from the object to the audience. The object becomes a means of extracting visitor response. Their experience is shaped by a sense of wonder, the unexpected connection, the "oh, wow" reaction.[16]

Visitors vary in age, education, interests, and motivations. How do we create experiences for all of them that will provoke curiosity, understanding, awe, or fun? Extensive research has gone into understanding different learning styles and designing exhibits that can reach the widest audience. The development of the Insect Zoo is an example of a successful and fun learning experience, one that uses powerful tools—living, breathing arthropods—as agents to change people's concepts of organisms, ecosystems, and conservation.

THE INSECT ZOO: AN NMNH INNOVATION

The first Insect Zoo opened as a temporary summer exhibit in the early 1970s and heightened visitor experience by using live arthropods—insects, spiders, scorpions, centipedes, and millipedes—to illustrate biological principles, along with interpreters to answer questions and give informal demonstrations. While fairly commonplace in zoos, teaching with live animals was not standard practice in museums at that time. Additional staff were needed to care for living organisms and to interpret them effectively through the daily hands-on demonstrations. People interested in working with insects and the public were recruited as Insect Zoo volunteers, and for many visitors, the volunteers were the only contact they had with museum staff. Hand-printed signs were written by science educators and could be changed easily if a more effective way to communicate were found. Visitors come to museums to see unique objects, and the Insect Zoo afforded them the novel opportunity to get close to an unfamiliar group of animals in a safe environment. It also gave them the chance to touch some things—a giant cockroach, for instance—that they would never have considered touching in an unmediated setting. By taking these small steps, the visitors' fear and loathing of the unknown turned to fascination, and their museum experience became memorable. They found the exhibit engaging and were so motivated to return that the museum opened the permanent hall in 1976.

Insects proved to be effective educators. Though vastly misunderstood, they have captured people's imaginations for centuries. It is difficult to be indifferent to creatures so unlike ourselves that affect such a large part of our lives. The Insect Zoo capitalized on people's fear of arthropods and used bugs as "hooks" on which to layer basic biological information. It worked. Teaching the physical characteristics of an insect is much easier when the learner is holding and touching a live grasshopper. Predator/prey relationships came alive with the daily tarantula feedings. The value of not being seen and some insects' intriguing defenses against being eaten were illustrated not with text but with real-life examples. Suddenly, the unknown was less frightening. Teachers, also, were discovering the intrinsic educational value of insects, and they worked with Insect Zoo staff to incorporate insects into their curricula. After a school trip to the museum, students often returned—many times with parents and siblings in tow. Some of those young students later became Insect Zoo volunteers, citing their class trip as inspiration for learning more. Yearly attendance soon climbed toward the one million mark.

After fifteen years, the exhibit became a victim of its own success. With many more visitors than it had been designed to handle, it looked worn and out-of-date. New exhibits were opening around the country that took advantage of the Insect Zoo's years of experience and improved on its mistakes. New methods for exhibiting live arthropods were being developed elsewhere, as well as new exhibit technologies in general.

The awareness that the Insect Zoo was lagging behind in this proved educational opportunity coincided with the museum's desire to exhibit organisms as integrated within their habitats.

> The urgency of environmental issues and the ways these issues interact directly with our on-going research requires that we interpret these troubling, politically sensitive, even controversial, issues for our public. These engaged exhibits and public programs will be known for their effective integration of accurate, objective, current scientific research and judgments with environmental educational leadership. Special emphasis will be placed on exhibits that explore the complex interconnections and interdependencies that characterize ecosystems and the impact and consequences of human activity on those ecosystems. . . . The new rhythm of the Museum's programs will strike a balance between an interest in the object itself and an interest in its functional relationship within dynamic living systems.[17]

As the museum's role in general has moved from displaying isolated specimens, we sought to do the same with the Insect Zoo. The old exhibit displayed insects as "bugs in boxes"; a new exhibit would reveal insects as an integral part of the biosphere and play a role in increasing people's awareness about elements that maintain the integrity of our natural world.

A NEW INSECT ZOO: THE NINETIES AND BEYOND

In developing a new Insect Zoo that would effectively address the present and future scientific needs of our audience, we relied on current theories on learning in informal educational settings. Our goal was to create lasting memories for a diverse audience. The learning model we chose was Bernice McCarthy's 4MAT System, based on a system developed by David Kolb of the Massachusetts Institute of Technology. Essentially, the 4MAT System recognizes that there are individual differences in learning and identifies four ways in which people process information: (1) concrete experience (feeling); (2) reflective observation (watching); (3) abstract conceptualization (thinking); and (4) active experimentation (doing). Schools tend to reach those who excel in style 2, for they "respond best to the traditional teaching strategy of lecturing."[18] Museum exhibits can accommodate all four types of learners: (1) the diverger, who integrates experience and answers the question "Why?" (2) the assimilator, who formulates concepts and answers the question "What?" (3) the converger, who practices and personalizes and answers the question "How does this work?" and (4) the accommodator, who integrates application and experience and answers the question "What can this become?"[19] The Insect Zoo as a learning environment offers visitors rich, multisensory experiences in which the presentation of ideas through novel specimens is a powerful tool in facilitating understanding of the world and their place in it.

Visitors must be motivated and engaged if they are to learn and want to return. Motivation and interaction are the basic elements of effective education in all settings.[20] But how does one motivate visitors to interact? Fun is an important part of the experience. If learning isn't enjoyable, most visitors will leave. Holding their attention is the responsibility of the writers, curators, and designers, who must work in concert to create an exhibit in which the enjoyment of exploration and social interaction depends on learning something from the exhibit.

For the design of the new exhibit, we drew upon our previous seventeen years of experience with our audience. We knew that visitors arrived with varying expectations. Some move through quickly, seeing as much as possible, while others wander until they see something that interests them. But they had many agendas in common: All were seeking novelty; most came in social groups—whether on a school trip, with family, or with friends; and they responded positively to living organisms, particularly those that invited sensory involvement. Text and two-dimensional displays were less successful. The challenge for us was to design an area that would both incorporate the successful elements of the old exhibit and put into practice our museum's philosophy, new exhibiting technology, and better science, in order to create more effective learning experiences.

Because we decided not to limit the number of visitors to the Insect Zoo, we had to design an interactive space that would withstand the punishment of its million or more annual visitors. It also had to be self-explanatory if a docent was unavailable for personal attention. We designed displays that offered several levels of interaction, as well as representative habitats. The O. Orkin Insect Zoo opened in September 1994.

Each major subject area in the exhibit reinforces the unifying theme of the Insect Zoo, "Designed for Survival." At the entrance, visitors are immediately introduced to the enormous diversity of arthropods, using a multitude of specimens from the National Museum's collections. Each subsequent display guides visitors through the mechanics of that diversity. "Explorations through Evolution, Adaptation, and Defenses" relates the arthropods' success in terms of how well they have solved the "problems" they confront in a sometimes hostile world. The story is completed in the final section, "Habitats," where visitors examine: (1) how those adaptations have been shaped by the driving forces of time and a wide variety of environments and (2) the roles arthropods play in the maintenance of their habitats.

The strengths of the old and new Insect Zoos lie in the appeal of watching living arthropods and the availability of volunteers to answer questions. But some arthropods remain inactive much of the time. To supplement this lack of activity and to better illustrate certain points, we integrated live animals with preserved specimens, models, and movable parts. Videos show sequences such as metamorphosis and certain defensive adaptations. The former two-dimensional panels are now in 3-D that invites touching. The text is more interactive and playful and relates to human experience whenever possible in order to personalize the information.

The Zoo has accomplished its goals if the visitor no longer sees insects and their relatives as the enemy but can view them as an incredibly diverse group of animals, making their livings in wonderful and varied ways, each in response to the challenges of its environment over millions of years. Our story is about the fit between habitat and organism.

Although it was clear that a new insect exhibit was needed, funds for such a large overhaul were not forthcoming. In the past, our exhibits were supported through government funds; now that those funds are scarce, we are seeking money from the private sector in order to accomplish our exhibit goals. Finding the right fit of donor to project is a creative endeavor, and the Insect Zoo was no exception. Normally, when looking to fund individual projects, we apply certain criteria to the businesses that are targeted; among those criteria are (1) they must have an interest in the subject matter and (2) they should be financially healthy. If the subject matter is insects, the field is narrowed down to the producers of chemical pesticides and the larger businesses that provide pest control services. We were fortunate to find a partner in Orkin Pest Control, whose participation made the exhibit possible. Orkin remained a silent and cooperative donor throughout the exhibit's development, and we retained complete control of its content and look. Financial support from outside donors does come with some strings attached, however, and corporations and individuals who fund museums expect their gifts to be visible to the public in some way. In return for the Orkin donation, the Insect Zoo was named for its founder, Otto Orkin. The company has made public education about beneficial and harmful insects a priority, and the Insect Zoo gives these efforts enormous exposure.

The Exhibit

Insects won't inherit the earth; they own it now.[21]

Among the million and more species of animal life on earth, the small insects and their relatives in the arthropod group are the most far-flung of all. There are more insects in more places all over the planet than any other living creatures.

Visitors to the O. Orkin Insect Zoo can explore the history and diversity of life in natural and human-influenced environments and learn about the evolutionary processes that created this rich biodiversity. The complex interconnections and interdependencies that characterize these environments are woven throughout. Here is a snapshot of the exhibit:

The entrance to the Zoo is a floor-to-ceiling mural of an arthropod's-eye view of the world in which insects and their relatives live. The scene is typical of an overgrown corner of a backyard, vacant lot, or park in the Washington, D.C., metropolitan area. Insect sounds fill the air. Sound was as much as consideration as the other exhibit elements, and a sophisticated sound track was designed specifically for the space.

Adaptations and Defenses

Insects and other arthropods could be called the most refined creatures in the natural world—or quick-change artists. Thanks to short breeding cycles, the most successful of them reproduce quickly and in great numbers, creating new generations that come into the world as well adapted as possible.

Surrounded by birds and other enemies, insects need many defensive weapons to protect themselves. How has the evolutionary process of natural selection influenced insect appearance and behavior? The exhibit shows how some insects communicate the message "We are not here" by near-perfect camouflage with their surroundings or by their resemblance to inedible objects. An interactive push-button display illustrates just how cryptic insects can be.

"Spiders as Stalkers" looks at the mightiest hunters of the arthropod clan. With or without their famous webs, their methods succeed against other insects that have a great advantage over the wingless spiders—flight.

Hives, Hills, and Nests: The Insect Societies

Although insects are among the most streamlined and well-engineered animals, their small size has led some species—termites, ants, and many wasps and bees—to band together in highly organized groups to share housing, care of young, work, food, and protection. This section displays desert-dwelling honeypot ants, Costa Rican acacia ants, and termites.

Gifts of Silk, Honey, and More

Insects offer an array of benefits. This section shows some of these "gifts," such as honey, silk, and dyes; the services that insects provide, such as pollination, decomposition, and food production (even for humans); and the roles insects can play in science and medicine. The Insect Zoo designed an activity that invites people to match an insect with its beneficial service or product.

Observation Beehive

We created a tree that houses a live beehive. A clear plastic tube is their route to the outdoor pollen and nectar sources. Visitors can watch the bees working in the hive and leaving the building in search of pollen and nectar. Like ants and termites, honeybees are social insects that rely on a division of labor to allow the hive to survive and grow.

Entomologists at Work

What do entomologists do? Most people don't know what it means to be an entomologist. A great deal of research on arthropods is conducted behind the scenes at NMNH. Entomologists collect insects, identify new species, and investigate their evolutionary relationships and their relationships with the rest of the natural world by collecting data in the field and studying one of the world's largest insect collections. In an effort to bring our science out to the public, a changing exhibit highlights individual Smithsonian entomologists and their research.

People are curious about what they can't see. Closed doors and solid walls seem to hide secrets about how exhibits and museums work. We have brought the back room of the zoo to the public through an observation window that provides a glimpse into the behind-the-scenes operation of the zoo.

How Dangerous Are They?

Although most insects and other arthropods are harmless, we can't ignore those who have had a negative impact on humans. Some are deadly, while others are simply annoying. To balance the exhibit, we have a section on the dangerous ones. Mosquitoes, fleas, and ticks are just some of the arthropods that can transmit diseases from one human to another. The bubonic plague was the worst disease epidemic in human history. The plague is spread from rats to humans via the Oriental rat flea. Lyme disease and Rocky Mountain spotted fever are carried by the deer tick and the dog tick, respectively.

At Home Everywhere

Insects and their relatives live almost everywhere on earth, from snow fields to the open ocean. Thanks to short breeding cycles and genetic flexibilities that allow them to modify features such as size, shape, and behavior, insects can adapt easily to constantly changing environments. The Insect Zoo re-creates five contrasting habitats—freshwater pond, mangrove swamp, desert, rain forest, and house—to show how insects have adjusted to different surroundings.

Our House, Their House

Of the five habitats, the most unexpected—and the one closest to home—is a house. Teaching the concepts of a habitat and its components is easier when it is easily recognizable as integral to everyday life. The house's walls, doors, and cabinets are opened to expose the permeability of its barriers and the ways in which we have unwittingly provided insects with ample opportunity to thrive and survive.

Rain Forests

Most Smithsonian scientists who study tropical biology do so in the tropical forests of Central and South America—the neotropics. Old World tropics stretch from Africa to Australia. The rain forest in our exhibit highlights plants and animals found in neotropical rain forests.

Rain forests cover just 7 percent of the earth's surface and contain almost half of all species of living things. Africa, Asia, Australia, Central and South America house these shrinking and biologically rich areas. We are losing rain forests at a tremendous rate each year. Figures of annual loss of rain forest areas equal in size to the state of Pennsylvania have been cited.

The diversity of life reaches its zenith in the canopy of the rain forest, where Smithsonian scientists estimate that there could be up to 30 million species of insects throughout the world. They are bursting with life. The riddle for rain forest plants and animals is how to share limited time and space and food.

The value of natural history museums is twofold: the acquisition of scientific knowledge and the dissemination of public information. Our goal as exhibit developers is to translate and transform a rich body of biological research into exhibits and public programs that will increase our visitors' awareness of the world around them and to teach them how to ask important questions about it. Our final products are not exhibits or programs but people—"transformed and enlivened, who leave us different than when they arrived; whose attitudes, beliefs, feelings and knowledge of the natural world and their place in it have been positively altered."[22] Our first step toward that goal is to design memorable experiences that utilize the natural links that exist between curiosity and play.

In the book *The Museum Experience,* John Falk and Lynn Dierking describe the importance of "meaningful learning"—the linking of new information to existing concepts and principles in a learner's body of knowledge. The network of connections and relationships so formed provides the framework on which to layer new information and facilitate the application of this new knowledge to new situations and problems. In museums, meaningful learning comes to visitors through their active relationship with objects—such as holding a large, living grasshopper, through reading labels, or through interactions with friends and docents. In this way, new information and ideas can be incorporated into their existing body of knowledge.[23]

Museums are ideal settings for meaningful learning because they are so rich in opportunities for diverse and novel multisensory experiences. The presentation of ideas through tangible objects, such as insects, is a powerful device for sense-making and, thus, understanding.[24] We have the opportunity to be part of the educational effort to restore an environmental ethic; to do so, our message must be personal. The habitat groups of the turn of the century educated people about selected segments of wildlife. We now need to show that organisms are all the more remarkable in combination. By learning how the threads of nature's diversity are intricately interwoven in our lives, we can begin to understand the consequences of our actions and inactions and work toward the restoration of our biological wealth.[25]

NOTES

1. R. Sullivan, *The Unity of All Creation: A New Paradigm for the National Museum of Natural History* (Washington: Office of Public Programs, The National Museum of Natural History, 1990), p. 1.

2. E. O. Wilson, *The Diversity of Life* (Cambridge: Belknap Press of Harvard University Press, (1992).

3. Ibid.

4. Clyde Fisher, "Carl Akeley and His Work," *Scientific Monthly* 27, no. 2 (1927).

5. E. G. Hancock, "A Surviving Display from William Bullock's London Museum, 1807–1818," *Museums Journal* 79, no. 1 (1979): 172–75.

6. K. Wonders, "Exhibiting Fauna—From Spectacle to Habitat Group," *Curator* 32, no. 2 (1989): 131–56.

7. Ibid.

8. Ibid.

9. Ellis L. Yochelson, *The National Museum of Natural History: 75 Years in the Natural History Building* (Washington: Smithsonian Institution Press, 1985).

10. Ibid.

11. Ibid., p. 62.

12. L. V. Coleman, *The Museum in America: A Critical Study,* 3 vols. (Washington: American Association of Museums, 1939), p. 51.

13. Wonders, "Exhibiting Fauna."

14. C. P. Blackmon, T. K. LaMaster, L. C. Roberts, and B. Serrell, *Open Conversations: Strategies for Professional Development in Museums* (Chicago: Field Museum of Natural History, 1988), p. 39.

15. J. C. Belland and H. Searles, "Concept Learning in the Museum," *Curator* 29, no. 2 (1986): 85–92.

16. Blackmon et al., *Open Conversations.*

17. "Vision 2000." Internal Document for the National Museum of Natural History. (1995).

18. J. H. Falk and L. D. Dierking, *The Museum Experience* (Washington: Whalesback Books, 1992), p. 103.

19. B. McCarthy, *The 4MAT Workbook: Guided Practice in 4MAT Lesson and Unit Planning* (Chicago: Excel, 1980).

20. Falk and Dierking, *The Museum Experience.*

21. T. Eisner, personal conversation with author, 1992.

22. Sullivan, *The Unity of All Creation,* preface.

23. Falk and Dierking, *The Museum Experience.*

24. Ibid.

25. Wilson, *The Diversity of Life.*

12

And Now for Something Completely Different

Reconstructing Duke Ellington's *Beggar's Holiday* for
Presentation in a Museum Setting

DWIGHT BLOCKER BOWERS

What is a museum exhibition? To ensure legitimacy with both the academy and the public, must an exhibition always consist of an array of objects, images, and labels that are artfully arranged in carefully illuminated vitrines? What if the artifacts in question not only imply but *demand* levels of curatorial interpretation and modes of presentation that simply cannot be delivered by conventional methods of museum exhibitry? Visual displays alone of sheet music, holographic scores, and theatrical manuscripts have little resonance or meaning for the average observer, for, as lyricist-librettist Oscar Hammerstein II wrote, "a song is no song till you sing it."[1] Therefore, communicating to museum audiences the significance and dynamism of these artifacts of performing arts history places new demands on the curator, requiring an interpretive approach that combines the scholarly with the impresarial, resulting in a nontraditional, "living" exhibition that conveys for a museum public the greatest possible communicative immediacy for the artifacts that form its basis.

In 1990, as part of my charge to develop research-based performances as director of the Division of Museum Programs at the National Museum of American History, I embarked on such a challenge: to resurrect and reconstruct the score for Duke Ellington and John Latouche's innovative but all-but-forgotten 1946 Broadway musical, *Beggar's Holiday,* for presentation at the Smithsonian. The manuscript artifacts that served as its foundation were discovered in various states of assembly among multiple boxes and folders in the newly acquired Duke Ellington Collection, housed in the museum's Archives Center. The collection, purchased by the museum in 1987 through a special congressional appropriation,[2] consists of the composer's voluminous personal archives of scores, papers, photographs, posters, and recordings, which he maintained throughout his long career. The Ellington Collection has offered points of departure for a number of interpretive strategies for a variety of museum audiences;[3] however, this was the first attempt to use the collection to reassemble and reinterpret one of the composer's theatrical efforts.

Although Ellington's extraordinary contributions to American music are indisputable and legendary, his work as a theater composer remains a fascinating mystery, primarily because it is rarely, if ever, revived in its original contexts. Furthermore, this body of achievement is largely ignored by both jazz scholars, who display greater interest in his orchestral compositions, and theater historians, who generally judge the swift (if undeserved) commercial failures of his stage works as a reflection of their artistic merits.[4] In my adaptation of *Beggar's Holiday* for presentation as a "living" exhibition, my tandem aims were to reveal a significant but largely unknown aspect of Ellington's oeuvre and to reintroduce audiences to a neglected treasure of the American musical theater.

In his autobiography, *Music Is My Mistress,* Ellington recalled the genesis of *Beggar's Holiday* as "a great experience" resulting in "a gorgeous play"; however, he lamented the fact that, although "it enjoyed a tremendous *succès d'estime*" among the Broadway cognoscenti, "the public was not really ready" for its flawed but striking attributes.[5] Ellington and poet-playwright John Latouche freely adapted their work from John Gay's 1728 London ballad opera *The Beggar's Opera*. Considered by many to be a direct antecedent of modern musical theater, Gay's work also provided the source for a revered 1928 version by Bertolt Brecht and Kurt Weill known as *Die Dreigroschenoper (The Threepenny Opera)*. My own interest in *Beggar's Holiday* and its theatrical heritage began in 1979, two years before I joined the staff at the Smithsonian and during the period when I was a graduate student pursuing a master of arts degree in theater history at the University of Connecticut. Searching for academic arenas to explore my interest in the evolution of the twentieth-century commercial musical theater, I developed a research paper titled "Variations on a Theme: The *Beggar's Opera* in Three Keys." Combining production histories with critical textual analyses, I examined the three extant versions of *The Beggar's Opera* within the contexts of the eras that led to their respective creations, citing similarities and departures in construction and theatrical execution.

I had no problem at all in securing bountiful data on both the original by

Fig. 12.1. The Smithsonian's American Song Company performs the first-act finale from *Beggar's Holiday,* "Tomorrow Mountain."

John Gay and the Brecht-Weill redaction, but my pursuit of solid historical/ critical documentation for *Beggar's Holiday* proved maddeningly difficult. Of the secondary sources located, the most illuminating were Gerald Bordman's exhaustive chronicle, *American Musical Theatre,*[6] which yielded a paragraph-long description of the original Broadway production; Daniel Blum's 1946 *Theatre World Annual,* which contained reproductions of three photographs documenting the Broadway company during a performance; and autobiographies by various members of the original creative team.[7] In the Billy Rose Theatre Collection at New York Public Library at Lincoln Center, I studied a slim clipping file of publicity materials and journal reviews and pored over an incomplete draft of Latouche's script. My attempts to contact surviving cast members proved impossible to achieve in the time period I had in which to develop my findings into a monograph.

By assembling the fragments of my research, I was able to reconstruct a barebones outline of the show's troubled production history. In brief, I learned that the creation of *Beggar's Holiday* began in 1945 under the guidance of Perry Watkins, an African American scenic designer, and writer-turned-producer Dale Wasserman. Together, they commissioned Ellington and Latouche to transform John Gay's portrait of eighteenth-century London's demimonde of highwaymen and trollops into a jazz opera about gangsters and molls set in a modern, unnamed American cityscape. Aside from Ellington and Latouche, the original production boasted such esteemed personnel as director John House-man, choreographer Valerie Bettis, designer Oliver Smith, and star Alfred Drake, heading a cast as talented as it was culturally diverse. Houseman's auto-biography, *Front and Center*,[8] re-created the chaotic pre-Broadway tryout, in which creativity, convivialty, and, above all, cash were in exceedingly short sup-ply. A study of the critical reviews that followed the Broadway opening in 1946 suggested a fascinating work still in progress—an observation supported by study of Latouche's script, which consisted of a brilliant, diamond-hard first act fol-lowed by a less-than-scintillating second act that simply ended rather than con-cluded. In fact, according to some accounts, the show never had a final scene and relied upon its actors to improvise dialogue based on a rough scenario.

All the research materials that I had collected proved enlightening, if incom-plete. One integral component was missing in my study—Ellington's score, which was never published in its entirety and never recorded commercially by its original cast. All that I found at both the New York Public Library and the Library of Congress was sheet music for half a dozen of its songs and several recordings by various popular singers of the show's ballads. Neither the sheet music nor the recordings gave much indication of the original theatrical con-texts for the songs. The overall spareness of data about the work available at the time left the final third of my research paper with a rather weak coda and me with a commitment to pursue further research on *Beggar's Holiday.*

In 1983, shortly after I joined the staff of the Smithsonian's Division of Per-forming Arts as a researcher and annotator on various archival recording proj-ects, I made the acquaintance of a recording company executive who had in his private collection several acetate recordings of the *Beggar's Holiday* score, featur-ing Ellington at the piano and performed by, among others, original cast mem-ber Alfred Drake. He explained that these discs had been made before the Broadway production solely as a way to entice potential financial backers. Al-though his sense of legal propriety kept him from making a audiotape copy of the recording, he happily played it over and over for me one April afternoon, giving me the opportunity to discern the infinite variety and joyous audacity in-herent in the music and lyrics. Hearing these timeworn recordings only prompted even more my impulse to find a way to experience in its entirety the score of *Beggar's Holiday* and to reintroduce the work for a variety of scholarly and public audiences. At last, five years later, with the Smithsonian's acquisition of the Ellington archive, the opportunity materialized to locate the missing components that would complete my research and yield the basis for an unconventional museum exhibition.

Before digging through the rediscovered musical manuscripts in the Ellington Collection, I, with the help of my intern, Russell Lehrer (who remained a godsend throughout the process), compiled a list of sixty song-and/or-dance numbers composed for *Beggar's Holiday,* only twenty-five of which were used in the Broadway production. This list was culled from three sources: the songs included in Latouche's draft script at the New York Public Library, the songs identified in the "Compositions" addendum for *Music Is My Mistress,* and the musical numbers listed in the playbills for the 1946 Broadway production. Armed with this compilation, we set forth to locate as many pieces of music from the score as possible. Throughout, archivists Deborra Richardson and Reuben Jackson were enormously supportive of our efforts.

Since much the Ellington Collection had yet to be cataloged, the musical manuscripts were in various stages of (dis)order. After several disappointing searches through boxes of unsorted materials, I struck gold, finding yet another draft of Latouche's script (with fragments of unused or revamped lyrics in various stages of development). Immediately, I compared the song titles in this script and its addendum of untitled lyric fragments with the songs on the list we had compiled, adding several new titles to the roster. Shortly thereafter, in other boxes, I began to unearth, one by one, holograph scores for the show's songs. Some of these were expressed in the neat, angular hand of a professional music copyist and contained full sets of lyrics to match the musical notes. Others were far less tidy, yielding only hastily scribbled melodic lines devoid of lyrics and identifiable only by a title scrawled at the top of the first page.

I started the reconstruction process by assembling a stack of all the holograph scores bearing complete (or nearly complete) sets of lyrics. I photocopied them, returned the originals to the archivists, and arranged the photocopies alphabetically in individual folders. I compared the lyrics in these materials with songs bearing identical or similar titles in the museum copy of Latouche's script. Quite often, this script contained additional verses and reprises for the songs that mated perfectly with the notated music. These were duly transcribed and placed in the appropriate folders. Next, I collected all the titled and untitled fragments of music and lyrics, photocopied them, returned the originals, and placed my copies in folders. Referring constantly to my compiled list of song titles, I started the painstaking process of locating and matching the lyrics in Latouche's script and lyric fragments with the titles and musical notation in these incomplete manuscripts. Eventually, I was able to consolidate music and lyrics for approximately 75 percent of these materials.

In a situation somewhat similar to one that beset the original production, I simply could not locate a suitable musical conclusion for the score. I did not find "The Hunted," identified in the Broadway playbill as the final song in the score, among the archival materials. The piece was described in reviews by New York theater critics as a climactic soliloquy for Macheath, the show's protagonist. Reviewing a pile of other Ellington-Latouche songs that I had traced to the year, if not the score, of *Beggar's Holiday,* I discovered a roughly sketched holographic copy of a song called "Live for the Moment." Its propulsive melodic line and devil-may-care lyric made it a perfect substitution for the missing song. I quickly realized that a project such as this, by both nature and necessity, must serve more than one Muse. Therefore, in this instance, I shifted my loyalties from Clio to Calliope, Thalia, and Melpomene, thereby favoring musical and dramatic effectiveness over substantiated historical accuracy.

The next step was to assemble the manuscript materials into a usable piano-vocal score. I organized the titles in a way that corresponded, for the most part, to the order in which they appeared in both the script and the listings for the Broadway production. This yielded a roster of approximately thirty-five songs and/or sketches for ballet music. Then I engaged in a marathon session at the museum's Steinway grand, playing through all the materials and noting any gaps that occurred in the assembled music and lyrics. My excitement steadily grew as I moved from song to song, slowly surrendering to the intoxicating appeal of exquisite ballads ("When I Walk with You," "Maybe I Should Change My Ways"), rhythmic character songs ("I Got Me," "Tooth and Claw," "Take Love Easy"), moody atmospheric pieces ("In Between," "Lullaby for Junior," "Brown Penny"), and devilishly clever ensemble numbers (including the Gilbert and Sullivan–esque "Chorus of Citizens," which opens act 2). The artful, varied mélange of musical theater styles contained therein was matched only by Leonard Bernstein's brilliant score for his 1956 operetta *Candide* (which also had several lyrics authored by Latouche). Above all, this "audition" process convinced me that the songs for *Beggar's Holiday* were all that I had hoped that they would be—unfailingly melodic and eminently theatrical. A public presentation of the score was essential in adhering to the museum's goal of diffusing knowledge about the Ellington legacy. Fired by my immense enthusiasm for a project that had been long a-borning, I set about formulating a version of *Beggar's Holiday* for a series of performances at the museum in February 1992.

Devising the format to display my findings proved a crucial element in the research-to-performance method. Like the development of traditional exhibitions, the mode of presentation was determined by four simultaneous factors: the need to present a cogent interpretive focus, the selection of artifacts to illus-

trate the curatorial point of view, the limitations of physical space and production, and the location of funding sources. In conceptualizing its intellectual
framework, I had decided, almost from the beginning, that the presentation
would be founded on a musico-theatrical performance of the show's score
alone. This decision was influenced by certain realities. First of all, the acquisition of the Ellington archive gave us rights to only the score materials, not to
the Latouche script; even if we could secure the rights for its performance, the
demands of the original script could not possibly be accommodated in the museum's small, 285-seat Carmichael Auditorium. Furthermore, the show required
a newly created script that would function similarly to traditional exhibition labels, assimilating and interpreting the show's history and providing an intellectual framework for the selected illustrative artifacts.

The physical limitations of the museum's available performance space also influenced the shaping of presentation format and script. The tiny, postage
stamp–size stage, devoid of either wings or flyspace, made it impossible to
achieve multiple scene changes or house a cast anywhere near the size of the
original Broadway company of more than fifty performers. Given these constraints, I decided to design the performance as a vehicle for a cast of twelve performers. Four actors would be selected to sing and portray the principal roles:
gangster Macheath; his henchman, Careless Love; Macheath's love interest, Polly
Peachum; and sinister bordello keeper, Miss Jenny. The actor who would serve
as the program's narrator would also portray, in a hoped-for *coup de théâtre,* the
comic mobster Hamilton Peachum. The remaining roles would be handled by
an ensemble of eight, who would also double as the chorus. Determining
the size and function of my cast allowed me to set about the construction of the
script. The concept for the script that I wrote set up the illusion that the performance was an early rehearsal for the original 1946 Broadway production.
Not only did this context provide opportunities to create a much-needed theatrical atmosphere, it also provided a logical theatrical explanation for the absence of full sets or costumes. The narrator figure that I had envisioned was
transformed into a fictional stage manager. As the only character to be given any
spoken dialogue, the stage manager became a physicalization for the interpretive
stance of the curator, which is conventionally in evidence in the labels of a traditional museum exhibition. Within the context of the dramatic conceit that I
had created, I was able to use the presence of the narrator to pilot the actors and
audiences through the course of the concert by periodically dispensing research-
based anecdotal commentary about the show's original cast and creative team,
providing background historical data, and effecting a connective relationship
among the songs by offering a brief scene-by-scene narrative.

Fig. 12.2. Petty crook Careless Love (Charles Williams, center) sings the lively "Wrong Side of the Railroad Tracks" with his cronies (Ken Jackson, left, and Jimmy Peters, right) while a bemused Macheath (Thomas MacKenzie, far right) watches.

To devise a budget for the undertaking, I tallied a list of potential production costs. These included personnel fees for twelve performers, a pianist–musical director, a director-choreographer, a costumer, a lighting designer, the museum's labor crew, a photographer, and a technician to provide audiovisual support services. Additional costs included costume rentals, lighting supplies, props, printing fees for program handouts, and advertising costs. The total was a modest $12,000. A proposal submitted to my museum's director, Roger G. Kennedy, resulted in securing most of the needed funding. The remaining funds required were granted from the museum's annual federal budget and the John Hammond Fund for the Performance of American Music, an endowment fund at the museum that supplements the presentation of musical outreach activity.

Among the unique requirements that distinguish the execution of this type of museum exhibition from a traditional one is the need to hire a group of professional interpreters (read: actors) to bring the selected artifacts and historical data to vibrant life. To select the cast, I conferred with my musical director, Howard Breitbart, and my director-choreographer, Dr. Ronald J. O'Leary. Dr. O'Leary, chairman of the directing program at the University of Maryland, and

Mr. Breitbart, a leading musical director in the D.C. theatrical arena, have been my frequent collaborators in developing research- and collection-based performances. We mutually agreed on an approach for choosing our cast from the pool of professional talent in the Washington-Baltimore area and sent out a call for auditioners. Aside from a strong commitment to preserve the multiethnic casting that had been such an important component of the 1946 Broadway production, we resolutely decided against the near-impossible task of casting the roles with actors who physically resembled their 1946 counterparts. Instead, our company was made up of performers with extensive experience in professional musical theater, as well as several University of Maryland students, who performed in the ensemble. Similarly, our costumes would not and, for both financial and legal reasons, *could not* resemble the originals by costumier Walter Florell. Our frocks would suggest generally the 1940s era rather than being character-specific.

With a fine cast and production team working in harmony, our rehearsals went smoothly. Each day of rehearsal was prefaced with discussions about the original production, the contexts for the musical numbers, and a viewing of appropriate photographs from the Ellington Collection.

Then, two days before we were scheduled to open, disaster struck. The National Museum of American History, the site of our projected performances, was immediately closed until further notice because of the sudden discovery of dangerous asbestos fibers in its ventilation system. Unlike traditional exhibitions, which have long-term commitments on staging spaces, our *Beggar's Holiday* presentation was virtually impossible to postpone and reschedule because of heavy subsequent commitments on the auditorium's schedule and those of our actors. Determined to proceed in my best "the-show-must-go-on" style, I, to my complete surprise, was able to secure a last-minute standby space for our performances in the considerably larger auditorium at our National Museum of Natural History (although the costumes, set pieces, and props remained locked up at the American History Museum). We scoured the city for places to conduct our final rehearsals. The possibilities ranged from facilities at the University of Maryland to an empty ballroom at a D.C. hotel. At 4:00 P.M. on the day before our first scheduled performance, I learned that the asbestos contamination had proved to be a false alarm and that the museum would reopen the following day, allowing us to proceed as scheduled. We quickly phoned all the local broadcast and newspaper sources to elicit their help in getting the word out to our patrons that *Beggar's Holiday,* which had lain untouched for nearly fifty years, would at last step out of Ellington's own archives and onto a Smithsonian stage.

The next morning, I was greeted by an extensive front-page article in the

Style section by *Washington Post* music editor Richard Harrington that documented our efforts to resurrect *Beggar's Holiday*. It was precisely the kind of thoughtful notice we needed to secure audiences for our experimental exhibition of the Ellington legacy. By noon, several hundred potential attendees had formed a serpentine line that snaked from the entrance to the Carmichael Auditorium to the museum's back door—a distance of six city blocks. When the doors opened at 1:30 P.M., the auditorium hastily filled, well beyond its capacity. After a brief greeting to our packed house, I sped to the control booth and activated the first light cue, which plunged the theater into darkness. Immediately the darkness was replaced by a second light cue, which bathed the tiny stage in a dim blue haze. The cast entered and began the opening song, a moody expression of ambivalence called "In Between." At the number's conclusion, the narrator entered and was greeted with polite applause; it wasn't until the end of the sixth number, the sultry "Take Love Easy," however, that the all-too-rare relationship between performers, material, and audience solidified. The spectators reacted to the song's performance with a two-minute ovation of applause and whistles, literally stopping the show. From that point on, we knew that the show that had experienced such a long and troubled history had, at last, landed on its feet, bringing our audience to theirs at the finale.

Following its initial series of concerts in February 1992, *Beggar's Holiday* was subsequently performed, under the museum's auspices, for an audience of three hundred D.C. students in a special outreach performance presented at, appropriately enough, the Duke Ellington High School for the Performing Arts. When the museum presented various artifacts from the Ellington Collection in the 1993 exhibition "Beyond Category: The Musical Genius of Duke Ellington," we revived *Beggar's Holiday* for four more performances, with largely the same cast and creative team. Since the 1992 presentations, I had conducted additional research in our archives and discovered more songs written for the score—two wonderfully cynical pieces called, respectively, "A Virgin's Like Ore from a Goldmine" and "Wanna Be Bad." An added bonus for the 1993 performances was that they were attended by Dale Wasserman, one of the show's original producers. Wasserman's hearty approval, coupled with that of our capacity audiences, reassured us of the value of our undertaking.

While using musical artifacts in research and collection-based performances is not a new endeavor at the Smithsonian (the period instrument collections have often been used in concerts), our "living" exhibition founded on the score for *Beggar's Holiday* blazed new paths in finding alternative methods for interpreting collections of musical scores and theatrical artifacts for museum visitors. They provide lively, accessible vehicles for scholarship and serve also as an effective outreach activity to attract new audiences to the museum's ongoing educational mission. Above all, these unique performances allow curators to display and interpret collections of musical manuscripts to their utmost, restoring them to the context for which they were originally created—to be interpreted through live performance.

NOTES

1. Oscar Hammerstein II and Richard Rodgers, "Sixteen Going on Seventeen," reprise, act 2, scene 5 (New York: Williamson Music, 1960).

2. The Ellington Collection was brought to the Museum of American History through the efforts of a number of its staff, headed by music curator John Edward Hasse, Archives Center director John Fleckner, and the museum's director, Roger G. Kennedy.

3. Among the projects that the Ellington Collection has yielded are two commemorative exhibitions, the publication series *Jazz Masterworks Editions,* which offers transcriptions of orchestral scores for performance by student ensembles, and performances of Ellington's big band charts by the museum's resident ensemble, the Jazz Masterworks Orchestra.

4. Four musicals for which Ellington supplied the scores were given major productions during his lifetime: *Jump for Joy* (1941, Los Angeles), *Beggar's Holiday* (1946, New York), *My People* (1963, Chicago), and *Pousse Cafe* (1966, New York). His music was used for *Sophisticated Ladies,* a posthumous tribute to his work that premiered on Broadway to acclaim in 1980.

5. Edward Kennedy Ellington, *Music Is My Mistress* (Garden City, N.Y.: Doubleday, 1973), pp. 185–86.

6. Gerald Bordman, *American Musical Theatre: A Chronicle.* (New York: Oxford University Press, 1979), pp. 554–55.

7. In addition to Ellington's brief discussion of *Beggar's Holiday* in his autobiography, *Music Is My Mistress,* it is also discussed in several other autobiographical texts, including *Front and Center* (New York: Simon and Schuster, 1979), by John Houseman, the show's original director, and *Mister Abbott* (New York: Random House, 1963), by George Abbott.

8. Houseman, *Front and Center.*

Contributors

RICHARD E. AHLBORN, curator of the National Museum of American History's Division of Culture History (since 1965), specializes in Hispanic American material culture of territory now part of the United States.

MARY JO ARNOLDI is the curator of African Ethnology and Art in the Department of Anthropology, National Museum of Natural History. Her research interests include both the history of museum collections and exhibitions of African materials, as well as the contemporary arts and performances of West Africa.

DWIGHT BLOCKER BOWERS is a performing arts historian in the Division of Cultural History at the Smithsonian's National Museum of American History. He is a three-time Grammy Award nominee for his Smithsonian Collection of Recordings releases.

LONNIE G. BUNCH is the associate director for Historical resources at the National Museum of American History. His research specialties are African American history; African Americans in the West, especially California; the history of the American West; and nineteenth-century social and urban history.

TOM D. CROUCH has served both the National Air and Space Museum (NASM) and the National Museum of American History in a variety of curatorial and administrative posts. He is currently chairman of the Department of Aeronautics at NASM. His publications include *A Dream of Wings: Americans and the Airplane, 1875–1905* (1981); *Blériot XI: The Story of a Classic Airplane* (1982); and *The Bishop's Boys: A Life of Wilbur and Orville Wright* (1989).

WILLIAM W. FITZHUGH is currently director of North American anthropology and director of the Smithsonian's Center for Arctic Studies. He is a specialist in circumpolar anthropology and archeology and has spent more than twenty years studying and publishing on arctic peoples and cultures in northern Canada, Alaska, Siberia, and Scandinavia.

AMY HENDERSON, a cultural historian at the Smithsonian's National Portrait Gallery, has curated exhibitions on music, Hollywood, and the media. She is the author of *On the Air: Pioneers of American Broadcasting* (1988) and *Red, Hot & Blue: A Smithsonian Salute to the American Musical* (1996), both published by the Smithsonian Institution Press.

ELLEN RONEY HUGHES is a historian in the Division of Cultural History at the National Museum of American History, specializing in American sport and leisure history, popular culture, and material culture. She has curated more than fifteen exhibitions, including Smithsonian's America, produced exhibit videos and CD-ROMs, and contributed to several exhibition catalogs. She is also the director of the American Sport Oral History Project.

ADRIENNE L. KAEPPLER is curator of oceanic ethnology at the Smithsonian's National Museum of Natural History and the author, most recently, of *Poetry in Motion* (1993).

RICHARD KURIN is director of the Smithsonian's Center for Folklife Programs and Cultural Studies, where he oversees the Festival of American Folklife, Smithsonian/Folkways Recordings, and a variety of cultural and education programs. He is chair of the program committee for the Smithsonian's 150th anniversary and past chair of the Smithsonian's Council of Information and Education Directors. He has curated and co-curated a number of exhibitions, including "Aditi" for the Festival of India.

SALLY LOVE has been with the National Museum of Natural History since 1982. She was director of the Insect Zoo from 1984 to 1993 and was the exhibit developer for the new Insect Zoo, which opened in 1993. She is currently developing other natural history exhibits, and she recently coordinated the museum's contribution to the "America's Smithsonian" traveling exhibit.

STEVEN LUBAR is chairman of the Division of the History of Technology at the National Museum of American History and was curator of the "World War II: Sharing Memories" exhibit.

WILLIAM L. MERRILL is the curator of the Western North American Ethnology Collections in the Department of Anthropology, National Museum of Natural History. His research focuses on the religion, worldview, and cultural history of American Indian societies in the southwestern United States and northern Mexico.

JANE MACLAREN WALSH is a museum specialist in the Department of Anthropology. Her main interest is in the archaeology and ethnohistory of central Mexico. She was coeditor of the Americas section of Timelines of the Ancient World and a curator of the exhibit and contributor to the volume Seeds of Change. She is codirector of a historical and archaeological project in Mexico studying the environmental and social consequences of European contact with native groups in the Valley of Toluca during the sixteenth century.

WILLIAM H. TRUETTNER is curator of painting and sculpture at the National Museum of American Art. He was co-curator of "The West as America" (1991) and "Thomas Cole: Landscape into History" (1994).

WILLIAM YEINGST is a domestic life specialist with the Division of Social History at the National Museum of American History. His research specialties are the history of American home life; American domestic furnishings; and youth and reform movements.

Index

Page references in italics refer to illustrations.

277